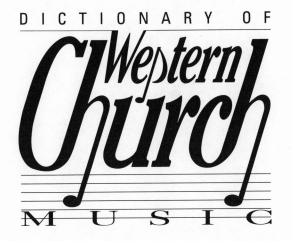

DICTIONARY OF Western Church MUSIC

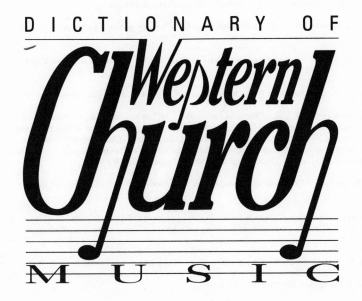

DICTIONARY OF Western Church MUSIC

BY

DAVID POULTNEY

American Library Association
Chicago and London   1991

Library of Congress Cataloging-in-Publication Data

Poultney, David.
    Dictionary of Western church music / by David Poultney.
       p.   cm.
    "List of sacred music periodicals": p.
    Includes index.
    ISBN 0-8389-0569-2 (alk. paper)
    1. Church music — Encyclopedias.   I. Title.
ML102.C5P77   1991
782.32´03 — dc20   91-12325

Printed in the United States of America.

95 94 93 92 91   5 4 3 2 1

Contents

126098

Music Examples

Preface

DICTIONARY OF WESTERN CHURCH MUSIC is intended for the use of those who provide music for worship services, including both professional and nonprofessional church musicians. It is also for those with occasional need for concise information regarding some aspect of sacred music: clergy and seminarians, scholars, librarians, and music students. Finally, it is for all those who love church music (and the broader field of religious music) and desire to learn more about it. As a practicing church musician for many years, I have often wished for a handy reference book of necessary, useful, and stimulating knowledge of the subject, a volume that could accompany me to and from church and, indeed, that I could read for pleasure as well as professional enhancement during times of relaxation. Knowledge about traditional liturgical practices and music can be difficult to acquire outside research libraries and large metropolitan churches. It is hoped that this single-volume reference source will provide that knowledge, or at least whet the reader's curiosity and offer guidance to more detailed information and reference sources within the field.

This book cannot and is not intended to cover in a comprehensive manner the vast subject of church music. It deals principally with the musical heritage of the following Christian traditions: Roman Catholic, Anglican and Episcopalian, Lutheran, Methodist, and Baptist. Its approximately four hundred entries are arranged alphabetically, with cross-references to related subjects. In addition to the expected material on terms and genres, there are eighty substantive essays on significant composers of church music. In their careers one can trace the history of church music and perhaps find inspiration in a brotherhood of the spirit. No apology is made for the preponderance of great composers or for the inclusion of composers whose religious music forms a small part of their output. No music used to praise God can be too good. However, a certain number of essays (principally for composers of the nineteenth and twentieth centuries) have been allotted to musicians of a more modest sort, whose resources and aims may more closely reflect the pragmatic musical needs of churches. One can also learn here how music that speaks a more popular language has always had its place in the worship service, from the SEQUENCE to evangelical HYMNODY, and from the Lutheran CONTRA-FACTUM to GOSPEL MUSIC. Today, a church musician should build a broad repertory and be able to recognize quality in many styles.

One fact that became clear in preparing this material is how large a quantity of choral and organ music of superior quality can be performed by modestly gifted but dedicated musicians. There are many preludes and simple chorale arrangements for organ manuals only, and there are many motets and anthems with modest requirements. In the absence of a modern performing edition, a pilgrimage to a university library, or the preparation of one's own edition of suitable music, is sometimes necessary. The reader should be able to discern from the essays and articles (and perhaps by listening to recordings) when the performance of the compositions referred to may be impractical. It is hoped that the serious reader will also pursue avenues leading to a broader knowledge of religious music outside the functional framework of the church service.

Various aids have been used to help the reader move from place to place in the book. These include various "key" articles for major historical periods, religious traditions, and genres. Within these articles and throughout the book, CROSS-REFERENCES are made to other subjects that may be of interest. The table that follows the Preface lists the significant composers chronologically by historical period under each of the major genres of church music. A list of musical examples is given in the order of their appearance to facilitate their location. Finally an index of compositions that are discussed at some length (and in some cases for which musical examples are supplied) has been provided.

I direct the reader's attention to two major musicological publications, the best of their respective kinds, and acknowledge my debt to them: *The New Grove Dictionary of Music and Musicians* (Macmillan, 1980, 20 vols.) and *The New Harvard Dictionary of Music* (Belknap Press of Harvard University Press, 1986). In these two sources the reader will find, as I have found, a clear bibliographical trail to more specialized literature in the field.

Debts of gratitude are also owed to Professor David Gehrenbeck of Illinois Wesleyan University for his suggestions, to Samuel Rogal of Illinois Valley Community College for drawing me into a joint project that eventually became this book, and to my parents for never being reluctant to drive a very young (and unknowledgeable) church organist to various drafty, usually snow-covered churches in Massachusetts many years ago.

The book is dedicated to all those who, like the author, give or have given their time, their talent, and their love in musical praise of the Lord.

Composers Arranged Chronologically by Genres

MASS	MOTET	MAGNIFICAT	PASSION	ANTHEM/SERVICE	CHURCH CANTATA	ORATORIO	ORGAN MUSIC
Late Medieval: 1175–1400							
Machaut	Machaut						
Dunstable	Dunstable						
Renaissance: 1400–1600							
Dufay	Dufay						
Ockeghem	Ockeghem						
Josquin	Josquin						
Isaac	Isaac						
Senfl	Senfl	Senfl					
Taverner	Taverner	Taverner					
Willaert	Willaert						
Morales	Morales	Morales					
Tallis	Tallis			Tallis			
Palestrina	Palestrina	Palestrina					
Lassus	Lassus	Lassus	Lassus				
Byrd	Byrd	Byrd		Byrd			Sweelinck
Victoria	Victoria	Victoria	Victoria	Tomkins			Titelouze

Baroque: 1600–1750

			Gibbons				Gabrieli, G.
	Gabrieli, G.						Frescobaldi
	Frescobaldi						
	Schuetz		Schuetz		Schuetz	Schuetz	Scheidt
	Scheidt	Scheidt					Buxtehude
Carissimi	Carissimi					Carissimi	
Charpentier	Charpentier	Charpentier			Buxtehude	Charpentier	Pachelbel
	Pachelbel	Pachelbel	Humfrey		Pachelbel		Couperin
Scarlatti, A.	Scarlatti, A.	Scarlatti, A.	Purcell	Scarlatti, A.		Scarlatti, A.	Grigny
	Couperin, F.	Couperin, F.					Walther
Telemann	Telemann	Telemann		Telemann	Telemann		Bach, J. S.
Bach, J. S.	Bach, J. S.	Bach, J. S.		Bach, J. S.	Bach, J. S.		Boyce
			Boyce			Handel	

Classical: 1750–1825

		Billings				
Haydn, F. J.	Mozart				Mozart	
Mozart						
Beethoven				Beethoven		

Composers Arranged Chronologically by Genres (continued)

MASS	MOTET	MAGNIFICAT	PASSION	ANTHEM/SERVICE	CHURCH CANTATA	ORATORIO	ORGAN MUSIC
Romantic: 1800–1920							
Schubert Berlioz Franck Bruckner Verdi	Wesley, S. Mendelssohn Bruckner Brahms Reger	 Bruckner		Wesley, S. Mason Mendelssohn Wesley, S. S. Stanford Maunder Parker	 Mendelssohn Maunder Parker Reger	 Berlioz Mendelssohn Franck Stanford Parker	Wesley, S. Mendelssohn Wesley, S. S. Franck Bruckner Brahms Reger
Twentieth Century							
Vaughan Williams Stravinsky Howells Poulenc Thompson Distler Britten David Duruflé Peeters Langlais Zimmermann Albright	Vaughan Williams Willan Howells Titcomb Poulenc Distler Hovhaness David Pepping Peeters Zimmermann	Parker Hovhaness Pinkham Penderecki Peeters Zimmermann Mathias	 Thompson Pinkham Penderecki Pepping	Vaughan Williams Willan Howells Titcomb Sowerby Thompson Hovhaness Mathias	 David Distler Britten	Vaughan Williams Zimmermann Albright	Willan Howells Sowerby David Distler Pepping Duruflé Messiaen Peeters Langlais Pinkham Zimmermann Mathias Albright

Introduction

Music has been regarded as indispensable in church services for so long that its role and the execution of that role by church musicians are often taken for granted. The organist establishes a devotional mood with preludes before the church service, interludes during prayer and the offertory, and a postlude after the closing benediction. In addition, there are hymns to be played for congregational singing – not an easy task when it is done properly – as well as accompaniments for the liturgical music, if any, for the anthem by the choir, or for music by a solo singer. The choir (or choirs) may be trained and led by a choir director, into whose hands also falls the responsibility for selecting the vocal music, purchasing it (and managing the budget), maintaining the choral library and the choir robes, and so forth. In many churches the same hands that play the organ also direct the choir. None of these duties is unusual; all have been carried out by dedicated church musicians for centuries, as may be seen in the following document, a legal contract for a position offered to Johann Sebastian Bach in 1708 (as translated by Hans T. David and Arthur Mendel in *The Bach Reader,* revised edition [Norton, 1966], pages 65–66).

> We, the undersigned fathers and members of the Council of Eight...testify that we have herewith appointed and accepted the honorable and learned Mr. Johann Sebastian Bach as organist of the Church of Our Lady, on condition that he be faithful and regular in attendance upon us and our Church, strive for a virtuous and exemplary life, above all cling faithfully all his life long to the unchanged Augsburg Confession, the Formula of Concord, and other symbolic confessions of faith, keep diligently to the altar of this Church and be devoutly

obedient to the Word of God, and thus demonstrate to the entire Congregation his confession of faith and Christian character.

Further, as concerns the performance of his official duties, he is obliged: (1) On all high holidays and feast days, and any others as they occur, and on the eves of such days, and every Sunday and Saturday afternoon, as well as at the regular Catechism sermons and public weddings, to play the large organ in furtherance of divine service to the best of his ability and zeal, and in such manner that at times the small organ and the regal also may be played, particularly on high feasts for the chorales and the figured music.

He is also (2) ordinarily—on high and other feasts, as well as on every third Sunday—to present with the Cantor and the choir students, as well as with the town musicians and other instrumentalists, a moving and well-sounding sacred work; and on extraordinary occasions—on second and third holidays [of the three each celebrated at Christmas, Easter, and Pentecost]—to perform short concerted pieces with the Cantor and the students, and also at times with some violins and other instruments; and to conduct everything in such a way that the members of the Congregation shall be more inspired and refreshed in worship and in their love of harkening to the Word of God.

But especially he is (3) obliged to communicate in good time to the Chief Pastor of our Church..., for his approval, the texts and music chosen....

Further he is (4) to take care to accompany attentively the regular chorales and those prescribed by the Minister, before and after the sermons on Sundays and feast days, as well as at Communion and at Vespers and on the eves of holidays, slowly and without unusual embellishment, in four or five parts, on the diapason, to change the other stops at each verse, also to use the fifth and the reeds, the stopped pipes, as well as syncopations and suspensions, in such manner that the congregation can take the organ as the basis of good harmony and unison tone, and thus sing devoutly and give praise and thanks to the Most High.

(5) Accordingly, he is hereby entrusted with the large and small organs, as well as the church regal and other instruments belonging to the church, specified in an inventory to be made out for him, and he is instructed to take good care

that the former are kept in good condition as regards their bellows, pipes, stops, and other appurtenances, and in good tune, without dissonance; . . . and if any of them are lost, or broken as a result of negligence, the damage is to be made good by him.

For these his efforts he is to receive annually from the church receipts a salary of. . . . In return for which he promises not to accept secondary employment during the present engagement, but to attend exclusively and industriously to his duties in this church.

Although moral character is prominently mentioned in the contract, probably for legal reasons, it receives far less attention from the church fathers than musical concerns. Indeed, the city fathers (since it was a municipal responsibility) go so far as to prescribe the choice of tempi, of organ registration, the nature of musical accompaniment, and the role of improvised ornamentation. Modern organists might be flattered at such attention to their playing; they would certainly be pleased not to have to earn most of their livelihood at some other job. The great surprise lies in what remains unstated (though certainly understood) in the contract: that the organist would compose a considerable amount of music for the church service. As this book unfolds, it will become clear how neglect of this unstated responsibility brought church music gradually, but inevitably, to its low ebb at the beginning of the twentieth century.

Western music was born and grew to maturity in the church, first as Gregorian CHANT, then as chant-based polyphonic MASSES and MOTETS, and eventually as freely composed CHORALE MOTETS, ANTHEMS, and Anglican SERVICES. When the court replaced the church as the principal music patron during the RENAISSANCE, some of the finest performers and composers elected to serve as church musicians. In the BAROQUE PERIOD, when the Italians and the French were turning increasingly to the aural excitement of opera or the new instrumental genres, the Germans applied these new elements of style to church music and the region enjoyed a remarkable outpouring of church CANTATAS and ORGAN MUSIC by great church musicians. The church, however, ceased after the Baroque period to provide a livelihood for major composers.

In spite of the lack of direct patronage from the church during the CLASSICAL PERIOD, there was still significant cultivation of traditional liturgical genres, especially of the Mass. But the church was beginning to serve, if nothing else, as a concert hall for performances of music. As a result, strong forces such as the CECILIAN MOVEMENT arose during the ROMANTIC PERIOD to arrest the application of contemporary styles to church music. Drawn as they were to grapple seriously with contemporary creative problems which were generally symphonic in nature, major composers—with some exceptions—found little opportunity to compose liturgical music; if they were moved to express religious feelings in music, the resulting compositions were conceived from the beginning for the public concert hall. Forced to adhere to outmoded aesthetic requirements, functional church music fell by default into the hands of less gifted musicians who increasingly just performed the music. If they did compose, they preferred not to deal with vital creative issues.

The music which had gradually been excluded from the church during the Romantic period informally and on aesthetic grounds soon became the subject of fixed policy in certain churches. The *Motu proprio* of Pope Pius X in 1903 established specific guidelines for Catholic church music that pointedly excluded many masterpieces from the past and thoroughly discouraged contemporary composers of quality from writing church music. However well-intentioned, the sanctification of church music brought musical creativity within the church by leading composers to a halt. Several prominent twentieth-century composers have shown interest in religious and liturgical music—some of them (such as PENDERECKI) within a sectarian approach—but seldom has the contemporary composer found in the church either a patron or a place of performance. Responsibility for the creation of new church music, the most significant aspect of the highly trained church musician's role—that which was understood but not stated in the contract quoted above—was nearly lost by the turn of the twentieth century. In Germany, where support existed for the KAPELLMEISTER tradition and for schools in which these musicians could be trained, church music experienced a resurgence in the twentieth century in the works of DAVID, PEPPING, and DISTLER. Imagine how the history of church music in the United States might read if there had been a comparable tradition in this country—one in which STRAVINSKY might have lived the life of "a small Bach,... composing regularly for an established service and for God...." (See the end of the essay on Stravinsky.)

Because music of the past falls most comfortably upon the ears of most congregations, many twentieth-century church musicians with professional training have neither created nor performed contemporary music. They have functioned rather as performers of an accepted corpus of music composed in a commonly recognized "sacred" idiom. Their proper role still appears to many people both inside and outside the church to be one of preserving a musical heritage handed down from the late nineteenth century. In these circumstances, however healthy and necessary the profession might seem, certain questions must be raised by those concerned about its future. What are the effects of neglecting the creative aspect of an art? How well trained for their tasks are performers who do not create music, or at least understand their art in a contemporary context?

Whether the profession of church musician is healthy is also a question that must be raised. Too often an historical account will cite exceptional contributions to church music, such as those of the Christiansens of Saint Olaf's Lutheran College or the publisher-editor-arranger-composer Edmund Lorenz, without assessing whether contemporary church musicians have emulated their creativity. The remarkable success of people trained in church music at Union Theological Seminary and its School of Music (now defunct) and at the Westminster Choir School has certainly earned the gratitude of everyone concerned with standards of music-making in the church, but one must ask whether the creation of a new and contemporary repertory has been a result. With the exception of certain metropolitan areas and university towns, the established denominational churches in the United States seem to rely increasingly upon part-time semiprofessionals, or if at all possible, entirely upon amateur musicians. Most church choirs are composed of all the members of the congregation who are willing to sing, regardless of their ability to sing or to read music. The repertory that can be performed with such groups is necessarily limited by the abilities of those who volunteer their services. In many cases, a church's music is in the hands of enthusiastic amateurs whose musical experience is solely in popular music. Given the current lack of trained musicians and the understandable reluctance of congregations that would neither appreciate nor reward their efforts to employ trained musicians, many churches outside of metropolitan areas cannot maintain even a modest program of traditional church music. Churches which can are faced with the question of how traditional church music can compete with the increasing acceptance of popular musical styles in the church, styles which to many people represent a lower level of creativity than that found in music of the past, but which are certainly alive and vital.

Aided by radio, television, and modern means of electronic reproduction, a new repertory of church music based on popular musicial idioms, and in some cases on "rock," has already established itself in many American churches. Accompaniment for willing but untrained soloists is sometimes provided, not by church musicians, but by electronic tapes. Rather than deplore that trend, an impartial observer might acknowledge that popular styles serve the purposes of worship at least as well as the largely sanctimonious repertory they replaced. Perhaps these styles can reach young people whose lack of music education has rendered meaningless any music composed in traditional idioms. A knowledgable observer might also recall how Martin LUTHER and John WESLEY transformed popular music into religious music, and how such distinctively American styles as evangelical singing (GOSPEL MUSIC) and the SPIRITUAL have played a significant role in the history of American music.

Are there any solutions to the fundamental problems that beset church music at the end of the twentieth century: the creative sterility of many trained church musicians and the need to communicate a spiritual message at least occasionally in popular musical idioms? The biographical articles in this *Dictionary* seem to suggest the need for a redefinition of the role and the status of the church musician. What is required is a wider recognition of the church musician as a minister of music, and of his or her work as a full-time professional responsibility requiring further education and training, particularly in the creative aspect of the art. Adequate remuneration is also required. Although they may cost nothing, enthusiasm and dedication cannot make up for lack of talent. There is no lack of talented people in music schools, conservatories, church-related colleges, and seminaries across the country who would render enthusiastic and dedicated service if given the opportunity. Most churches manage to afford what they want. More churches need to want well-regulated and comprehensive music programs under the direction of a professional educated in a wide range of styles (including folk and popular) and able to make use of both trained and amateur volunteers.

The pessimism which surrounds the sorry decline of the church musician's role through the centuries need not prevent the modern church from reversing that trend. Attracting to the profession talented and creative young church musicians who use contemporary styles in an appropriate way that involves all of their volunteer musicians could mark the beginning of a new era in church music. Once again, as in the days of Martin Luther and John Wesley, music could rally the faithful to new heights of spiritual awareness and dedication to the causes of the church. There is no better stimulus than music to inspire a congregation towards a new openness and honesty and a renewed spirit of love and spontaneous giving. An optimistic observer looking in the right places may find that some of the necessary changes in the nature of church music and the role of the church musician are already taking place.

Signs of health in twentieth-century church music are evident in the various ways in which contemporary, and at times avant-garde (forward looking) musical techniques have been used in music for the worship service. Avant-garde techniques are found in impressive works by composers such as Daniel PINKHAM. Pinkham's setting to music of words from Genesis entitled "In the Beginning of Creation" (Ione Press) requires a chorus to sing different melodies at the same time, to speak in unison, to whisper, and to create new clusters of sound by singing random pitches together; electronic sounds on tape supplement the live performance by mixed chorus. Improvised speaking of a text from Romans by members of a chorus creates a striking effect in D. Duane Blakley's "Be Strong in the Lord" (Harold Flammer, Inc.). Here there is also use of a prepared electronic tape, as well as an opportunity for players of keyboard, brass, and percussion to improvise "evil noises." In yet a third example chosen from among many, the composer Leslie Bassett uses electronic tape to supply an accompaniment for a choral piece entitled "Collect." Although the choir sings in a traditional manner, the style of the music is of the twentieth century.

Many composers, including those mentioned above, have extended themselves to communicate with church audiences and to make performance of their music possible by nonprofessionals. A second new direction finds forward-looking musical techniques combined with the performance of traditional music to striking effect. In her arrangement of the well-known folk hymn "Amazing Grace" (Carl Fischer, Inc.), Marie Pooler allows for the use of a unison treble choir, a mixed chorus in four voice-parts, organ (or piano), handbells, and recorder (or flute) — all of them sanctioned by tradition. Her arrangement also calls for improvisation within clearly specified parameters affecting the rhythm and the order of the pitches; the performers (or more likely the director) are given a choice during the performance among three alternatives, according to the mood or the occasion.

Infusion of new musical elements into the service need not displace well-loved traditional music. If discrimination is used in the choice of music, there is room for both the past and the present in music by the choir, the organist, and the congregation. Church hymns offer a place for the new as well as the tried-and-true. Arrangements of familiar hymns, among them "This Is My Father's World" and "For the Beauty of the Earth," have been published by Buryl Red (Broadman Press) with special attention given to the musical abilities of children and youth. Jane Marshall has also composed anthems specifically for children's voices. Adults as well as young people are considered in Helen Kemp's collection of hymns, carols, and songs entitled *Hymns Plus* (Hinshaw Music Company). Hymns for the congregation (or for choirs) that focus upon life in the present rather than familiar metaphors from the past may be found in such collections as the *Contemporary Hymn Book* of David Yantis and in the works of Sebastian Temple, Jim Strathdee, and Ray Repp, among others. Perhaps hymnody, as in the past, can be one aspect of the worship service that sets aside the social, economic, and racial barriers that often separate churches and cause them to forget their common cause in the work of the Lord. The church musician need not carry out extensive research to become acquainted with the new reportory for the church service. Publishers of church music welcome inquiries and gladly furnish information and catalogs of their publications, whether they are new or traditional. (See appendix 1.)

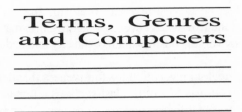

Terms, Genres and Composers

a cappella — Italian for "in the chapel," meaning that a composition should be performed according to the usual practice in the chapel of a religious or noble court. Because independent parts for instruments were not included in scores until the Baroque period, the term *a cappella* was interpreted by later musicians to mean that singers of earlier polyphonic music should not be accompanied by instruments. This usage of the term became common among post-Renaissance composers and musicians, and the supposed practice in earlier music lay behind the return to motets for unaccompanied voices in the works of such Catholic composers of the Romantic period as BRUCKNER. Modern composers who mark a piece or a passage *a cappella*, intend that it be sung unaccompanied. The problem in the use of the term stems from the fact that instruments were used in chapels long before they were given independent parts or were otherwise indicated in the score; their use followed the practice in a particular chapel. Recent studies in performance practice have established that, outside of Rome, available instruments were commonly employed in the Renaissance church service to double the vocal parts of music by DUFAY, JOSQUIN, and LASSUS. Modern choir directors need not withhold necessary accompaniment from their singers under the impression that they are upholding a universal Renaissance performance practice.

Abendmusik (pl., Abendmusiken) — A German word that means "evening music." In the Baroque period it referred to concerts of church music given on Sunday evenings at Saint Mary's Church in the North German city of Luebeck. From modest beginnings featuring organ music and a variety of sacred vocal works, these concerts developed under the direction of Dieterich BUXTEHUDE into oratorios that were performed over the course of the five Sunday evenings before Christmas. The concerts were sponsored by various businessmen of the city and endured until 1810.

Agnus Dei—A threefold invocation for forgiveness that derives from the Bible (John 1:29). It was one of the last sections adopted as part of the Roman Catholic MASS Ordinary, which it concludes. Composers of polyphonic music found the inherent tripartite structure and parallel construction of phrases in the "Agnus Dei" an invitation to musical expansion.

Agnus Dei qui tollis peccata mundi, miserere nobis.	Lamb of God, who takest away the sins of the world, have mercy on us.
Agnus Dei qui tollis peccata mundi, miserere nobis.	Lamb of God, who takest away the sins of the world, have mercy on us.
Agnus Dei qui tollis peccata mundi, dona nobis pacem.	Lamb of God, who takest away the sins of the world, grant us peace.

Albright, William (1944–)—An American organist, pianist, and composer who has been a leader in the creation of a contemporary repertory of American organ music. During extensive tours as a pianist and an organist, he has specialized in new music and comissioned some works himself. As a composer, he has won several awards and shown an enduring interest in American popular music. Among his teachers in composition was MESSAIEN, whose influence may be heard in the colorful timbres and chromatic language of Albright's early works and perhaps in his choice of extramusical religious subjects (e.g., the "Toccata Satanique" movement in *Organbook* II, 1971). Timbre has remained one of the composer's principal means of expression. The use of prerecorded electronic tape, as in "Last Rites" (*Organbook* II), reflects his interest and research in electronic sounds as associate director of the electronic music studio at the University of Michigan. In other works he has made use of multimedia resources. His ebullient humor is featured in a passage of improvisatory wandering in *Organbook* III (1978) that is written in the spirit of an inebriated Sunday School organist. Unlike so many of his colleagues among contemporary composers, Albright has maintained a balance between the new and the traditional, between atonal and tonal, and between abstract concern for texture as a means for articulating structure and the value of music as a form of communication.

The starting point for organists whose primary concern is church music should be the first of Albright's three organbooks. Like its namesake, the French *livre d'orgue, Organbook* I (1967) contains short works of liturgical utility and almost etude-like working out of strikingly contemporary musical ideas. Among his vocal works are "An Alleluia Super-Round" (1973) for eight or more voices; Mass in D (1974) for chorus, congregation, organ, and percussion; *Chichester Mass* (1974) for chorus; psalm settings entitled "David's Songs" (1982) for soloists and chorus; and an oratorio, *A Song to David* (1983), for soloists, two choruses, and organ.

alla breve—Italian for "at the breve," indicating that the music that follows the sign ¢ is to be performed in two half-notes (actually two breves, thus 2/2 time) rather than in four quarter-notes (4/4); often referred to colloquially as "cut" time. Music composed before 1700 frequently calls for performance *alla breve*, thereby moving with the half-note as the beat rather than the quarter-note, and producing a faster tempo than may seem (to the modern musician) to be implied. Use of the sign is one of the few performance aids contained in early music, which ordinarily offers neither tempo markings nor indications of expression. In a modern edition, the church musician often finds the note-values of the original composition halved, so that he or she may use the familiar quarter-note as the beat.

Alleluia—The Latin equivalent of *hallelujah*, meaning "praise ye the Lord." The word occurs frequently in the Bible and in the Roman Catholic liturgy; in the Mass Proper, an Alleluia is sung before the Gospel is read for much of the year.

alternatim—A Latin word referring to the singing of a liturgical text alternately by soloist and choir, or by choir and organ, or by other contrasting means. In the Medieval church, PSALMODY was often sung antiphonally; when ORGANUM came into use, it was sung by soloists in alternation with choral plainchant. *In alternatim* vocal performance was commonly used for the MAGNIFICAT and for HYMNS and SEQUENCES through the Renaissance, while the use of organ music (often improvised) for alternate verses of text in the Mass reached its height in the Baroque period. In the Lutheran church, the practice of alternation frequently found the congregation taking a role by singing verses of a chorale tune in unison, while the choir, or perhaps the organ, supplied verses in polyphony. Beginning with the famous *Geystliches gesangk Buchleyn* of 1524 by Johann Walther, many collections of polyphonic chorale settings were intended for some type of alternation practice. Although its use declined in the Baroque period, there has been a revival of the *alternatim* practice in twentieth-century Lutheran churches.

Amen—A Hebrew word meaning "so be it," often used at the end of prayers and hymns. Its occurrence at the close of the GLORIA and the CREDO of the MASS became an occasion for composers to display their mastery of counterpoint. It also serves to remind modern musicians that the power and beauty of music found expression at a time when music was nominally secondary to the liturgical word.

Anglican liturgy—The Church of England originated with Henry VIII's break with the Roman Catholic Church in 1532. Not surprisingly, many aspects of Anglican worship resemble that of its predecessor. Anglican church music, on the other hand, has been governed from its inception by the adoption of the English vernacular, by a noteworthy fidelity to textual clarity, and by the use of the BOOK OF COMMON PRAYER. The problem of supplying music for the new church led at first to the use of Latin motets in English translation by such composers as TALLIS. PSALMS, CANTICLES, HYMNS, and ANTHEMS make up the largest part of the Anglican musical repertory, with a special place reserved for four canticles: "TE DEUM" and "BENEDICTUS" (sung during MORNING PRAYER), and "MAGNIFICAT" and "NUNC DIMITTIS" (sung during EVENING PRAYER). In addition, a special form of chant evolved that differs greatly from Gregorian CHANT; Anglican chant is based on short formulas harmonized in four voices, to which the text of a psalm or a canticle is adapted. Many Anglican chant formulas unfold in two balancing phrases, some in as many as three. Fitting the words to the music of the chant formulas has always been a task requiring rehearsal.

By the seventeenth century, three principal musical kinds of Anglican service had evolved, corresponding to the three principal liturgical rites: Morning Prayer, Holy Communion, and Evening Prayer. (For their components, see SERVICE.) There also arose in the parish churches an imperative need for a simpler kind of anthem that could be sung by a volunteer choir of mixed voices, as opposed to the elaborate cathedral music that required trained soloists and choirs. Similarly, a strong nineteenth-century movement towards making room in the service for congregational singing created a surge of interest in the hymn. The most noteworthy result of this interest was the publication of HYMNS ANCIENT AND MODERN in 1861. (See also the entries for TAVERNER, TALLIS, BYRD,

TOMKINS, GIBBONS, HUMFREY, PURCELL, BOYCE, SAMUEL WESLEY, MENDEL-SSOHN, SAMUEL SEBASTIAN WESLEY, MAUNDER, STANFORD, VAUGHAN WILLIAMS, HOWELLS, and BRITTEN.)

Annunciation—The announcement of the INCARNATION by the angel Gabriel to the Virgin Mary. The term also refers to the church festival for that event, which was traditionally held on March 25. It was apparently taken over from the Greek church some time before the late seventh century. Among the chants of the MASS PROPER for the Annunciation are the Gradual ("Diffusa es") and the Offertory ("Ave Maria"), both of which were given polyphonic settings by PALESTRINA.

anthem—A religious but nonliturgical composition in English for choir (and sometimes for solo voices as well). It serves the same role in Protestant churches as does the MOTET in the Roman Catholic Church.

The term "anthem" appears to have been in use before the sixteenth century, perhaps as early as the eleventh century, as a corruption of ANTIPHON. Indeed, the sixteenth-century anthem served in the Anglican rite as a votive antiphon at the conclusion of MATINS and EVENSONG. When the genre began to be used regularly after the establishment of the Anglican Church, some anthems were simply translations of Latin motets. The style of the anthem, however, tended to be more concerned with conveying the prosody and the sense of the text, and thus the anthem was more chordal and less melismatic than the motet of the period. Among the leading Renaissance composers of the anthem were Christopher Tye (c.1500-1572) and Thomas TALLIS (c.1505-1585).

Towards the latter part of the sixteenth century, musical settings of metrical psalms began to alternate verses written for soloists with accompaniment with choral passages, creating a form known as the verse anthem. So popular was it in the examples by William BYRD (1543-1623), Thomas Morley (c.1557-1602), and others that it began to outnumber the anthem proper in the early sixteenth century. Its leading proponents were Thomas TOMKINS (c.1572-1656), Thomas Weelkes (c.1575-1623), and Orlando GIBBONS (1583-1625). Gibbons, an outstanding church organist and member of the CHAPEL ROYAL (the king's musical establishment), composed both full anthems and verse anthems. In them the anthem becomes more dramatic through textural contrasts, and through more declamatory text setting and greater sectionalization of form. In his verse anthem entitled "See, See, the Word Is Incarnate," an extraordinary account of the life of Jesus, Gibbons achieved contrast by varying the soloists in each verse, and unified the sections through the subtle use of recurring motives rather than the use of repetition, which was customary. (See example 1.)

EXAMPLE 1. Orlando Gibbons, "See, See, the Word Is Incarnate" (meas. 80–85)

See,   O   See   the   fresh   wounds,   the

fresh   wounds, the go - ring blood,

The stylistic innovations of the Italians in the early Baroque period, principally monody and the basso continuo, made little impact in conservative England until after the period of the Commonwealth. Then, composers who had been abroad, such as Matthew Locke, brought back Continental practices and made the Chapel Royal for a time central to the development of English cathedral music. No Englishman of the period, including Pelham HUMFREY and John Blow, reached the heights of Henry PURCELL (1659–1695), whose masterful synthesis of his predecessors' techniques in the anthem and uniquely personal fusion of Italian, French, and English style traits found expression in sixty-three anthems, fifty of them verse anthems. Although the independent use of instruments in interludes or in an obbligato manner makes Purcell's verse anthems resemble the German church cantata and renders their performance difficult in a modern church setting, no such excuse keeps churchgoers from hearing the expressive five- to eight-voice polyphony of his full anthems.

With the greater emphasis upon the opera house and the concert hall in early eighteenth-century England came a decline of the Chapel Royal and of church music, despite some worthy anthems by such Englishmen as William Croft, Maurice Greene, and William BOYCE. Hovering over all musical activities was the overwhelming presence of George Frideric HANDEL (1685–1759), nearly all of whose twenty-one anthems were composed in his grandest oratorio manner for special festive occasions. The eleven anthems composed for the Duke of Chandos between 1716 and 1718 were among the first works Handel set on English texts; they are therefore appropriate for placing in clearer perspective Purcell's accomplishments in this sphere.

The later eighteenth century and most of the nineteenth century witnessed a great deal of anthem composing of a generally mediocre and uninspiring kind, despite the noteworthy efforts of Samuel WESLEY (1766–1837) in composition and in reviving the music of J. S. Bach. It was simply not a very rewarding period for either church music or the church musician. In *A Few Words on Cathedral Music* (1849) SAMUEL SEBASTIAN WESLEY (1810–1876), son of Charles, wrote that there was not one English cathedral with "a musical force competent to embody and give effect to the evident intentions of the Church with regard to music." Although the second half of the century produced such popular and generally competent church composers as John Stainer (1840–1901) and John MAUNDER (1858–1920), the rebirth of English church music did not truly begin until the turn of the twentieth century. It came, significantly enough, largely through the efforts of Charles STANFORD (1852–1924), a dedicated composer and teacher of composition who did not limit himself to the field of church music.

The anthem made its way to America in the eighteenth century, both in collections brought from England and in editions by American compilers such as Andrew Law. It became American in the works of such native New Englanders as William BILLINGS (1746–1800). (See example 2.) It reached a level of quality as high as that of Europe in an isolated colony of Moravians in Pennsylvania. (See MORAVIAN CHURCH MUSIC.) For the most part, however, the nineteenth century in America, as in England, witnessed numerous mediocre anthem publications, many of them simply adaptations of existing European music with English words or, if original, of questionable quality. Among the many composers and compilers of anthem collections, only two will be mentioned: Lowell

EXAMPLE 2. William Billings, "An Anthem for Easter" (meas. 23–30)

Now   is   Christ   ris - en from the   dead   and be -

come   the   first   fruits of   them   that slept.

MASON and George F. Root. Mason's highly influential publications of hymns and anthems began in 1822 with *The Boston Handel and Haydn Society Collection of Church Music*, while Root published his popular collection entitled *The Diapason* in 1860. Raising the level of composition in American church music could not be achieved until, as in England with Stanford, a well-trained composer and teacher took an interest in the medium. In the United States that man was Horatio PARKER (1863–1919).

Major twentieth-century composers have rarely found employment in the church, and writing anthems for practical church use has seldom engaged their attention. Among the exceptions in England have been Ralph VAUGHAN WILLIAMS (1872–1958) and Herbert HOWELLS (1892–1983), both students of Charles Stanford, as well as Edward Elgar, Michael Tippett, and Benjamin BRITTEN. In America, the quality of musical training in seminaries and music schools has brought a relatively high level of music to urban and suburban churches that have been willing to support a church music program run by professional church musicians. Among church composers of particular significance for their anthems are the Canadian Healey WILLAN (1880–1968), H. Everett TITCOMB (1884–1968), and Leo SOWERBY (1895–1968). Among the American composers born after the turn of the century who have made noteworthy contributions to the Protestant anthem are the church composers Gordon Young and Jane Marshall.

Twentieth-century church music has proved to be one of the few areas in which female composers were free to make significant contributions. American composers not known mainly for their church music, among them Virgil Thomson, Alan HOVHANESS, and Ned ROREM, have also contributed anthems for use in churches able and willing to perform the musical styles of the later twentieth century.

The outstanding source for information about the anthem remains Elwyn Wienandt and Robert Young's *The Anthem in England and America* (Free Press, 1970). For a list of anthem composers, see the table, Composers Arranged Chronologically by Genre, preceding the Introduction. A List of American Publishers of Church Music is given as appendix 1.

antiphon—A liturgical chant used as a refrain in psalmody, as processional music, or with reference to special texts on the subject of the Blessed Virgin Mary.

antiphonal—Used as an adjective, it describes performance by alternating choirs; as a noun, it commonly refers to the Roman Catholic liturgical book that contains the chants, including antiphons, for the Office, a daily series of services.

aria—An Italian word for a formal vocal piece by a soloist with accompaniment. In church music, arias form important components of the ORATORIO, the church CANTATA, and the MASS. The aria plays an important role in the cantatas of J. S. BACH and the oratorios of HANDEL.

arioso—A passage in a vocal work that lies stylistically between the aria and the recitative, being less formal than the former and more lyrical than the latter. In an ORATORIO or church CANTATA, a passage in arioso style often follows declamatory recitative and precedes an aria.

Ascription—In the Roman Catholic Mass, the Ascription precedes the SANCTUS and consists of the following words: "Therefore with angels and archangels, and with all the company of heaven, we laud and magnify thy glorious name, evermore praising thee, and saying: Sanctus...."

Ave Maria—Latin for "Hail, Mary." The words begin an important Roman Catholic prayer; the music constitutes an ANTIPHON.

Bach, Johann Sebastian (1685–1750)—A seminal figure in the history of church music, Bach systematically mastered the traditional structural principles, styles, and genres of his time, from CHORALE, TOCCATA, and

FUGUE to the church CANTATA and PASSION, imbuing them with his consummate contrapuntal craftsmanship and his uniquely expressive intensity. Although he was respected by his contemporaries as a composer in the contrapuntal style, his reputation during his lifetime was earned principally as a great organ virtuoso and a noteworthy consultant on the construction of church organs.

Bach's respect for and mastery of tradition in music arose quite naturally from his position among six generations of family musicians, most of them instrumentalists and many of them organists; in addition, he lived his entire life within a relatively small region in central Germany, somewhat removed from the leading musical centers of the time. Born in Eisenach, he received an excellent humanistic education there and subsequently in Ohrdruf, where he was sent after his father's death in 1695. Until 1700, he lived with his oldest brother, Johann Christoph, who had studied organ with Pachelbel. His schooling was completed at Saint Michael's in Lueneburg, where he served from 1700 to 1702 as a choirboy and probably became acquainted with the music of Georg Boehm and the great organ virtuoso J. A. Reincken.

Bach's career followed a logical progression from lesser positions to positions of increasing importance and greater professional demands and responsibilities. As a young man, he served as a church organist at Arnstadt (1703–1707) and Muehlhausen (1707–1708); a highlight of this period was his journey to Luebeck to hear the great organist and church composer Dieterich BUXTEHUDE. Finding his attempt to upgrade church music in Muehlhausen blocked, he accepted the position of organist at the court of Weimar. His responsibilities and his concern with secular music increased in 1714, when he became Konzertmeister in Weimar, and reached their apex during his years as Kapellmeister to Prince Leopold of Coethen (1717–1723). Bach's imprisonment by the Duke of Weimar before he was allowed to proceed to Coethen offers a degree of insight into his self-assured and assertive nature, which had already been indicated by the disagreements with church officials (and with his choristers and instrumentalists) that marked his previous positions. His relationship with the musical Prince Leopold, however, was both happy and harmonious; as in Weimar, Bach was in Coethen able to study the music of the leading composers and extend his mastery of secular musical genres. Only when the Prince's impending marriage threatened Bach's prominent place at the court did the composer once again turn his attention towards church music.

When Bach accepted the position of Kantor at the Thomaskirche in Leipzig in 1723, he must have regarded it as an opportunity to achieve goals in the composition of church music that he had been unable to accomplish earlier in his career. That he was not chosen until several others, including Telemann, had rejected the position should have given some warning of the problems that would beset him. As Kantor in Leipzig, Bach was to supply music for the principal church services held in the four major churches of the city on Sundays and feast days; there were also important subsidiary services to cover, as well as an opportunity to earn extra income by supplying music for weddings and funerals. Bach's responsibility was not as organist but as director of the musicians, who ordinarily numbered about sixteen singers (boys from the Saint Thomas School) and perhaps eighteen instrumentalists (who included boys from the same group, civic musicians, and students from the university). Unfortunately, after Bach had devoted only a few years to his task—a period noteworthy for the creation of a great number of church cantatas—bitter disputes about the extent of his authority, especially his power to select from among the boys for his musicians, undermined his position and shattered his lofty aspirations.

Although Bach retained the post of Kantor until his death, after about 1730 he was drawn once again to secular music. In spite of his move to Leipzig, he attempted to maintain his connections with musical life in the courts. He retained the title of Kapellmeister at Coethen until 1728; subsequently, he became Kapellmeister for the Saxe-Weissensfels court and then, in 1737, court composer at Dresden. More significant was his assumption in 1729 of the post of director of the Collegium Musicum at the University of Leipzig. With the exception of the period from 1737 to 1739, this voluntary chamber group of university students and professional musicians absorbed much of Bach's interest until 1741, by which time he seems to have become less concerned with achieving worldly success.

The music of Bach's last decade reflects his absorption with abstract musical values unfettered by the demands of church or chamber. The final versions of works such as the Passions, the completion of the Mass in B Minor, and the organ arrangements known as the *Schuebler* Chorales fulfilled his personal needs; *Clavieruebung* III, the collection of revisions known as the "Eighteen Chorales," (BMV 669–689), the Canonic Variations on "Vom Himmel hoch," and the unfinished "Art of Fugue" represent an aging master's legacy in each of the genres represented. Although he was denied the recognition as a composer that he deserved during his lifetime, Bach nevertheless must have thoroughly enjoyed his visit to the court of Frederick the Great in 1747; perhaps (from a worldly standpoint) the most noteworthy event of his life, this encounter resulted in the publication of the *Musikalisches Opfer* (Musical Offering).

Bach began his career as a church organist and remained active as an organ composer and a virtuoso performer throughout his life. Such was his musical exuberance as a young man that he was reprimanded for confusing the congregation at Arnstadt by his extraordinary manner of accompanying the chorales. The majority of Bach's chorale settings were gathered by the composer himself into four collections: the *Orgel-Buechlein* (with forty-six small-scale, liturgically-oriented settings); the twenty-one chorale movements in the *Clavieruebung* III; the six *Schueb-ler* Chorales (at least five of which originated as cantata movements); and the so-called "Eighteen Chorales" that he gathered and revised late in his life. The organ chorale served a wide variety of purposes during Bach's time; it could be played as an independent piece in the service, as a prelude or an interlude to congregational chorale singing, or in place of the congregation during alternate stanzas of a chorale. In addition, it could have been performed outside the service during an organ concert.

Among Bach's freely composed works for organ, there is less order and far less agreement on chronology. A tendency to construct movements in pairs seems clear; the opening movement of the pair, variously titled PRELUDE, TOCCATA, or even FANTASIA, generally unfolds in an improvisatory manner that is perfectly complemented by the contrapuntal severity of the succeeding fugue movement. A number of Bach's most outstanding compositions exemplify this aesthetically satisfying combination, among them the Toccata and Fugue in F Major (BWV 540) and the Prelude and Fugue in C Major (BWV 547). Some exceptional works offer three movements, such as the magnificent Toccata, Adagio, and Fugue in C Major (BWV 564) composed at Weimar. Although the freely composed works may have been intended primarily for concert performance or for pedagogical purposes, they may also have served as preludes and postludes to church services. (See examples 16a–c.) For a comprehensive introduction to the organ works of Bach, the reader is referred to *The Organ Music of J. S. Bach*, by Peter Williams (Cambridge University Press, 1980–84, 3 vols.); a numbered list (the source of the BWV numbers) may be found in the invaluable thematic catalog of all Bach's works by Wolfgang Schmieder, *Thematisch-systematisches Verzeichnis der musikalischen Werke Johann Sebastian Bachs: Bach-Werke-Verzeichnis* (6th ed., Breitkopf & Haertel, 1977).

Vocal compositions for the church constitute more than half of the many volumes required to publish Bach's complete works. Among them are approximately two hundred CANTATAS, two PASSIONS, three ORATORIOS, several MASSES, a MAGNIFICAT, a number of MOTETS, and many sacred songs. Five complete cycles of cantatas (more than three hundred works) were composed for the church year; nearly two-thirds of them have been preserved. Most of the church cantatas were written between 1723 and 1730 at Leipzig, when Bach threw himself wholeheartedly into the creation of what he referred to as "well-regulated church music." Extensive research into watermarks on manuscript paper, handwriting of copyists, and the specific calendars of the Leipzig church year has revealed that Bach composed his first cycle of cantatas (each of which number about sixty) for 1723-24, the second (a chorale-based cycle) for 1724-25, the third over the longer span of 1725 to 1727, and the fourth during 1728-29; the fifth, reflecting the composer's disillusionment with his situation, occupied much of the next decade and often involved re-use (with revision) of earlier works, a method known to scholars as parody technique. It was Bach's custom as a composer to adopt traditional practices rather than to invent new forms; therefore, the diversity of his cantatas and their place in the history of church music may perhaps be best understood by referring to the standard history by Friedrich Blume entitled *Protestant Church Music* (Norton, 1974).

Bach's cantatas remain largely unknown and unperformed in contemporary churches because of the wide variety of their instrumentation and their need for virtuoso vocal and instrumental soloists. In the composer's time they were performed before and after the sermon in the Lutheran service. Bach's contribution to the genre stems not only from the quality of his music, but also from the noteworthy manner in which he constructed and unified these large-scale works. In the Reformation cantata entitled "Ein' feste Burg ist unser Gott" (A Mighty Fortress Is Our God, BWV 80), for example, Bach arranged eight movements so that the first, fifth, and eighth are four-voice choruses featuring the famous CHORALE melody; on either side of the center of the work are independent recitatives and movements for soloists in which the chorale tune does not appear. As for Bach's varied treatment of the chorale, the first chorus constitutes a grand chorale fantasia, the fifth a ritornello form with orchestral interludes between phrases of the chorale, and the eighth an unadorned four-voice setting; in addition, the second movement of the cantata offers both a unifying ritornello and the chorale melody treated as a CANTUS FIRMUS.

The other large sacred vocal compositions of the Leipzig years, among them the *St. Matthew Passion,* the *Magnificat,* the *Christmas Oratorio,* and the Mass in B-Minor, represent the highest level of Baroque development in their respective genres; they also reveal an unappreciated Bach turning from the composition of functional church music for the liturgy to religious music for concert performance or for his own pleasure.

Although the lack of understanding and support from his contemporaries certainly affected the nature and the quantity of Bach's output, its quality remained unaffected and served as a standard for succeeding generations of composers. Today, in an era of informality and of preference for commercially successful popular styles, the church music of Bach remains in the repertory wherever there are musicians who feel equal to its challenge. Just as the music of Palestrina has come to represent a proper style for the Roman Catholic church, so the music of J. S. Bach now serves as a model for Protestant church music.

Baptist church music—Although the Baptist church was founded in North America in 1639, it was not until the early eighteenth century that the powerful effect of music began to overcome English Baptists' opposition to congregational singing. Soon hymn singing began to supersede psalm singing in importance, the hymnals being strongly influenced by the general rise of English hymnody. Well before the division of the Baptist church into northern and southern groups in 1845, the two regions had adopted different hymnals that reflected their spiritual and cultural differences. Only with the emergence of GOSPEL MUSIC in the nineteenth century did the two segments of the church join their efforts to produce *The New Baptist Hymnal* (1926), which nevertheless could not compete in the South with the immense popularity of a kind of gospel song quite different from the folk hymn that remained popular in the North.

Opposition to instrumental music and choral music in the Baptist church took longer to overcome than opposition to congregational singing, and it greatly impeded the development of these arts, especially in the South. In the twentieth century, a welcome trend towards elevating the role of music in the Baptist service has resulted in the formal recognition of church music and the establishment of music ministry programs at leading Baptist seminaries. (See also PSALMODY, HYMNODY, and GOSPEL MUSIC.)

Baroque period—A term referring to the era between about 1600 and 1750. Although this was a time of religious conflict between Catholics and Protestants, church music experienced a great flowering in its traditional forms (the MOTET and the ANTHEM), and especially in the new genres (ORATORIO and the church CANTATA) that came about with the gradual adoption of monody after 1600. The period also proved to be a golden one for the composition of ORGAN MUSIC. (For the names of the major composers of Baroque church music, consult the table, Composers Arranged Chronologically by Genre, that precedes the Introduction.)

Beethoven, Ludwig (1770–1827) – So far had the prestige of vocal music, and especially of vocal church music, fallen during the later stages of the Enlightenment that Beethoven was able to establish himself as the principal successor to Haydn simply on the strength of his instrumental works. Although the composer had ample opportunity to become familiar with the traditions and repertory of church music during his years at the elector's court in Bonn, where he received his musical training as an organist, it was not until the first decade of the nineteenth century that he composed an oratorio and his first Mass.

Christus am Oelberge (Christ on the Mount of Olives) was composed hastily in 1803 for a concert which also featured three instrumental works. The oratorio reflects a degree of caution and a dependence upon tradition characteristic of the composer's first efforts in a new genre. On the one hand is the work's debt to opera, seen principally in Beethoven's highly dramatic treatment of the part of Christ, whose agony in the garden, arrest, and confrontation with Peter form the highlights of the plot; on the other hand, also not quite fully assimilated, is the closing fugal chorus, which draws on the Viennese contrapuntal tradition. The first performance was not entirely successful. After revising his oratorio, first in 1804 and then for publication in 1811, Beethoven still took care to refer to it as "my first work in that style as well as an early work." Of greater significance are the composer's two Masses. In them his goal was to reconcile, without the distraction of operatic expression of emotion, the largely conventional structures and ceremonial character of the Viennese Mass with his hard-won mastery of the Classical symphonic ideal.

Beethoven's Mass in C (Op. 86) was composed in 1807 for the same patron, Prince Nikolaus Esterhazy II, and for the same occasion, the name day of the Prince's wife, as the last six Masses by Haydn. It is possible that Haydn had something to do with his former pupil receiving the commission. Beethoven's worst fears concerning the inevitable comparison were realized when both the rehearsal and the first performance went badly, and Prince Esterhazy did not like the Mass. Among traditional features of the Mass in C are its setting for four soloists, standard four-voice choir, orchestra, and organ, and the basically conventional structure of the individual movements of the Mass Ordinary. There is fugal writing where it would be expected at the end of the Credo and in the Hosanna. The composer has also learned from Haydn's example how to employ the soloists as a unit or accompanied by the choir, rather than in solo arias, and how to achieve unity within, between, and among movements by means of a symphonic reliance upon thematic development and large-scale tonal coherence. Like Haydn, Beethoven places a cyclical return of the Kyrie theme at the end of the Agnus Dei. He most likely displeased his contemporaries and Prince Esterhazy with his subjective approach to key words and phrases of the text, and in his newly characteristic use of greater contrasts than had been known of key, timbre, dynamic levels, and articulation. During his extensive efforts at publication of the Mass, which finally took place in 1812 with a dedication to Prince Ferdinand Kinsky, Beethoven wrote: "Notwithstanding the utterly frigid attitude of our age to works of this kind, the Mass is especially close to my heart."

When Beethoven completed the last of his three religious works, the *Missa Solemnis* (Op. 123), he felt that it was his masterpiece. Unlike the previous church works, it seems to have been born of an inner need as well as in response to an appropriate occasion, the installation of his friend, the Archduke Rudolf, as Archbishop of Olmuetz in 1820: "The day on which a High Mass composed by me will be performed during the ceremonies solemnized for Your Imperial Highness will be the most glorious day of my life." With some interruptions, the composer was to labor over the Mass from 1819 until 1823, pouring into it the results of extensive liturgical, linguistic, theological, and musical research and making it, in a truly Romantic manner, a personal testament. His concern for musical exegesis, or the interpretation of words and meanings of the Mass text, goes even further than in his Mass in C, resulting in a composition of enormous length and even more numerous, more abrupt, and greater contrasts of mood and style. The orchestra is called upon much more often than before for tone-painting, both symbolic and expressive. The quartet of soloists also serves the composer as a means for subjective interjections, a surprising number of them of a traditional nature. A special effort is required to unify such diversity. In both the Gloria and the Credo, for example, the composer employs recurring themes and short orchestral ritornellos in a symphonic manner; the Agnus Dei unfolds in a rondo-like structure. In his *Missa Solemnis*, Beethoven achieves a remarkable synthesis between the Classical symphonic ideal and traditional church music of a celebratory, not a functional, kind.

bells — Handbells and tower bells have been used in the church since about the fifth century, although finely crafted sets of tuned bells date from only about the twelfth century. Tower bells rang for worship services and tolled for the dead, as well as marking the hours and signalling townspeople about various emergencies. Mechanisms for ringing bells automatically were developed in the fourteenth century, and were followed in the fifteenth and sixteenth centuries by the CARILLON.

Benedicamus Domino — Latin words meaning "Let us bless the Lord." It was a favorite chant among Medieval composers, who used various of its melodies as the basis for polyphonic compositions. The text occurs in the Roman Catholic liturgy at the end of COMPLINE and, occasionally, as a substitution for the "Ite missa est" at the end of the MASS.

Benedicite — Latin for "Bless ye (the Lord)," the opening of the Canticle of the Three Children in the Fiery Furnace, which is found in the Apocryphal additions inserted in the third chapter of the Book of Daniel.

benediction — In a general sense, a blessing; church services customarily close with a benediction. In the Roman Catholic church the term refers to a worship service in which the congregation is blessed with the Host.

Benedictus — Part of the SANCTUS of the Mass Ordinary, the Benedictus came to be set as a separate movement (eventually featuring vocal soloists) in elaborate polyphonic settings of the MASS.

Berlioz, Hector (1803–1869) — One of the most original of Romantic composers, Berlioz is generally regarded by twentieth-century music historians as the leading French composer of the nineteenth century. During his lifetime, however, he did not find success at the Paris Opera, his primary goal, and he was largely ignored by the leading concert-giving society in Paris. To make a living he was forced to write a great deal of music journalism and criticism and to undertake numerous concert tours in Germany, England, and Russia. Considering the conservative state of affairs in the commercial music world at the time, it is not surprising that although Berlioz composed some noteworthy music on sacred texts, it does not constitute church music, and he never considered being a church musician. When he was drawn to express his decidedly unorthodox religious feelings, he made use of several liturgical texts, but his settings were not intended to function within a worship service. It is significant that his monumental Requiem Mass (*Grande Messe des Morts*, 1837) was not commissioned by or for the church, but by the government minister of the interior. A second masterpiece on a liturgical text, his *Te Deum* (1849), was first performed not in a church, but at the Exposition Universelle of 1855. Both of these works were conceived and carried out on a vast scale for tenor soloist, large choruses, and large orchestras, without a thought for their liturgical roles in the church. In the *Requiem,* an already large orchestra is augmented by eight pairs of timpani and four groups of added brass at the four corners of the orchestra. When they are employed in the "Tuba mirum" (The Trumpet Blasting), it is in the service not of church doctrine but of the composer's personal vision of the Last Judgment. In the *Te Deum,* a children's chorus of six hundred is required in addition to a soloist, double chorus, orchestra, and organ. In both works, movements of unprecedented grandeur are set in perspective by wonderfully intimate movements, as in "Quid sum miser" in the *Requiem.* The third noteworthy composition on a religious subject by Berlioz is *L'enfance du Christ.* Composed in 1854, it offers an account of the "childhood of Christ" in three parts: "The Dream of Herod," "The Flight into Egypt," and "The Arrival at Sais." Unlike the earlier works, this religious piece requires no special resources – only soloists, chorus, and normal orchestra. As in earlier works, but now with quite a different subject, the composer sought what he termed "accuracy of expressive content." Although the religious music of Berlioz has found little place in the church, the experience of hearing these works performed well in the concert hall might well convert a music lover.

Billings, William (1746–1800) – Born in Boston, Massachusetts, and largely self-educated, Billings may well have been the outstanding native American composer of the eighteenth century. In spite of his unprepossessing appearance and lack of training, he was able for some years to support himself by composing and teaching singing in some of Boston's finest churches. In 1770, he published 120 vocal settings of the psalms in *The New-England Psalm-singer*; this was the first book of psalm tunes by one American composer and also the first collection of music devoted entirely to American music. Although Billings later deprecated this collection, it proved to be influential and it contained some of his best-known tunes, among them "Chester" and "Amherst." Five other tunebooks by Billings followed, the most popular of them appearing in 1778 under the title *The Singing Master's Assistant.* More than two-thirds of this collection consisted of new compositions, some of them of a patriotic or humorous nature, in keeping with his role of singing master. Among the most impressive sacred pieces are the psalm tune "Majesty" ("The Lord Descended from Above"), the anthem entitled "I Am the Rose of Sharon" and the composer's moving paraphrase of Psalm 137 ("Lamentation over Boston"). Of the later collections, *Music in Miniature* (1779) contained only psalm tunes; *The Psalm-singer's Amusement* (1781) offered perhaps Billings's most outstanding anthems; *The Suffolk Harmony* (1786) included settings of universalist religious texts quite unlike texts used for standard hymns; and *The Continental Harmony* (1794) made available a selection of works from various periods of his career.

Altogether, Billings composed approximately 350 works, the majority of them settings of psalms or hymns. Anthems and fuging tunes each number about fifty; the latter group represents an Anglo-American tradition in which at least one section of a piece offers contrapuntal entries with textual overlap. All of the composer's works are written for four-voice chorus; in the psalm and hymn settings, however, he encouraged the curious practice of having some sopranos double the principal tenor melody (as well as having tenors double the soprano line an octave lower. Some of Billings's works were published singly, among them anthems for Easter and for Thanksgiving; the Easter anthem is said to have been the most popular anthem by an American composer of the time. (See example 2.) Unfortunately, the later collections by Billings were not so well-received as the early ones, and he found it increasingly necessary to work at other trades to make a living; *The Continental Harmony* represented a charitable undertaking sponsored by various musical societies to ameliorate his financial distress.

BMV (or BVM)—Abbreviation for the Latin words *Beatae Mariae Virginis*, meaning Blessed Virgin Mary.

Book of Common Prayer (Booke of Common Praier)—The basic liturgical text of the Church of England. First issued in 1549 and then revised significantly in 1552 and 1662, it contains the daily Offices of MORNING PRAYER and EVENING PRAYER, the order of COMMUNION, and such other rites as Baptism, Matrimony, and Burial as well as the Psalter and the Ordinal. Its use was suspended from 1553 to 1558 (the reign of Mary I) and from 1645 to 1660 (the time of the Puritan Commonwealth). In 1980 a supplement designed to be used in conjunction with *The Book of Common Prayer* appeared, entitled *The Alternative Service Book*. (See also the entries ANGLICAN LITURGY and SERVICE.)

Boyce, William (1711–1779)—One of the leading native-born composers in eighteenth-century England, Boyce not only composed dramatic music, songs, sonatas, symphonies, and church music, but also edited a significant three-volume anthology entitled *Cathedral Music*. The composer served for most of his life as a church organist, eventually becoming in 1758 one of three organists of the CHAPEL ROYAL. From 1755 he held the post of Master of the King's Musick. His church music, which seems not, on the whole, to equal his instrumental works in interest, includes more than sixty ANTHEMS, twenty-two HYMNS, one ORATORIO, ten organ VOLUNTARIES, and some liturgical music for the Anglican SERVICE. There is doubt as to his authorship of the best-known among the anthems, "O, Where Shall Wisdom Be Found?" In the later part of his life, which was marked by increasing deafness, Boyce chose not to modify his essentially Baroque style along Classical lines.

Brahms, Johannes (1833–1897)—Although he never held a church position, Brahms was one of the few major composers of the nineteenth century to write a significant amount of music suitable for use in church. In part his compositions with religious texts represent his orientation towards tradition, particularly his fascination with the contrapuntal art of the Renaissance and Baroque periods; in part they exist because the composer served for some years as a conductor of choral groups for which he composed some music. Several works for female chorus, for example, date from the period 1859 to 1862, during which Brahms founded and conducted such a group in Hamburg. When in 1863 he succeeded for a year to the position of director of the Vienna Singakademie, he undertook a series of *a cappella* works for mixed choir. His religious choral works were thus performed in the concert hall rather than in the church. His religious orientation was unorthodox, resting upon his love for and knowledge of the Bible rather than upon institutional doctrine. As conductor from 1872 to 1875 of the orchestra and chorus of the Vienna Gesellschaftskonzerte, he presented both Catholic and Protestant church music with regard only for its quality, an approach that surprised Viennese concertgoers.

Whether from inclination or from the desire to compose suitable music for immediate use, Brahms composed a considerable number of motets, as well as part-songs to Biblical or to chorale texts. Among the early small-scale works are the *Geistliches Lied* (Sacred Song), Op. 30 ("Lass dich nur nichts dauern"), for mixed choir in four voices with organ or piano accompaniment, and Psalm 13, Op. 27 ("Herr, wie lange"), for female choir with organ or piano. The former demonstrates the contrapuntal mastery of the composer as early as 1856 in its use of double canon at the interval of a ninth. Unaccompanied early works with religious texts include three *Geistliches Choere* (Sacred Choruses), Op. 37, for female choir, and two five-voice motets for mixed choir published as Opus 29. The former work invoked the spirit of Palestrina, thus receiving a warm reception from those involved in the CECILIAN MOVE-

MENT, but the motets revealed his thorough knowledge of the music of J. S. Bach. The first motet, "Es ist das Heil uns kommen her" (The Grace of God Has Come to Man), makes use of both chorale and fugue writing, while the second, "Schaffe in mir" (Create in Me), precedes each of its two fugues with a canon. Among the early religious works that call for instrumental accompaniment, the most striking also recalls the style of Bach; "Begraebnisgesang" (Burial Song), Op. 13 ("Nun lasst uns den Leib begraben"), for mixed five-voice choir, wind instruments, and timpani, reveals the composer coming to terms with the theme of death and resurrection, a subject that remained close to his heart.

As in the finest of the early compositions to religious texts, so in the smaller works from later in Brahms's career, mastery of counterpoint and evocation of a traditional style (now that of the late sixteenth and early seventeenth centuries) never inhibit his musical expression. The first of two unaccompanied motets from Opus 74, "Warum ist das Licht gegeben" (Why Is Light Given), reveals use of both chorale technique and canon, but now with greater freedom and without eclipsing the composer's individuality. The second, "O Heiland, reiss die Himmel auf" (O Savior, Rend the Heavens Apart), offers an impressive series of chorale variations. Brahms's last collection of motets, also unaccompanied by instruments, was published in 1890 as Opus 110. The third (and last) of them, "Wenn wir in hoechsten Noeten sein" (When We Are in Deepest Need), displays a magnificent synthesis of personal expression with antiphonal writing in the early Baroque Venetian tradition. (See example 3.)

Foremost among the composer's religious music is *Ein deutsches Requiem* (A German Requiem), Op. 45, one of the towering musical creations of the nineteenth century. It is not a Mass but rather a Protestant Requiem that Brahms shaped lovingly on words that he selected from Martin Luther's translation of the Bible to offer consolation to those left grieving. Completed in 1868, the composition occupied Brahms for more than a decade. In it, he wrote for soloists, mixed chorus, and full orchestra for the first time. On its seven movements he lavished all that he had learned from tradition and the full measure of his own unique, yet fundamentally Romantic, expressive genius.

Brahms's organ music, like his choral music, reveals his strong affinity for tradition and his ultimate synthesis of traditional means with his own musical language. In 1856 and 1857 he composed several preludes and fugues in the spirit of the Baroque period, among them a chorale and fugue on "O Traurigkeit, O Herzeleid" (O Heart-Breaking Sadness). When his life was drawing to a close, the composer returned to the genre

EXAMPLE 3.   Johannes Brahms, "Wenn wir in hoechsten Noeten sein," Op. 110, no. 3 (meas. 60–65)

with the eleven chorale preludes of Opus 122, works that should be known by every church organist. The last composition by Brahms before his death in 1897 was a chorale setting of "O Welt, ich muss dich lassen" (O World, I Must Leave Thee).

Breviary—The Roman Catholic liturgical book containing the texts for the OFFICE; see also ANTIPHONAL.

Britten, (Edward) Benjamin (1913–1976)—An outstanding British composer, Britten wrote prolifically in a wide variety of forms, the most successful of which were his operas and art songs. Works like the song cycle *Serenade* (1943) and the opera *Peter Grimes* (1945) soon entered the standard repertory, bringing with them a degree of economic independence rare for a twentieth-century composer. For Britten, this meant that he could increasingly concentrate his efforts on expressing his strong ethical and moral concerns in his music. Personally unconventional, although fundamentally conservative in his musical language, Britten generally avoided conventional church music as a medium for his message of peace and tolerance, preferring to appeal directly to a wider community. Functional church music, such as his *Te Deum* of 1934 (not completed until 1961) and the *Missa Brevis* of 1959, is rare among the larger number of concert works on religious texts. Cantata-like compositions are particularly prominent in the composer's early years. They included: *A Boy Was Born* (1933), a challenging set of chorale variations for unaccompanied choir; *A Ceremony of Carols* (1942), an enduringly popular cycle of Christmas carols for boys' voices and harp; *Rejoice in the Lamb* (1943), a festival cantata in the spirit of Purcell for four soloists, chorus, and organ; and *Saint Nicolas* (1948), a cantata for tenor, adolescent choruses, string orchestra, piano duet, percussion, and organ. With the exception of *Cantata Misericordium* (1961), a Latin setting of the parable of the Good Samaritan, Britten's later years found him employing dramatic music to reach his audience, as in *Noyes Fludde* (1957), a setting of the Chester Miracle play for both children's and adults' voices, chorus, orchestra, and chamber ensemble. The three parables composed for performance at Orford Church during the Aldeburgh Festival— *Curlew River* (1964), *The Burning Fiery Furnace* (1966), and *The Prodigal Son* (1968)— constitute a unique revival of medieval LITURGICAL DRAMA, inspired no less by Western plainchant than by the stylized ritual of Japanese Noh drama. Perhaps the greatest among Britten's religious works and his strongest denunciation of war was composed for the consecration of Coventry Cathedral in 1962; set for three soloists, chorus, boys' choir, organ, chamber orchestra, and full orchestra, the *War Requiem* achieves its unconventional immediacy through the interspersal of the war poems of Wilfred Owen among the liturgical texts that make up the REQUIEM MASS.

Bruckner, Anton (1824–1896) — Only after a long period of training did Bruckner emerge as one of the major Romantic composers of church music. Until he was forty years old, he appeared to be just another provincial Austrian schoolteacher, organist, and choirmaster. During his years as organist at the monastery of Saint Florian and subsequently at the cathedral in Linz, he mastered the traditional elements of his style by composing approximately thirty-five functional works for the Roman Catholic Church, among them five MASSES (one left incomplete), two REQUIEM MASSES (one lost), a MAGNIFICAT, and many Latin MOTETS. In 1863, he encountered the music of Wagner, an experience which set him free creatively and led directly to the masterpieces of his maturity. The transformation is only somewhat less amazing if, as Robert Simpson suggests, the composer had gradually evolved in his organ improvisations a personal idiom that had not yet found expression in his compositions.

The first composition of Bruckner's maturity as a composer was his Mass in D Minor of 1864, a large-scale work for four soloists, chorus, organ, and orchestra. It was followed in 1866 by a Mass in E Minor, in which the composer acknowledges the ideals of the CECILIAN MOVE-MENT, even to the use of unaccompanied choral passages and a theme by Palestrina in the Sanctus; nevertheless, the hand of the Romantic master is revealed in the varied textures and harmonies that Bruckner secures from his chorus of singers in eight parts and his ensemble of fifteen wind instruments. The Mass in F Minor, like the Mass of 1864, is a large-scale composition for soloists, chorus, organ, and orchestra. Not completed until 1868, and composed on a grand scale that suggests the concert hall, it brought to an end the period of Bruckner's absorption with the Mass. In 1867, Bruckner's career had taken him to Vienna, the center of musical Europe, where his duties were largely to teach harmony and counterpoint at the Vienna Conservatory (later at the University of Vienna) and his mission was to become a significant composer of symphonies.

Among the sacred compositions of Bruckner's later years are several that by themselves place him among the best of Romantic composers for the church. On a grand scale for soloists, chorus, and orchestra are his *Te Deum* (1884) and Psalm 150 (1892); more functional but of no less quality are a number of Latin motets, among them "Os justi" (The Mouth of the Just, 1879), "Christus factus est" (Christ Was Made Obedient, 1879, revised for unaccompanied chorus in 1884), and "Virga Jesse floruit" (The Rod of Jesse Blossomed, 1885). His organ music, mostly preludes, does not reach the same level, apparently the victim of his extraordinary skill in improvisation.

burden—The refrain of a CAROL.

Burgundian period—The years from about 1419 to 1477, a time in which both sacred and secular music flourished at the court of the Dukes of Burgundy. The outstanding composer of the time was Guillaume DUFAY.

Buxtehude, Dieterich (c. 1637–1707)—Regarded by his contemporaries and by subsequent scholars as the outstanding and most influential composer of organ music of the seventeenth century, Buxtehude also excelled in sacred vocal music, particularly in what is now loosely termed the church CANTATA. Probably born in Danish-governed Holstein to a family that had moved there from Germany, he was educated by his father, an organist and schoolteacher, whom he succeeded as organist at Helsingborg in about 1657. From 1660 to 1667 he served as organist at the Marienkirche in Helsingor. In 1668 he competed for and won the important position of organist at the Marienkirche in the North German city of Luebeck. There for forty years he diligently supplied organ music and appropriate vocal music on Sundays and feast days for the principal morning service and the afternoon service as well as for Vespers on the preceding afternoon. On five Sundays a year, he also gave the famous concerts known as ABENDMUSIKEN.

Buxtehude's music was preserved largely in manuscript copies—the organ music in numerous scores or in tablature, and the vocal works in a relatively small number of sources. The keyboard manuscripts of the period offer a mixture of sacred and secular genres without specifying either the instrument or the purpose of the music. Strictly speaking, the worship service provided little opportunity for organ music; in churches that maintained use of the traditional liturgy, however, it became customary to replace parts of the Ordinary or the Proper with organ music, and it was always in order to perform organ music (or indeed a motet or sacred concerted piece) during Communion.

The composer's approximately fifty settings of CHORALE melodies, particularly the small-scale CHORALE PRELUDES that offer just one stanza of the chorale as an introduction to congregational singing, constitute his most clearly functional organ compositions. In "Durch Adams Fall ist ganz verderbt" (Through Adam's Fall), for example, the chorale melody appears with ornamentation in the top voice, accompanied by three parts, the lowest one for organ pedals; the sorrowful character of the music, with its affective use of chromaticism, expresses the meaning of the first verse of the chorale text. (See example 4.) Buxtehude's larger compositions on chorale melodies reflect the virtuosity of this generation of North German organists, their skill at improvisatory self-expression, and the wonderful tonal resources of the North German Baroque organ. In the composers's CHORALE FANTASIA on "Nun freut' euch, lieben Christen gmein" (Now Rejoice, Dear Christians), the seven phrases of the chorale serve as a foundation for an expansive setting in ten clearly articulated and richly varied sections.

EXAMPLE 4. Dieterich Buxtehude, "Durch Adams Fall," BuxWV 183 (meas. 19–23)

Buxtehude's approximately forty free organ works—those without CANTUS FIRMUS—represent the composer's unique synthesis of style traits from both northern and southern Germany. Idiomatic toccata-like passages alternate in an unsystematic manner with more clearly structured fugal sections, as in the Praeludium in E Minor (Buxtehude-Werke-Verzeichnis 142); in this instance, the preludial and improvisatory sections are overshadowed by three subtly interrelated and masterfully worked out fugues. In the great Praeludium in C Pedaliter (BuxWV 137), a stunningly virtuosic opening toccata section and modulatory fugue are followed by a closing *chaconne* (a variation form) and improvisatory coda; once again, unity is achieved through motivic relationships among the sections.

Nearly all of Buxtehude's more than 125 extant vocal works were composed on sacred texts. Today they are generally referred to as church cantatas, although most of them belong to the traditional categories of the sacred vocal concerto (usually for one solo voice), the strophic chorale setting in homophonic style, and the sacred aria. When the composer combined elements from different categories into a unified work with several independent movements, he created church cantatas in the modern sense. They include works for a large ensemble ("Laudate pueri"), dialogue cantatas ("Herr, ich lasse dich nicht"), ode cantatas ("Jesulein, du Tausendschoen"), and even a small number of chorale cantatas ("Wachet auf, ruft uns die Stimme"). In the words of Friedrich Blume in *Protestant Church Music* (Norton, 1974, p. 275), "None of his contemporaries could rival the penetration of Buxtehude's expressiveness or the richness of his methods of text interpretation or his romantic lyricism. At the same time, he was the most advanced musician in respect to style."

BWV—These letters form an abbreviation for *Bach-Werke-Verzeichnis* (Bach Works List), a comprehensive thematic catalog of the works of J. S. Bach by Wolfgang Schmieder. (Schmieder, or S, numbers are the same as BWV numbers.) Musicians must be acquainted with the BWV numbers (and with other such bibliographic tools) in order to identify works that bear only a generic title, such as Prelude and Fugue in C or Toccata and Fugue in d. (For example, Bach's much played Toccata and Fugue in D Minor is BWV 565 not BWV 538, the less well-known work by the same title). Consultation of the Schmieder catalog will supply the BWV numbers of many works in common use in the church but not identified by the editors or publishers.

Byrd, William (1543–1623)—Widely recognized by his contemporaries as the finest composer of Tudor England, Byrd mastered the chief styles of his time, particularly the art of counterpoint of the Netherlands. His career led him from Lincoln Cathedral, where he served as organist and choirmaster from 1563 to 1572, to the CHAPEL ROYAL in London, where he stayed for the remainder of his life. There, despite his staunch Roman Catholicism, he excelled in church music as well as consort songs, madrigals, and music for the virginal. His influence on musical life stemmed not only from his music, but also from his license to print and sell music in England, which he held with Tallis from 1575 until 1596, and from his efforts as a teacher.

For the Anglican rite Byrd composed two SERVICES, two settings of the MAGNIFICAT and NUNC DIMITTIS (sometimes referred to as his second and third Services), various LITANIES, PRECES, RESPONSES, and nearly sixty ANTHEMS. His Great Service contains the usual seven items of the Services of that era, set for five to eight voices in a generally contrapuntal manner that displays all of his consummate mastery; especially noteworthy is his care to vary the texture, as well as the number and timbre, of the voices within and among the various movements. The so-called "Short Service" contains all the usual items and a Sanctus; its name comes from the basically simple chordal setting of the words. Byrd's anthems are of two kinds, traditional motet-like full anthems (e.g., "Arise, O Lord") and concertato-like verse anthems ("Behold, O God"). In the latter type of anthem, which may owe its origin to Byrd, passages for solo voice or voices with accompaniment are set in contrast to those for full choir. "Christ Rising Again," a verse anthem published in 1589, displays a characteristically subjective approach to the text involving detailed tone-painting as well as contrasting timbres, textures, and meters. The composer's anthem texts were drawn most often from the psalms, and less frequently from nonbiblical religious poetry, optional Anglican Collects, and various CAROLS.

Byrd's Latin church music stands comparison with the best ever composed in that language. There are three MASSES, in three, four, and five voices, each apparently freely composed and each an example of the motto-type Mass. The two books of motets entitled *Gradualia* comprise not just GRADUALS, but thirteen complete settings of the Mass PROPER, including one for Christmas, one for Easter, and several for the Blessed Virgin. Among the MOTETS are some of his masterpieces. Works like "Ave verum" (Hail, O True Body), "Exsurge Domine" (Arise, O Lord), and "Emendemus in melius" (Let Us Atone) reveal both his extraordinary sense of structure and his acute sensitivity to his texts. In Byrd's setting of "Emendemus in melius" (from the *Cantiones sacrae* of 1575), form is determined by the liturgical text, which is a proper for Matins on the first Sunday in Lent. Part 1 presents man as a sinner seeking salvation, while part 2 embodies a plea for deliverance through God's mercy. Each phrase of text receives its own melodic and harmonic setting, and each phrase is clearly articulated by cadences, which often fall in rhythmically unexpected places. Texture is a major form-giving element since each part begins with chordal declamation, followed by carefully graded levels of increasing rhythmic activity, until a climax is reached just before the end. Truly contrapuntal writing is reserved for the cadences in such a way that the second, shorter part receives the most striking melodic material, the most elaborate use of counterpoint, and the strongest cadence in the composition. (See example 5.)

EXAMPLE 5. William Byrd, "Emendemus in melius," *Cantiones Sacrae* (meas. 47–54)

Calvin, Jean (Eng., John; 1509–1564)—Founder of the Reformed (or Calvinist) Church, Calvin recognized and feared the power of music and carefully sought to limit its use in the service to unison singing of psalms and some New Testament CANTICLES translated into the vernacular. The decline of church music was inevitable with such an attitude, since significant composers were excluded from serving the church. The most famous early Calvinist psalmbook was the Geneva PSALTER of 1562.

camp meeting—An informal gathering for the purpose of religious revival. It originated in the United States among itinerant eighteenth-century preachers and largely frontier or lower-class participants. Religious ballads, popular HYMNODY, and revival SPIRITUALS were used along with impassioned oratory to create an emotional catharsis and an assurance of salvation. (See also GOSPEL MUSIC.)

canon—Latin for "rule," this term refers to the manner in which a melody is turned into a polyphonic composition by successive overlapping entries in various parts. As a strict form of imitation, canon can be found in church music as early as the thirteenth century; it reached its height in sacred music during the Renaissance as a favorite technique of the great Franco-Flemish composers. The word "canon" also refers specifically in the Roman Catholic MASS to the prayer said after the SANCTUS to consecrate the elements of COMMUNION. In yet another meaning, a canon is a priest attached to a specific cathedral.

Canonical Hours—The Roman Catholic services that, until the Second Vatican Council, consisted of the eight daily parts of the Divine OFFICE: MATINS, LAUDS, PRIME, TERCE, SEXT, NONE, VESPERS, and COMPLINE. The liturgical books containing these prayer offices are, for the nonmonastic clergy, the *Roman Breviary*, and for ascetic monastic orders, the *Monastic Breviary*. Although Martin Luther opposed the length and complex structure of the Office, Matins and Vespers were retained in his *Deutsche Messe* (German Mass), and have been revived in several contemporary American Lutheran versions.

cantata—In the context of church music, the term most frequently refers to the Protestant church cantata, a composition in several movements for soloists, chorus, and orchestra (or organ). The church cantata served as the principal music of the Lutheran service, usually being linked closely by subject to the sermon and heard before and after it in the church service. The chorale cantata is a special kind of church cantata based wholly or in part upon a CHORALE melody.

It is important to realize that, used by itself, *cantata* (derived from *cantare*, meaning in Italian "to sing") properly refers to an Italian vocal genre in which a soloist or pair of soloists sing, usually on the theme of secular love, with continuo accompaniment. The Italian secular cantata came into being in the early seventeenth century as a realization of monody (expressive accompanied solo singing) for the chamber. Unlike opera, it was not staged and it did not call for an orchestra. Prominent among the ranks of its composers were Alessandro Scarlatti and, during his years in Italy, George Frideric Handel. Following the Italian model, the secular cantata in the vernacular also flowered in eighteenth-century France in works by composers like Louis-Nicolas Clérambault and Jean-Philippe Rameau. Significantly, the genre did not become a favorite of the Germans, who preferred to apply the new style to Latin religious texts that had previously served for polyphonic motets. As early as the works of Heinrich SCHUETZ (1585–1672) may be found sacred "concertos" that adopt the Italian style of separate sections in monodic style with instrumental accompaniment, as in the *Symphoniae Sacrae* (Sacred Symphonies) of 1629. (See example 6.) The use of a traditional German chorale melody may also be found in the early seventeenth-century sacred vocal concerto, as in the works of Johann Hermann Schein and, subsequently, those of Andreas Hammerschmidt and Franz Tunder.

Perhaps the outstanding composer of cantata-like, or concerted, church music in Germany before Bach was Tunder's successor in Luebeck, Dieterich BUXTEHUDE (1637–1707). His Sunday evening sacred

EXAMPLE 6. Heinrich Schuetz, "Anima mea liquefacta est," SWV 263, *Symphoniae Sacrae* I (meas. 65–72)

EXAMPLE 6, continued

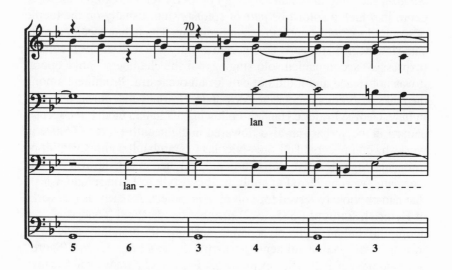

concerts (known as ABENDMUSIKEN) won widespread acclaim, and at different times drew both Handel and Bach to his services at Saint Mary's. In his sacred concerts, Buxtehude made use of the new, freer texts and styles of Italian dramatic music as well as the traditional strophic character of the German chorale, which resulted in a powerful alternation of recitatives and arias on the one hand and choruses and chorales on the other.

In Leipzig a strong tradition of church cantatas was established before the time of Bach by Johann Kuhnau and Friedrich Wilhelm Zachow. Their works were usually adapted from the Bible or the Lutheran liturgy and made use of chorales as well as of recitatives, arias, duets, and choruses. So indispensable to Protestant church life did the cantata become in the eighteenth century that many composers wrote at least five hundred such works and some, including such esteemed masters as Christoph Graupner and Georg Philipp TELEMANN, wrote more than one thousand.

The body of cantatas (few of them called such by the composer) by J. S. BACH constitutes an unparalleled wealth of Protestant church music. More than two hundred of his approximately three hundred cantatas, most of them for the church, have been preserved. It may have been Bach's intention to compose five complete cycles for the liturgical year, two of them chorale cantatas. Only about thirty cantatas date from before his appointment in 1723 at Leipzig, and most date from his first two decades in that city.

The church cantatas of Bach follow no standard form. Their texts are generally based on the new, more freely poetic model introduced by Erdmann Neumeister, in which paraphrases of liturgically appropriate biblical verses alternate with meditative glosses on the same themes, both taking forms and meters suitable for either recitative or formal numbers, such as aria or chorus. Most begin with an extended chorale fantasia for chorus and orchestra, which is succeeded by recitatives and arias or duets in no particular pattern; the ending is frequently a simple four-voice chorale harmonization for chorus and congregation. Their glory lies in Bach's transcendent use of all the expressive forms and devices of High Baroque music and his unique synthesis of German and Italian stylistic traditions.

Not surprisingly, the period after Bach proved considerably less fruitful for the cantata. Not only did the church decline as a patron of music, but purely instrumental forms like the symphony and the sonata, rather than church music, became the testing grounds of major composers. Such was emphatically the case during the Classical period, when Haydn, Mozart, and Beethoven contributed a few minor works to the genre. By the nineteenth century the church cantata had almost entirely lost its functional character and status and had become virtually a small-scale oratorio. Furthermore, at the same time that many composers were abandoning the term "cantata" for works that it might properly be applied to, it was increasingly used as a generic word for miscellaneous kinds of compositions, including liturgically proper ones such as the Stabat Mater, and secular ones with little or no connection to the historical cantata. In the examples by the principal Protestant composer of the era, Johannes BRAHMS, the cantata became basically a work for chorus and orchestra on a poetic text of a serious but not sacred nature. Only in England, with its strong tradition of choral singing, did the cantata retain some of its former importance, but even there the genre was often of a secular nature and not totally distinguishable, except by being smaller, from the oratorio.

In the twentieth century the term "cantata" has been used more freely by composers—perhaps not always when it would seem appropriate—while the general public appears to use it at random. For example, Carl Orff described as a "scenic cantata" his *Carmina Burana*, a setting for soloists, several choirs, and orchestra of a collection of Medieval secular texts. Nevertheless, noteworthy compositions with clear links to the sacred heritage of the genre remain, outstanding among them the sacred cantatas of Ralph VAUGHAN WILLIAMS and the chorale cantatas of Hugo DISTLER. (See example 7.) The turn towards evangelistic religion and gospel songs in the United States does not bode well for formal and functional genres such as the church cantata in the era of its glory. Those who wish to delve further into the history of the genre will find two sources especially helpful, Friedrich Blume's *Protestant Church Music: A History* (Norton, 1974) and Friedhelm Krummacher's article entitled "Cantata" in *The New Grove Dictionary* (vol. 3, 702-713).

Cantemus Domino—Latin for "Sing ye to the Lord," the opening of the canticle of Miriam and Moses, as found in Exodus 15.

Cantica de tempore—See DE TEMPORE HYMNS.

canticle—From the Latin for "song," this term refers to a lyrical chant on a biblical text not taken from the Psalms. The greater canticles (*cantica majora*) in the Roman Catholic liturgy are drawn from the New Testament; two of them are the MAGNIFICAT (sung at VESPERS) and the NUNC DIMITTIS (sung at COMPLINE). The lesser canticles (*cantica minora*), which are drawn from the Old Testament, include the "Cantemus Domino" (Sing to the Lord; Exodus 15:1-19) and "Confitebor Tibi" (Trust in the Lord; Isaiah 12). Canticles are also sung in the Lutheran service: the Magnificat, for example, is appropriate at Vespers and on all festivals.

cantiga—Spanish for "song," particularly with reference to Medieval monophonic songs about or in praise of the Virgin Mary.

EXAMPLE 7. Hugo Distler, *Wo Gott zum Haus* (opening of chorale stanza)

cantillation—The practice of chanting the text in Jewish religious worship. Cantillation was apparently done in free rhythm following notated accent marks and using stereotyped melodic formulas.

cantional style—A term referring to the homophonic style in which CHORALE melodies are set in a CANTIONALE.

Cantionale—A Latin word for a collection of Protestant CHORALE settings, most of which offer the melody in the soprano part, accompanied by three lower voices in simple chordal fashion. The basic format was established by Lucas Osiander's *Fuenfzig geistliche Lieder und Psalmen* (Fifty Sacred Songs and Psalms) of 1586, and it was followed by a great number of publications for the next twenty-five years, perhaps most significantly in collections by Hans Leo Hassler and Michael Praetorius. The cantionale settings were frequently used in alternation with unison congregational singing. (See ALTERNATIM.)

cantor—Latin for "singer." In the Roman Catholic service a cantor sings certain parts of the MASS. In Lutheran usage the cantor (or Kantor) directed the music program, which included teaching school and recruiting singers, as well as composing music. J. S. BACH served as a cantor in Leipzig. The Jewish cantor (*chazzan*) was the chief bearer of the religious ritual.

Cantorei (or Kantorei)—A term used originally for the musical establishment at a church or court, but since the sixteenth century applied to various kinds of singing groups, choir schools, and instrumental ensembles.

cantoris—The cantor (or precentor) of an English cathedral, second in rank to the dean (*decani*). Because the dean and the cantor sat on opposite sides of the chancel, the two parts of the divided choir were referred to as the *decani* choir and the *cantoris* choir.

cantus firmus—A Latin term referring to the common practice in church music of using a pre-existing melody, often a Gregorian CHANT, as the basis for a new polyphonic composition. In a cantus firmus MASS one pre-existing melody, sacred or secular in origin, unifies the sections of the Mass ORDINARY, as in the works of composers from DUFAY to VICTORIA. In the Lutheran Church, CHORALE melodies were commonly used as cantus firmi, as in the CHORALE PRELUDES and church CANTATAS of J. S. BACH.

cantus gregorianus—Latin for "Gregorian CHANT." By itself, the word *cantus* also refers to the highest, or soprano, voice in a polyphonic composition.

canzona—Italian for an instrumental song (modelled after the French chanson) played in either secular or sacred contexts. The most famous examples of ensemble canzonas are the forty or so by Giovanni GABRIELI, which were composed in CONCERTATO style for various instruments in a loosely shaped series of sections. The keyboard canzona was also performed during the church service. Those by Girolamo FRESCOBALDI unfold in three to six imitative sections linked by short passages of a contrasting character.

Capellmeister — See KAPELLMEISTER.

carillon — A set of approximately twenty-five to forty tuned BELLS which are played from a keyboard and pedalboard. The earliest carillons were built in the late fifteenth century in the Netherlands, where the best builders have been based. In the United States, interest in carillons has grown during the twentieth century; after 1950, technology led to the development of the electronic carillon.

Carissimi, Giacomo (1605–1674) — A highly significant Italian composer of ORATORIOS and secular cantatas, Carissimi played a major role in the early history of both genres. Born near Rome, he assumed in 1629 the position of maestro di cappella at the Roman church of Sant'Apollinare, whose reputation for excellence he continued for the rest of his life. In 1637 he became a priest. After about 1650, he is known to have on occasion directed the music at the Oratory of the Most Holy Crucifix, the center for Latin oratorio in Rome, and he also directed musical activities for a time at the residence of the exiled Queen Christina of Sweden. Accounts and letters by his contemporaries reflect the composer's fame, and such noteworthy students as the Frenchman Marc-Antoine CHARPENTIER and the German Christoph Bernhard took their knowledge of oratorio back to their own centers of culture.

Carissimi's liturgical music would not, by itself, have distinguished him from other Roman composers of the time. Of the three Masses that can be attributed to him with certainty, only one (*Missa a quinque et a novem*) displays in its contrasting textures a modern spirit. His numerous motets, on the other hand, are mostly composed in monodic style for a few voices and basso continuo. Seldom are their texts liturgical, as in the past, and some of them are large enough to be shaped in a series of contrasting sections. About thirty-five of them feature dialogue between different persons, and thus form a group of works known as dialogue-motets. Research has shown that compositions of this kind were often performed in the Mass during this period as substitutes for ANTIPHONS, GRADUALS, and OFFERTORIES.

The larger dialogue-motets by Carissimi are what came to be called oratorios, a term derived from their principal place of performance. Their basis in scripture and Latin text might also have resulted in the name *historia*. Despite the confusion in terminology, a difficulty compounded by the loss of all of the composer's original manuscripts, approximately fifteen works by Carissimi are commonly referred to as oratorios, among them *Jephte*, *Jonas*, *Judicium Salomonis*, and *Abraham et Isaac*. *Jephte* tells the Old Testament story (Judges 11) of an Israelite general who, in exchange for victory, vows to sacrifice the first person to greet him upon his return home. Carissimi uses a narrator (either a bass or an alto) to link the various parts of the story together, and he gives the chorus a substantial role by having them either comment upon the action or take the part of the soldiers or the Israelites. Expressive solo singing (known as monody) conveys the dramatic turn from triumph to despair as Jephte is greeted by his beloved daughter, and leads finally to her celebrated lament with chorus, which concludes the oratorio.

carol — In its twentieth-century meaning, a carol is a simple strophic song on a religious text usually associated with Christmas or Easter, whether the text is in English, Latin, German (properly a *Weihnachtslied*), or French (a NOEL). Medieval carols were verse and refrain structures of English origin on any subject, but were most often about Christmas or the Virgin Mary. Some were danced as well as sung. In contrast to the prevailing popular character of the genre, a polyphonic carol, also on a wide variety of subjects, flourished during the Renaissance. The popular and informal nature of the carol caused its suppression by the Puritans in England; therefore, the tradition of the carol had to be revived in nineteenth-century England and disseminated anew by such collections as *Christmas Carols New and Old* (1871) and the *Oxford Book of Carols* (1928).

cathedral music — A term referring to the relatively elaborate style of Anglican church music traditionally cultivated in the cathedral and formally espoused as a model during the Oxford Movement, in contrast to the simpler music of the parish church.

Cecilia — Although Saint Cecilia has been venerated since the late fifth century, her designation as patroness of music, which dates only from the late fifteenth century, is apparently unfounded. Nevertheless, Saint Cecilia's Day became the focal point of musical celebrations in France, England, Italy, and Germany, which resulted in such significant compositions as the Odes to Saint Cecilia by PURCELL and HANDEL.

Cecilian movement — In the Roman Catholic church, the name of Saint Cecilia united opposition to the adoption of a secular musical idiom in church music of the eighteenth century; the movement for reform in church music gained strength in the nineteenth century, and led to the publication of Renaissance church music and renewed interest in Gregorian CHANT. The Allgemeine Caecilien-Verein, founded in 1869 by Franz Witt and subsequently sanctioned by the Pope Pius IX, made a significant contribution by supporting the need for authentic editions of chant, as well as the cultivation of church choirs, congregational singing, music education for the clergy, and, prophetically, of church music in the vernacular. However, by its dedication to a revival of sixteenth-century counterpoint and its rejection of contemporary elements of style, the Cecilian movement lost an opportunity to help fashion a vital twentieth-century repertory of church music. In the United States, the Cecilian influence led to the formation of an American Society of Saint Cecilia, which published the magazine *Cecilia* (1874–1964), and then of the Society of Saint Gregory of America, which published *The Catholic Choirmaster*. In 1964 the two societies merged as the Church Music Association of America, which — through its magazine *Sacred Music* — seeks to carry on the Cecilian ideals.

centonization — A term used to describe the patchwork manner in which certain types of Gregorian CHANT appear to have been created (or perhaps orally transmitted) so that chants similar in function and mode share the same melodic formulas.

change-ringing — Tower bells in English churches are traditionally rung in a series of mathematically possible orders called a method, the earliest of which developed in the fourteenth century.

chanson spirituelle — French for "sacred song," the term refers to a special variety of late Renaissance chanson by both Catholic and Protestant composers. Among the most significant contributors to the genre were Claude Le Jeune and Orlandus LASSUS. Many *chansons spirituelles* were created simply by replacing the original secular text of a chanson with a religious text. (See CONTRAFACTUM.)

chant (plainsong, plainchant; in Latin, *cantus planus***)** — Used with specific reference to religious song, the word "chant" suggests monophonic rendering of a sacred text by an individual or a choir in a manner that does not detract from the words through emphasis on tune, meter, or vocal technique. (See also ANGLICAN LITURGY.)

Chant has served a religious purpose in many cultures, both Eastern and Western. For those interested primarily in the history of Western music, it suffices to point out that for the first thousand years of the Christian era, almost the only Western music that was preserved was sacred chant. Furthermore, Christian chant, most notably Gregorian chant, served as a principal foundation of polyphony until the close of the Renaissance. The nature of that great body of once functional religious music and its use in the liturgy form the principal subject of this essay.

Early Christians were Jews who attended both synagogue services and their own private services; therefore, it is not surprising that the repertory, melodic style, and performance practice of European Christian chant reveal its Eastern heritage as clearly as does the Christian church's adoption of a yearly cycle of services as the basis of its liturgy, and of Bible reading and psalm singing as significant elements of worship. Like the influence on Christianity from Classical Greek culture, the Jewish influence on Christianity was largely transmitted through the Eastern Orthodox, or Byzantine, church and is still reflected in the music of the Armenian, Coptic, Ethiopian, and Syrian Christian churches today. Just as remnants of the magical role of music in prehistoric times found their way into the Christian liturgy in the East, so elements of earlier bodies of chant are deeply embedded in Gregorian chant, which has long served as the official liturgical music of the Roman Catholic church. Chant texts that include Greek words (such as "KYRIE ELEISON"), chants created after Byzantine models, and the steady stream of men and women of the church from East to West all document influence from the Eastern Christian church.

In addition to its Eastern heritage, Gregorian chant was presumably influenced by several kinds of Western chant that either preceded or developed alongside it. Among them were Gallican chant (in Medieval France), Celtic chant (in Medieval Ireland, Scotland, parts of England, and some places on the continent), Mozarabic (or Hispanic) chant (in Medieval Spain), and Ambrosian chant (still in use in the archdiocese of Milan). Except for Ambrosian chant, for which the earliest manuscripts date from the twelfth century and cannot be assumed to represent the period or the efforts of Saint Ambrose, little or no music exists for these liturgies.

The early history of the Latin liturgy in Rome remains virtually unknown. It seems that the transition from Greek to Latin during the third and fourth centuries brought with it stricter regulation of the liturgy until, by the sixth century, prayers, readings, and chants for both the Mass ORDINARY and PROPER were rigidly prescribed. Similarly, the rise of monasticism brought standardization to the daily observances of the OFFICE, particularly through the influential rules established by Saint Benedict (480–543). Lacking a precise means to notate pitches and rhythms, church musicians had to preserve music by oral tradition during the early Medieval centuries. The earliest extant manuscripts containing Gregorian chant do not appear until the ninth century, and there is no way to know how closely they followed earlier models. It is possible that the notation of a chant represents one of many closely related versions that resulted from oral improvisation along well-established melodic and modal guidelines. Despite constant attempts to unify liturgical and musical practices, not until the eleventh century was there essential agreement on the Gregorian version, and not until the sixteenth century did most of the variations disappear.

The contributions of Pope Gregory I to the musical development of the liturgy remain unclear and wholly secondary to his assertion that the Roman pope had universal supremacy as the head of Christendom. Perhaps he simply carried on the process of organizing and regulating the liturgy; he certainly did not compose many, if any, of the so-called "Gregorian" plainchants himself, and he did not found the papal choir. Nevertheless, when Gregory I established papal authority in England, he laid the groundwork for the eventual adoption of the Roman liturgy by the Carolingian kings in the latter part of the eighth century—a momentous step for Western Christianity.

For five centuries after the coronation of Charlemagne in 800, the history of Western music, which was principally the history of church music, took place largely within the Franco-German domains that constituted the Carolingian Empire. With the weakening of the papacy, especially in the tenth century, Gallican elements clearly influenced the Roman Catholic liturgy, even as it was practiced in Rome. The impact of the northerners upon music may have been just as great. The earliest Gregorian chant manuscripts that contain musical notation all come from the empire, not from Rome. The extent to which Roman musical practice was ever established in the Carolingian empire is questionable; not only did the liturgical books sent from Rome in the eighth century contain no music, but highly regarded singing schools, such as those at Metz and Saint Gall, already existed to challenge the few singers imported from Rome. The Roman need for liturgical books of music seems to have brought Gallican chant (or perhaps "Gregorian chant" modified by centuries of use in the Franco-German empire) to Rome itself. That might help to explain the existence among Roman manuscripts of another, earlier body of chant quite distinct from Gregorian and presently called Old Roman chant.

The musical nature of Gregorian chant melodies reveals its Eastern ancestry in that, like Jewish chant, its melodies are drawn from a common fund of short melodic patterns appropriate for a specific pitch mode, a process known as CENTONIZATION. Through their choice and arrangement of traditional melodic patterns, their extensions and elaborations upon those patterns, and perhaps through insertions of some new material, the creators of chant exercised their anonymous artistry at a level higher than that of other commonly used Medieval methods of expanding the body of chant. These methods merely parodied existing chants or adapted them to new words. Development of a large body of chant through centonization helps explain why so many chant melodies fail to observe the rules of modal theory. So does the fixing of a systematic arrangement of the modes after a considerable number of chants had already been composed. According to the system of the church modes, there are two sets of four church modes based on the pitches d, e, f, and g; the range, reciting (r) tone, and final (f) tone (or cadence tone) of each mode are shown. (See example 8.)

EXAMPLE 8. Church modes

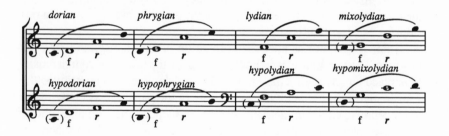

Gregorian chant has historically served several purposes in the Roman Catholic Church service, the principal one being to convey more audibly and richly the Scriptural readings and prayers, and the PSALMS and CANTICLES of the Office. As in the INTROIT, the OFFERTORY, and the COMMUNION of the Mass, music could accompany a procession or other liturgical event. Finally, music could stimulate an attitude of devotion, as in the GRADUAL, the ALLELUIA, and the TRACT of the Mass, or the RESPONSORY of the Office.

The various musical styles of chant are largely determined by its liturgical functions. Chant employed for Scriptural readings, for example, makes use of a reciting tone, which is one repeated pitch with occasional tones on either side to mark the beginnings and the ends of textual phrases. It represents not so much a musical composition as a formula for speech-song that can accommodate and articulate text of virtually any length and structure, so long as cadences are placed at appropriate places. Other chants recited largely on one pitch include COLLECTS, EPISTLES, and DOXOLOGIES. (See example 9a.)

EXAMPLE 9a. An epistle from the Mass: "Carissime"

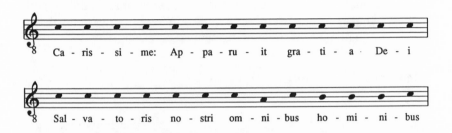

Somewhat more artistic – a quality arising from the poetic nature of their texts – are the nine PSALM TONES. Each has its own reciting tone, but because of the ANTIPHON that follows, each has several different terminal cadences. Because psalm verses are written in pairs, each psalm tone has its own intermediary cadence (or mediation) at the end of the first line of each pair. Since an antiphon is sung both before and after the psalm, the mode of the antiphon determines the choice of psalm-tone formula to be used. (See example 9b.)

EXAMPLE 9b. Psalm-Tone 2

On a somewhat higher musical level, but still circumscribed by the use of a reciting tone, stands the chant style employed for singing the canticle of the Office. In keeping with the greater importance and solemnity of this canticle, the chant style used is more ornate, with a slightly larger vocal range, and the use of somewhat more varied cadences.

Chant that accompanies a liturgical event is musically more elaborate than psalm tones. Instead of one note for each syllable (a syllabic style), there are usually several (a neumatic style); chant settings of the Offertory occasionally contain many notes per syllable (a melismatic style). The excerpt that follows (which is taken from the introit antiphon "Puer natus est") illustrates the customary neumatic style found in introits, offertories, and communions, all of which are part of the Mass Proper. Before the reduction of the length of the Mass that began in the tenth century, each of these types of chant extended to much greater lengths, depending upon the solemnity of the occasion. The introit melody illustrated here would originally have been chanted in the manner of an antiphon both before and after several psalm verses, the number of verses being determined by the length of the processional. (See example 9c.)

EXAMPLE 9c. An introit antiphon: "Puer natus est"

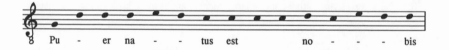

Chant of a meditational or devotional character constitutes the third large category of Gregorian plainsong. It is characterized by the use of a melismatic style, which results in somewhat more emphasis upon the music rather than the text. Nevertheless, the text is set in a manner appropriate to its liturgical function rather than for subjective expression of the words. The example illustrated is taken from a gradual, another type of chant from the Mass Proper whose performance was abbreviated over the years, in this case by omitting the return of the opening respond after the verse. (See example 9d.)

The melismatic chants, which might contain as many as twenty-five or more notes over certain syllables, were performed in a responsorial manner, with a highly skilled soloist being answered by a choir. Included among such chants are responsories, Alleluias, tracts, and Kyries. The neumatic chants usually featured half the choir alternating with the other half in antiphonal fashion. Among the antiphonal chants are antiphons, introits, and chants of the Mass Ordinary. A chant sung throughout without alternation among performers, as in psalmody, is said to be sung direct. Both collects and prefaces are performed in a direct manner by a solo celebrant. Like the contrasting styles used in

EXAMPLE 9d. An Office psalm: "Psalm 109"

Di-xit Do - mi-nus Do-mi-no me _

setting the text, styles of performance varied in the course of a service according to the importance of a chant, its place in the service, the season of the year, and the solemnity of the occasion.

Chants for the Ordinary of the Mass originally had somewhat less importance than chants for the Proper, and they remained simpler in style. They were originally sung by the congregation, whereas the Proper chants were intended for performance by skilled soloists and a trained choir. Over the years, however, trained singers and choirs were introduced in the sections of the Ordinary, settings became more elaborate, and the musical forms themselves — partly in response to textual repetitions — became more complex. Except for the beginnings of certain chants (such as the Gloria and the Credo), performance of chants for the Ordinary is more freely varied than that for the Proper, ranging from one choir throughout (as in the Sanctus) to antiphonal choirs, and including responsorial alternation between soloist and choir as well.

Chants for the Mass and the Office, including those used in the illustrations of chant styles in examples 9a–d, form the body of the present-day Gregorian repertory. They may be found in various LITURGICAL BOOKS. A selection of music for both the Mass and the Office is contained in the LIBER USUALIS, its focus being the principal feasts of the church year. All of the chants used in the Mass during the entire LITURGICAL YEAR are included in the GRADUAL; those for the Office (with the exception of Matins) are found in the ANTIPHONAL. Texts for the Mass appear in the MISSAL, those for the Office Hours in the BREVIARY. Additional books containing certain kinds of chant are also available. An important example is the KYRIALE, in which are printed all the chants for the Mass Ordinary. A useful book for the church musician is the TONARY, in which chants are arranged according to their modes. Some of the liturgical books that contain chants preserve the square neumatic notation and the four-line staff that came into use during the eleventh and twelfth centuries. This method of notation resolved one of the great difficulties that beset those who sought to preserve chant and to unify its use in the service. Gregorian notation from about the eleventh century clearly indicates the pitches that should be sung. On the other hand, as may be seen in example 9e, neither square notation using neumes nor modern notation provides the singer much assistance with rhythm.

EXAMPLE 9e. An offertory from the Mass: "Deus, Deus meus"

Medieval notation

De - us,   De - - us me _ _ _ _ _ _ _ _ _ _ _ _ _ _ _ _ _ _ us,

Modern notation

De - us,   De - - us me _ _ _ _ _ _ _ _ _ _ _ _ _ _ _ _ _ _ us,

The rhythmic aspect of Gregorian chant remains the greatest obstacle to its performance. Controversy on the subject has not brought opposing factions any closer to a common solution. In the examples that have been given, all notes have been shown as being of equal value. The modern-day interpretation accepted by the Roman Catholic church (and printed in its publications) is that of the monks of the Benedictine abbey of Solesmes in France. They assert that essentially all notes in chant are of equal value except for dotted-notes. (Unfortunately, dotted notes do not appear in Medieval chant manuscripts.) Drawing upon rather conclusive evidence from the Medieval period, opponents of an evenly flowing chant assert that Gregorian chant originally used long and short note-values. However, these scholars (known generally as mensuralists) find themselves in sharp disagreement as to how the long and short notes should be realized in measured note-values. Study of the original manuscripts indicates that as the pitches of chant became more clearly written, subtle rhythmic signs (of uncertain meaning) were gradually abandoned. It is therefore possible that performance in equal note-values may represent a corrupt practice of the later Medieval period. No simple answers may be expected to so complex a question as the performance of chant.

Like other great monuments of religion and culture, Gregorian chant has faced challenges from a world in which times and conditions change.

The description of chant just completed has largely left unaccounted for an ongoing creative impetus in monophonic church music that did not reach its peak until the twelfth century and found only a partial outlet in setting the texts of the Mass and the Office. One source of inspiration for new music in the later Middle Ages came from the enormous growth in the number of feast days celebrated during the church year. The late Medieval emphasis on the cult of the Virgin Mary, for example, brought about new feasts in her honor and a number of Marian antiphons that found a permanent place in the liturgy of the Offices.

Another principal source of change was troping, a characteristic Medieval process of interpolating new music or new texts, or both, into the liturgy. To emphasize the importance of special feast days, church musicians troped or embellished the standard liturgy in three basic ways: (1) by making melismatic additions to existing chants, an early practice that might have existed for many centuries through improvisation; (2) by making textual additions to existing chants; and (3) by inserting new phrases consisting of both text and music before or between the phrases of a given chant. Much remains to be learned about the nature and use of tropes in the Middle Ages. The addition of text to the Kyrie of the Mass Ordinary by troping is illustrated in example 9f.

Because the main outlines of the liturgy had become fixed around the chants of the Mass and the Office (which by no means protected them

EXAMPLE 9f. A troped Kyrie

from tropes), much of the effort of later Medieval composers was expended on new genres such as the SEQUENCE, the CONDUCTUS, the VERSUS, and the LITURGICAL DRAMA. Sequences, for example, had been composed in great numbers and widely adopted as part of the Mass before the Council of Trent caused all but four of them to be removed from the liturgy in the sixteenth century.

Attempts to reform chant have proved almost as great a threat to its preservation and integrity as growth from within. When the Council of Trent commissioned a comprehensive revision of chant in the late sixteenth century, a project that culminated in the publication of the Medicean Gradual of 1608, the result was a thorough simplification and modification that did not faithfully represent the Medieval chant heritage. Later attempts at chant reform, including a considerable number undertaken during the nineteenth century, also fell far short of their avowed goals. Indeed, despite the prodigious amount of research underlying the twentieth-century editions approved by the church, they too must be regarded more as functional liturgical publications than as scholarly, critical editions. Even as research of a highly specialized kind continues, holding out the prospect of solving some of the fundamental problems surrounding chant, major steps have been taken that threaten its continued functional existence. The Second Vatican Council, which met from 1962 to 1963, produced a document (*The Constitution of the Sacred Liturgy*) that has resulted in significant revision of the very structure of the Mass and the Office, as well as of the liturgical year. Attempts to involve the congregation in the service have resulted in new liturgical practices and in the translation of the Mass into modern vernacular languages. Whether or not this results in new traditions that will someday be of great historical importance, the enduring message may be how difficult it is to arrest the growth of the liturgy solely for the scholarly and aesthetic pleasure of later generations. It may well be true that the task of restoring chant to the supposed purity of a unified early practice at a point arbitrarily chosen in time cannot succeed. Readers interested in learning more about the history of Gregorian chant will find an excellent starting point in the book entitled *Gregorian Chant* by Willi Apel (Indiana University Press, 1958).

Chapel Royal—An English term used specifically for the professional singers and organist employed by the king of England. In ordinary musical usage, the term "chapel" (*cappella* in Latin and Italian, *chappelle* in French, *Kapelle* or *Capelle* in German) refers to the entire musical establishment—instrumentalists as well as singers—of a nobleman or prelate. Most chapel musicians supplied both church music and secular music for their patrons. Because they attracted the finest musicians, chapels played a prominent role in the history of Western music from the late Medieval period through the Baroque period.

Charpentier, Marc-Antoine (c. 1645–1704) — This composer was one of the most significant French composers of sacred music of not only the Baroque period, but of any period. That he never succeeded in obtaining royal posts commensurate with his ability may well have helped to channel his energies into religious rather than dramatic music. As a young man, Charpentier studied for several years in Rome with Giacomo CARISSIMI, the reigning master of the oratorio and the cantata. There he assimilated the Italian traits that lay at the heart of Baroque style, and to some extent incorporated them in his own music. Upon his return to France, he became master of the large musical establishment maintained by the Duchess of Guise, a post that he probably retained until her death in 1688. At about this time he assumed leadership of music at the principal Jesuit church in Paris, for which he composed many of his religious works. Even more prestige came with his appointment in 1698 as *maître de musique* of Sainte-Chapelle in Paris. Composed for performance there were such masterpieces as the oratorio *Judicium Salomonis* (The Judgment of Solomon); "In te Domine speravi" (In Thee, Lord, I Trust) (Psalm 70); and *Missa Assumpta est Maria*.

Charpentier was a prolific composer of sacred music for churches, chapels, and convents. According to H. Wiley Hitchcock (*The New Grove Dictionary*, vol. 4, p. 164), there are 11 MASSES, 207 MOTETS (among them 36 ORATORIOS), 84 psalm settings, 10 MAGNIFICATS, 54 lessons and RESPONSORIES for Tenebrae, 37 ANTIPHONS, 19 HYMNS, 9 settings of the Litany of Loreto, 4 settings of the TE DEUM, and 4 sequences. Very few of these were published during his lifetime, but they may be expected to appear in increasing number and frequency with wider knowledge of his achievement.

chazzan — A Hebrew word referring to the CANTOR or precentor in the Jewish worship service.

chiesa — Italian for "church," thus used to identify an instrumental composition to be performed therein, for example, a *sonata da chiesa* by Archangelo Corelli.

chironomy — Derived from the Greek word for "hand," the term refers to the practice of teaching and leading singers through the indication of pitches by hand signals.

choir—A term with several meanings, the most common being a mixed group of singers (with more than one on a part) gathered for the performance of church music; most often such a group will be composed of sopranos, altos, tenors, and basses (SATB). However, a choir may be composed of women only (a treble choir), of men, of men and boys (as was customary in the church before the eighteenth century), or of boys alone. A group of similar instruments playing together is also called a choir (e.g., a brass choir), and the music played by any choir may be secular instead of sacred.

choirbook—A term used by scholars for a manuscript arranged so that an entire choir could sing from it, usually with the soprano above the tenor on the left-hand page, and the alto above the bass on the right-hand page. Manuscripts in choirbook format were common in the fifteenth and sixteenth centuries and could be large enough to be placed on a stand before the singers.

chorale—A congregational HYMN used in the German Protestant Church after its break with Roman Catholicism in the early RENAISSANCE. To encourage worship by the people, chorale texts were in German and were strophic. The melody for a chorale was often taken from a folk song, from an existing vernacular hymn, or from Gregorian CHANT, and then given a sacred text—a process called CONTRAFACTUM. Some chorale texts and possibly some melodies were composed by Martin LUTHER himself. Collections of chorales and chorale settings began to be published in 1524 and grew to a large number in the BAROQUE period; some organized chorale melodies by their use in the LITURGICAL YEAR. During the Reformation, chorales were often sung in the Lutheran Mass at the Introit, after the Alleluia, after the Latin Credo, after the sermon, and at the beginning of, during, and after the Communion. After Luther's death, chorale texts came to stress personal appeals to God rather than public expression of thanksgiving, while unison singing and choral settings with the chorale melody in the tenor began to lose favor to soprano-dominated settings. (See CANTIONAL STYLE.) Baroque composers of ORGAN MUSIC, of MOTETS, and of church CANTATAS for Protestant churches came to depend upon chorale melodies as CANTUS FIRMI, a process that reached its artistic culmination (though by no means its termination) in the great masterpieces of J. S. BACH.

chorale cantata—A church cantata in which several, perhaps all, of the movements are based on the same CHORALE melody. In J. S. Bach's Cantata No. 80, for example, Luther's famous hymn "Ein' feste Burg ist unser Gott" (A Mighty Fortress Is Our God) serves as the basis for four of the eight movements. (See also the article CANTATA.)

chorale fantasia—A composition, usually for organ, freely based on the inventive use of a CHORALE melody, as in J. S. Bach's "Fantasia super Christ lag in Todes Banden" (Fantasy on Christ Lay in the Bonds of Death, BWV 695). (See also FANTASIA and ORGAN MUSIC.)

chorale motet—An elaborate treatment of a chorale melody in which each phrase is treated successively as a point of imitation. The genre began as early as 1524 in a collection by Johann Walther, reached a high point with J. S. BACH (e.g., *Jesu, meine Freude*, BWV 227), and then lay almost forgotten until the twentieth-century revival represented by the work of Hugo DISTLER.

chorale partita—A set of variations for organ on a CHORALE melody. The number of variations normally equal the number of verses in the chorale. One of the great contrapuntal masterpieces from late in J. S. Bach's career is a set of five canonic variations for organ on the hymn "Vom Himmel hoch" (BWV 769).

chorale prelude—An organ piece that is based upon a CHORALE melody; originally chorale preludes often introduced congregational singing of the chorale. Today, a chorale prelude often introduces the Protestant worship service, during which the chorale may or may not be sung by the worshippers. Chorale preludes vary widely in size and character, ranging from the exemplary models for the beginning organist contained in J. S. Bach's *Orgel-Buechlein* (Little Organ Book), to the extended settings of the collection known as the "Eighteen Chorales" (BWV 669–689). (See the article ORGAN MUSIC.)

choraliter—A Latin term for music in the unmeasured style of CHANT, as opposed to mensural (or measured) music.

Christian Year—See LITURGICAL YEAR.

Christmastide—The season of the Christian year that begins with Christmas Day and lasts until the eve of EPIPHANY. It is preceded by a period of preparation called Advent.

church bells—See BELLS.

church modes—See the article CHANT.

Classical period—As used by historians, the term refers to the years between 1750 and 1800 (or from about 1720 to 1820), a time featuring such great composers as HAYDN, MOZART, and for some scholars, BEETHOVEN. Church patronage of music declined markedly in the Classical period, while musical leadership passed from church music to such secular genres as the symphony, sonata, and string quartet. (See the table, Composers Arranged Chronologically by Genre, that begins on page xiii.

Collect—A short prayer that precedes the reading of the EPISTLE in the Roman Catholic Mass Proper. It may be chanted or spoken.

Communion—The final item of the Mass Proper. Originally an example of antiphonal PSALMODY, it has consisted of an ANTIPHON without verses since the twelfth century. The Second Vatican Council prescribed that verses be sung until all communicants have received the sacrament, at which time the lesser DOXOLOGY is sung. In the Anglican church, Holy Communion is one of the three principal SERVICES. (See also HOLY COMMUNION.)

Compline—The last of the eight services that constitute the Roman Catholic OFFICE, Compline is celebrated (generally only in monastic communities) at the end of the day, just before bedtime. Among the musical items in Compline are several PSALMS, a HYMN, one of the MARIAN ANTIPHONS, the "NUNC DIMITTIS," and the "BENEDICAMUS DOMINO."

concertato—An Italian term from the seventeenth century that refers to textural contrast achieved through use of both vocal and instrumental choirs in the new Baroque style. The greatest seventeenth-century composers in the concertato style were Monteverdi and SCHUETZ. (See example 6.)

concerto—An instrumental genre that emerged in the Baroque period. It was normally secular, but occasionally—as in the *concerto di chiesa*—heard in the church. Both the solo concerto (for instrumental soloist with orchestra) and the concerto grosso (for several, often a trio of, instrumental soloists with orchestra) were frequently heard in the church in the BAROQUE period, as in the concerti grossi of Arcangelo Corelli.

conductus—A Medieval Latin song, often religious in character but not set on liturgical texts. Its name apparently indicates use in processionals during the service and on ceremonial occasions. The earliest conducti, which are located in twelfth-century manuscripts, are monophonic. The thirteenth-century polyphonic conductus set on a religious text represents the earliest church music not based upon Gregorian CHANT.

contrafactum—A Latin term indicating that the original text of a composition, in general a secular one, has been replaced by a sacred text. The practice was common before the sixteenth century, as demonstrated in the chanson (which became a CHANSON SPIRITUELLE) and the Lied (which was transformed into a Protestant CHORALE). Some collections of psalm tunes, such as the *Souterliedekens* of 1540, consisted largely of popular folk melodies.

Council of Trent—An important Roman Catholic council that met over many years (1545–1563). Among other things, it made bishops responsible for seeing that composers did not engage in such unsuitable musical practices in the worship service as making liturgical texts unintelligible or using a secular tune as a CANTUS FIRMUS.

counterpoint—A special form of POLYPHONY in which the parts retain their individuality rather than dissolving into chordal harmony. The term derives from the expression "note against note," whereby a second line is added to an existing CANTUS FIRMUS. Counterpoint is said to be free when the separate parts do not share the same thematic material, imitative when they do.

Counter-Reformation—The movement of reform, and especially of resurgence, that took place within the Roman Catholic church in the late sixteenth and early seventeenth centuries.

Couperin, François (1668–1733)—The leading French composer of the early eighteenth century, François Couperin came from a renowned musical family. A student of his father and uncle, both of whom were noteworthy organists, he served as organist at the church of Saint Gervais from 1685 to 1733. In 1693 he succeeded the famous organist Jacques Thomelin, another of his teachers, as organist and *maître de chapelle* (master of the chapel) of the CHAPELLE ROYALE. Although his fame rests principally upon his secular music, particularly on the suites for harpsichord, the trio sonatas, and the solo sonatas, Couperin composed church music that represents him and at least one aspect of the aristocratic church music of his time at its best. In the words of Wilfrid Mellers (*François Couperin and the French Classical Tradition* [Dover, 1968], p. 153),

Couperin "in his church music does not attempt to emulate La Lande's massive dignity," but "he rivals, perhaps even excels him in the ability to express an intimate spirituality, a purity of feeling and a sense of wonder which are the prerequisites of a religious view of experience."

The church music of Couperin was composed during the last years of the reign of Louis XIV, from 1690 to 1715. His two ORGAN MASSES represent the composer at the age of twenty-one, paying tribute to his training and achieving a synthesis of the major trends in style of the time: a restrained contrapuntal manner in the tradition of the Netherlands and Germany; an Italian-inspired use of passionate chromaticism and expressive dissonance; and a native French preference for dance-like rhythms. Both Masses unfold in short episodic movements for organ, at times without clear reference to the appropriate plainchant melodies. (See example 10.) The larger one, *Messe pour les paroisses* (Mass for Parish

EXAMPLE 10. François Couperin, "Tierce en Taille," *Messe pour les paroisses* (meas. 22–27), *(Pièces d'orgue)*

Services), was intended for use on principal feasts when the plainchant setting "Cunctipotens genitor Deus" was sung for the Ordinary, since this chant appears as a CANTUS FIRMUS in the opening measures of the Kyrie, Gloria, Sanctus, and Agnus Dei. As its Offertory, this Mass contains a remarkable movement not unlike an operatic overture: a slow opening section featuring powerful suspensions, a more active section in fugal style, and a vigorous gigue-like conclusion.

Most of the vocal church music of Couperin was not published during his lifetime; at least twenty-seven MOTETS belong to this category (one of them a MAGNIFICAT), and some titles are known to have been lost. Among the published works are three collections of what Couperin termed VERSETS, eighteen cantata-like motets, and one collection of LAMENTA-TIONS. Although chorus and instruments are occasionally required by Couperin, most of the works are composed for soloists with accompaniment by organ (and perhaps bass viol). All are composed to Latin texts. Perhaps the most noteworthy among them are the three Lamentations (Leçons de Ténèbres), which feature rhapsodic melismatic passages for the Hebrew letters. In structure, all of Couperin's vocal church music consists of an alternation of recitative and aria with interspersed passages of arioso and instrumental ritornellos; in style, they represent a thoroughly French and somewhat spiritualized synthesis of the style of the Baroque Italian CANTATA.

Credo—An affirmation of Christian faith, properly known as the Nicene Creed, the Credo was the last part of the Mass Ordinary incorporated into the Roman Catholic liturgy. Its formal acceptance dates from the eleventh century, the same time as the earliest manuscripts that contain plainchant settings. Its place in the liturgy is after the Gospel and before the Offertory. Polyphonic settings have frequently found the text divided into separate sections or movements, and otherwise given special treatment because of its length and its dogmatic assertions. By far the longest of texts in the Mass Ordinary, only its beginning is given below.

Credo in unum Deum,	I believe in one God,
Patrem omnipotentem,	the Father Almighty,
Factorem coeli et terrae,	Maker of heaven and earth,
visibilium omnium et invisibilium.	and of all things
	visible and invisible.

David, Johann Nepomuk (1895–1977)—David was an Austrian composer who played a significant role in the BAROQUE-inspired resurgence of twentieth-century organ composition, organ performance, and organ-building. He began his career as an organist, became professor of composition (1934) and later director (1939) at Leipzig Conservatory, then served as director of the Salzburg Mozarteum (1945–1948), and finally as professor of composition (1947–1963) at the Musikhochschule in Stuttgart. Although most of the many instrumental works composed at the beginning of David's career have been lost—some in the bombing of Leipzig in World War II—he by no means became a specialist in church music; among his works are eight symphonies, two violin concertos, much chamber music, songs, and piano pieces. His musical language rests firmly upon a love for counterpoint that is reflected in his reliance upon ostinato techniques, variations, and above all the technique of composing on a CANTUS FIRMUS. Born a Catholic, he nevertheless used the Protestant CHORALE in much of his church music. Although his harmonic vocabulary often features quartal chords, tone clusters, and Schoenberg-inspired serial writing, it remains for the most part within the realm of an expanded tonality.

Organ music, which stretches over his entire career, comprises the bulk of David's creative output. It is deeply rooted in his knowledge of BACH, BRUCKNER, and REGER. A number of the early works are not based on a cantus firmus, among them a Ricercar in C Minor (1925), a Chaconne in A Minor (1927), a Toccata and Fugue in F Minor (1928), and a Prelude and Fugue in D minor (1930). As early as 1928, however, two hymn settings (on "Pange lingua" and "Veni, creator spiritus") reveal that he has taken up the challenge of composition on a cantus firmus. In 1932, he began publishing his *Choralwerk*, which at the beginning (the first five volumes) were just a random series of thirty-two CHORALE PRELUDES, PARTITAS, FANTASIAS, TOCCATAS, PASSACAGLIAS, FUGUES, and other types—all based on cantus firmi; by 1962, *Choralwerk* had grown to twenty-one volumes. Other organ compositions include *Introit, Chorale, and Fugue on a Theme of Anton Bruckner* (for organ with nine wind instruments) from 1939; a Partita on B-A-C-H (1964); and a Kleine Chaconne fuer Orgel (Little Chaconne for Organ) on "Nun komm, der Heiden Heiland" (1959) in which the recurring OSTINATO theme is the first line of the chorale melody. (See example 30.)

The composer's sacred vocal music presents an ecumenical picture, with some settings of Protestant chorales, motets, and chorale cantatas as well as some Catholic settings of the MASS, a STABAT MATER, a REQUIEM, and some other works based on plainchants. He began his chorale settings in the *a cappella* tradition of Leipzig, as in his large-scale motet for eight-part mixed chorus "Ex Deo nascimur" (1936). Among the best known are the five chorale motets on cantus firmi entitled *Deutsche Messe* (1952); each of the movements is composed in a different manner, including both chordal writing and counterpoint. The melodies are drawn from the Ordinary of the German Mass: Kyrie, Gott Vater in Ewigkeit (Lord, God, Eternal Father), Allein Gott in der Hoeh sei Ehr (To God in the Highest Alone Be the Glory), Wir glauben all an einen Gott (We Believe in One God), Jesaja, dem Propheten das geschah (Isaiah, The Prophet Saw), and Christe, du Lamm Gottes (Christ, Lamb of God).

De profundis—The opening words (in the Latin of the Vulgate edition) of Psalm 129. In the King James Bible (where the psalm is numbered 130), the words are translated as "Out of the depths." The psalm has often been set to music, either as an independent composition or as one of the seven PENITENTIAL PSALMS. One of the most famous settings is that by Orlandus LASSUS.

De tempore hymn—The hymn "of the time," that is, the hymn that is most appropriate for the specific day and season in the church year. In the Lutheran church, it is also referred to as the "gradual hymn," because of its position in the service. There are a number of plans, both official and unofficial, for the use of *de tempore* hymns in the Lutheran church.

descant—In common usage, the term refers to a vocal part added as a free counterpoint above the melody of a HYMN.

Deutsche Messe—A term referring to Martin Luther's revision and translation of the Roman Catholic MASS. Published in 1526 as *Deutsche Messe und Ordnung des Gottesdienst* (German Mass and Order of the Holy Service), it encouraged congregational singing by its inclusion of CHORALES, while it retained the major features of the Roman Catholic Mass.

dialogue—Compositions whose texts call for performance by two or more characters in alternation became important in the early seventeenth century under the name *dialogus* (Latin) or *dialogo spirituale* (Italian), both of which served as forerunners of the ORATORIO. In Germany, sacred dialogues were composed by SCHEIDT and SCHUETZ, among others. The term also occurs in some French organ music of the seventeenth century in which different manuals alternate in contrasting timbres.

Dies irae—The Latin words (meaning "Day of wrath") that open the SEQUENCE of the REQUIEM MASS. The text, attributed to Thomas of Celano, describes Judgment Day. The music became part of the Roman

Catholic liturgy in the sixteenth century, when it was officially accepted by the Council of Trent; it was frequently quoted with programmatic purpose by Romantic composers, as in the closing movement of the *Symphonie Fantastique* by Hector Berlioz.

discant—A term derived from the Latin word *discantus*, meaning "singing apart." It refers to passages in Medieval polyphony in which the voices move in similar rhythms, as opposed to ORGANUM. The great master of discant style was PEROTIN.

Distler, Hugo (1908–1942)—A leading figure in the twentieth-century German revival of BAROQUE genres and styles, Distler encountered the music of SCHUETZ and J. S. BACH as a student at Leipzig Conservatory. There he studied with two of the leading figures associated with the return to the sound and structure of the German Baroque organ. Stimulated by his experiences, he became church organist in Luebeck, where in 1935 he restored the organs at the Jakobikirche. He also worked with the church choirs and began to compose the choral works upon which his reputation rests. Much of his succeeding career was spent teaching and directing choirs in Stuttgart and Berlin, where in 1942 he became director of the Berlin State and Cathedral Choir.

 Distler's sacred music for choir and his music for the organ were composed in the spirit of the Baroque music that he loved. Despite their twentieth-century rhythms and harmonies, the structures, the CHORALE melodies, and the use of tone-painting and ostinato figures reveal their heritage, as do the very genres that he favors. Among the organ works are two PARTITAS on chorale melodies, two trio sonatas for organ, and a collection of small-scale chorale settings. The sacred vocal works include a German Mass and a number of short Masses (with just Kyrie and Gloria), numerous chorale MOTETS (many of them to be sung, supposedly as in the past, A CAPPELLA), chorale CANTATAS, an incomplete PASSION according to Saint John, and several collections whose titles recall the works of Heinrich Schuetz: *Geistliche Konzerte* (Sacred Concertos), *Geistliche Chormusik* (Sacred Choral Music), and *Die Weihnachtsgeschichte* (The Christmas Story). (See example 6.)

doxology—A liturgically proper expression of glory to God used in various forms in many churches; "Praise God from whom all blessings flow" begins the doxology used in many Protestant services. The Roman Catholic service contains a Greater Doxology (the GLORIA of the Mass) and a Lesser Doxology (GLORIA PATRI), which is sung after the INTROIT, most CANTICLES, and the psalms of the Office:

Gloria Patri et Filio	Glory be to the Father and to the Son
et Spiritui Sancto;	and to the Holy Ghost;
sicut erat in principio,	as it was in the beginning,
et nunc, et semper,	is now, and ever shall be,
et in saecula saeculorum.	world without end.
Amen.	Amen.

Dresden Amen—A well-known polyphonic setting of a traditional melody (by the late eighteenth-century composer Johann Gottlieb Naumann), which was sung at the royal chapel in Dresden. Its most noteworthy uses were by MENDELSSOHN in his *Reformation Symphony* and Richard Wagner in his opera *Parsifal*. (See example 11.)

EXAMPLE 11. Dresden Amen as quoted by Mendelssohn in *The Reformation Symphony* (Symphony No. 5)

Dufay, Guillaume (c.1400–1474)—A Franco-Flemish composer celebrated during his lifetime and long afterwards as the greatest composer of his era, Dufay contributed prominently to church music through his corpus of approximately ninety MOTETS and hymn-settings, and particularly through his development of the cyclic MASS as a major musical genre. His leading role in the creation of the expressive lyrical melodies and triadic textures of the Burgundian chanson was increasingly reflected in his liturgical music. Through the patronage of the Bishop of Cambrai, the young composer (and apparently priest) learned his craft in Italy, serving between 1428 and 1433 in the papal chapel and at such leading European courts as those in Ferrara and Burgundy. With the exception of a lengthy stay in Savoy, he spent the years after 1440 back in Cambrai, where he had been appointed canon in 1436.

Dufay composed at least eight complete settings of the Mass Ordinary and many more individual or paired texts from it. The majority of the Masses, which are normally set in four voices, employ in the tenor a recurring cantus firmus, generally drawn from chant and paraphrased (as in *Missa Ave Regina coelorum*); in the case of *Missa Se la face ay pale*, however, one of the composer's own chansons served as the source for his CANTUS FIRMUS. The custom of basing a Mass on a secular tune may have begun with Dufay; his setting of *Missa L'Homme armé* may have been the first in a long series of settings by significant Renaissance composers. The composer's motets feature a traditional type constructed in isorhythmic fashion and a song-like type not far removed from the FAUXBOURDON style so frequent in his many hymn settings. Late in Dufay's career came a freer and more flexible and expressive kind of motet that ranks with his finest achievements. "Ave Regina coelorum" (Hail, Queen of Heaven), a motet in four voices, was composed in about 1464. Based on a free paraphrase of the Marian antiphon, it is shaped by the composer in two large parts: the first contains two sections in triple meter, while the second (which unfolds mostly in duple meter) comprises three sections. Unity among the sections stems from their proportional balance, from a style generally reliant upon free counterpoint, and especially from the underlying liturgical cantus firmus. Dufay thought enough of the piece to insert his own name into the text and to stipulate its performance at his deathbed; when that proved impossible, it was sung at the composer's funeral. (See example 12.)

Dunstable, John (c.1390–1453) – Dunstable was the first Englishman to rank among the outstanding composers of his time. Relatively little is known about his career. Since he became a famous mathematician and astronomer, he must have studied science as well as music. He may have served the Duke of Bedford, who had English holdings on the continent; he may also have spent some years in Italy. Most of his music was preserved in European manuscripts and most of his reputation was created by European theorists. But no evidence exists to firmly link the composer with any cathedral, or with the CHAPEL ROYAL or any other patron. As for Dunstable's music, only about fifty compositions can be positively ascribed to him, nearly all of them on sacred texts. They include sections of the MASS Ordinary (some of them grouped in cycles of two to four items), Latin MOTETS (many of them on texts dealing with the Virgin Mary), and isorhythmic polytextual motets. The texture, and therefore the difficulty, of the compositions varies greatly, ranging from traditional accompanied melody in three voices to complex isorhythmic patterns in three or four voices. The most influential of his works, those on which his influence upon the Burgundians rests, emphasize full triads in root position or in first inversion, and careful control of dissonance. It is

EXAMPLE 12. Guillaume Dufay, "Ave Regina coelorum" (meas. 30–36)

possible that the credit for composing in this style should be shared with Leonel Power and other members of the English School of the period.

Duruflé, Maurice (1902–1986) — A French organist who composed a a very small number of works, most of them for the church. He was an organ student of Charles Tournemire, Louis Vierne, and Eugene Gigout; he commemorated the first two in the 1950s by publishing several reconstructions of their improvisations for organ. Between 1922 and 1928 he won first prizes in organ, harmony, fugue, accompaniment, and composition at the Paris Conservatory, where he returned to serve as professor of harmony from 1943 to 1967. As an organist, Duruflé assisted

Tournemire at Sainte Clotilde until 1930 and then spent the rest of his career as organist at Saint Etienne-du-Mont. He was also active as a concert organist for many years, his tours bringing him on occasion to the United States.

Duruflé's music is characterized by restraint and, in the church works, by his use of CHANT and chant-like melodies in suitably harmonic and contrapuntal settings. He began composing in an idiom rooted firmly in the works of Fauré, Dukas, and Ravel and changed very little over the years. His first major work for organ is Prélude, Adagio and Chorale Variations on the chant "Veni Creator" (Come, Creator, 1930); dedicated to Vierne, it established Duruflé's reputation and deserves a place in the repertory. A second composition in three movements (Prélude, Sicilienne, and Toccata) followed in 1934; entitled *Suite*, it makes much greater technical demands on the organist, particularly in the Toccata. Finally, in 1943, the composer honored the memory of a young French organist-composer who died in World War II with Prelude and Fugue on the Name of Jehan Alain; here, the closing movement, one of the Duruflé's finest, is a double fugue.

Among Duruflé's few vocal works is his most famous composition, *Requiem for Soloists, Choruses, Orchestra and Organ* (1948). In many ways it resembles Fauré's famous work of that name—certainly not a poor model. Its outstanding moment is perhaps the "Domine Jesu." There are also four Latin MOTETS on Gregorian melodies for unaccompanied chorus (1960) and a MASS entitled *Messe "Cum Jubilo"* for baritone solo, unison men's choir, orchestra, and organ (1967). Well-suited because of its modest demands for liturgical use, the Mass is based on Gregorian chant and remains close to the style of the Requiem. (See example 35.)

Eastertide—The primary festival of the Christian liturgical year, beginning with VESPERS on the eve of Easter and ending with Vespers on the eve of PENTECOST. It is preceded by a time of preparation called Lent.

ecclesiastical modes—See CHANT.

Epiphany—The feast of Epiphany which is celebrated on January 6 in the liturgical year, commemorates three events: the Baptism of Jesus, the visit of the Wise Men to Bethlehem, and the Miracle at Cana.

Episcopal church music—The roots of the Protestant Episcopal church in the United States lie in the Church of England. As in England, there has been marked contrast in the United States between the use of music in large cathedral-like churches and its use in local parish churches. The importance of a fairly elaborate liturgy and of English traditions helped metropolitan Episcopal churches establish and maintain high musical standards, whereas music in smaller Episcopal churches came to resemble that found in other Protestant churches in the United States. In the later twentieth-century, the Association of Anglican Musicians has aided the cause of church music and musicians; at the same time, the Episcopal Church has joined the trend towards encouraging greater congregational participation and introducing the use of more popular or folk-like musical styles. (See also ANGLICAN LITURGY and the entries for PARKER, SOWERBY, and WILLAN.)

Epistle — From the Latin for "letter," the term refers to the New Testament Epistles, which form the basis for readings or recitations in various liturgies. Instrumental pieces to be performed after the Epistle have been composed by FRESCOBALDI and MOZART, among others.

Epistle sonata — A movement in sonata form intended for performance after the reading of the Epistle during the Mass. The most noteworthy examples are the seventeen church sonatas for various combinations of instruments with organ by MOZART.

Eucharist — A Greek word for the "giving of thanks," as in the Last Supper of Jesus. The word is thus used to refer to the Holy Communion service.

euouae — These letters constitute the vowels of the liturgical words *seculorum Amen* (the closing portion of "world without end, Amen"), which represent a standard closing formula in the Roman Catholic liturgy.

Evangeliary (Latin, *evangeliarium*) — An early Roman Catholic liturgical book containing the readings for the Gospels.

evangelistic music — Music of a personal and emotional kind whose intent is to heighten the sensitivity of the flock, strengthen their feelings of belief, and rally them to do what an evangelist conceives to be the "work of the Lord." Spontaneous songs that result from impassioned preaching at evangelistic meetings are termed "ejaculatory hymns." Due to its success in the broadcast media, GOSPEL MUSIC has attracted new songwriters and performing groups heavily influenced by their experience in secular musical styles.

Evening Prayer—Another term for VESPERS, an evening service whose roots lie in the Jewish evening sacrifice. The most noteworthy musical event of Vespers is the singing of the MAGNIFICAT or of the NUNC DIMITTIS.

Evensong—See ANGLICAN LITURGY.

fantasia—An Italian term for a free, imaginative composition for solo instrument or instrumental ensemble. In some cases, the word refers to unwritten, improvised music. The genre flourished in the sixteenth and seventeenth centuries. As a church composition, the fantasia for organ was cultivated by such great masters as SWEELINCK and BUXTEHUDE; in one of the most noteworthy types of fantasia, composers displayed their contrapuntal ingenuity in the use of a CHORALE melody. (See example 13.)

EXAMPLE 13. Jan Sweelinck, "Allein zu Dir, Herr Jesu Christ" (meas. 158–161)

fauxbourdon—A controversial French term referring to a Renaissance church music technique whereby a given CANTUS FIRMUS is performed in three voice-parts moving principally in first inversion triads. The master of *fauxbourdon* was Guillaume DUFAY.

ferial—Although the word comes from the Latin for "festive day," it is used in the Roman Catholic church to refer to days that are not feast days. In the Anglican service, simple harmonized settings of the responses are termed "ferial."

Folk Mass—A trend towards encouraging the participation of the congregation in the music of the Mass has marked the latter half of the twentieth century. In 1956, the *Twentieth-Century Folk Mass* by Father Geoffrey Beaumont was composed in the popular idiom of the people. It was followed by the *American Folk Song Mass* by Ian Mitchell, the *Missa Luba* (an African Mass), and other works that have prompted church musicians everywhere to re-examine their mission and the effectiveness of their repertories.

Formula Missae—The Latin Mass as modified and published by Martin LUTHER in 1523. Luther's intent was to preserve the traditional order of service while purging or simplifying various objectionable elements. The influence of the Formula Missae may be seen in current Lutheran practice.

Franck, César (1822–1890)—Belgian by birth, Franck survived exploitation as a child prodigy to carve out a significant career as a church musician, teacher, and composer. Having turned to the organ and to teaching by economic necessity, he assumed his first important post in 1858 as organist at the church of Sainte Clotilde. Subsequently, in 1871, he became professor of organ at the Paris Conservatoire, where the quality and devotion of his students (among them d'Indy and Chausson) lifted him to a position of eminence in French music. Although Franck and his followers thought his grand oratorio in eight parts entitled *Les béatitudes* (1879) to be his chief masterpiece, most critics have found it to be an uneven achievement, although better than his earlier *Ruth* (1846, rev. 1871) and *Rédemption* (1872, rev. 1874). With certain exceptions (e.g., the Offertory, "Quae est ista"), much the same seems to be true of his many sacred choral works, among them a Solemn Mass (1858) and a Mass in Three Voices (1860); to the latter was appended in 1872 the composer's famous "Panis angelicus" (Bread of Angels), originally a tenor solo with accompaniment by organ, harp, violoncello, and double bass. Franck's fame as a composer rests largely upon a relatively few symphonic, chamber, and keyboard works written in the last twelve or so years of his life. In them he finally brought his chromatic harmonic vocabulary into balance with his preference for working out short germinal motives within an overall cyclic unity.

Outstanding among Franck's works for organ, which stand in the forefront of a new school of French organ music, are *Six pieces* (1862) and *Trois chorals* (1890). After hearing a concert in 1866 that featured the former collection, Franz Liszt praised Franck in the following words: "These poetic pieces have a clearly marked place alongside the masterpieces of Johann Sebastian Bach." In the *Six pieces* the composer was able to capture for the first time the essence of his renowned gift for improvisation. The *Trois chorals* were inspired by the works of Bach, but they were not written in the spirit of imitation. The first, composed in E major, and the second, in B minor, both offer several variations on their quite different themes; the third choral seems closer to an organ fantasy. (See example 14.) As always with Franck, the registration is carefully specified and requires an organ with stops very much like his own Cavaille-Coll to sound authentic.

EXAMPLE 14. César Franck, "Choral in A Minor," *Trois chorals* (meas. 97–99)

Frescobaldi, Girolamo (1583–1643) —The outstanding Italian keyboard composer of the early Baroque period, Frescobaldi was born in Ferrara and grew up while Luzzasco Luzzaschi, his teacher, and the famous madrigalist Gesualdo were active at the court of the music-loving Duke Alfonso II. With Gesualdo when he arrived in 1594 came the progressive Neapolitan keyboard style, an important influence for the young Frescobaldi. As something of a child prodigy, Frescobaldi apparently served as organist of the Ferrarese Accademia della Morte in 1597 and for some time afterwards. In 1604, if not sooner, he took up residence in Rome, where he became organist in 1608 at Saint Peter's Cathedral. Except for a period from 1628 to 1634 spent as court organist in Florence, Frescobaldi not only retained his prestigious post at Saint Peter's for the rest of his life, but also enjoyed the patronage of such eminent patrons as Cardinal Pietro Aldrovandini (until 1621) and Cardinal Antonio Barberini (after 1637), among others.

The achievement of Frescobaldi was to bring to their peak the Renaissance keyboard genres, especially the TOCCATA and the RICERCARE, within an advanced early Baroque rhythmic and harmonic language. While remaining faithful to his contrapuntal heritage, he adopted in his keyboard music the expressive vocabulary of the madrigal and its reliance upon irregular rhythms and affective ornamentation. This remarkable synthesis is first achieved in his first book of toccatas (Rome, 1615), which seems an attempt to capture in notation his improvisatory genius. The second book of toccatas (Rome, 1627) displays works of even greater length and complexity. It also contains his first liturgical organ music based on chant and the first toccatas composed specifically for the organ, these being for the Elevation of the Mass. Since Italian organs of the Renaissance and Baroque periods only rarely had organ pedals, the style of Frecobaldi's music must determine its suitability for the church. As for his vocal church music, there exist more than thirty motets and at least two Masses; according to scholars who have studied them, they are of far less interest than the keyboard works.

The most important edition of Frescobaldi's church music was published in 1635 in a famous collection entitled *Fiori musicali* (Musical Flowers). In it are found various kinds of keyboard pieces arranged so as to supply music for three ORGAN MASSES in the following manner: toccatas in the place of introits, instrumental movements to play for the Kyrie; canzonas in place of the Gradual; ricercari (some with toccatas before them) to play during the Offertory, toccatas for the Elevation, and a canzona or a ricercare after the Communion. In style, the later works do not as yet present a clear picture, since so few are known. The toccatas for the Elevation of the Host offer an intimacy and sense of mystery as masterful in their way as the contrapuntal complexity of the late ricercari and the inventive freedom and scope of the capriccios. In the "Toccata cromaticha per l'Elevatione" (Chromatic Toccata for the Elevation) in E minor (for the *Messa della Domenica*), for example, the music unfolds meditatively in a series of modulatory episodes unified by the recurrence of prominent rhythmic motives and the return of the slower harmonic rhythm of the opening section. Its rhapsodic structure is emphasized by the composer's rich harmonic idiom, in which chromaticism has dispelled the church modes without falling into the predictable progressions of functional harmony. (See example 15.)

Frescobaldi was an influential teacher and an even greater model for succeeding composers of keyboard music. Through his great German

EXAMPLE 15. Girolamo Frescobaldi, "Toccata cromatiche per l'Elevatione in e," *Fiori musicali* (meas. 1–6)

pupil Johann Jakob Froberger, his works became the most copied and most influential of all keyboard music, not only in Italy but in Germany as well, during the second half of the seventeenth century. Their impact remains audible in the works of Bach's great predecessor Dieterich BUXTEHUDE, and the young Bach himself is known to have copied the collection *Fiori musicali* by hand.

fuging tune—An eighteenth-century manifestation of imitative counterpoint in English and American hymn or psalm tunes, as in the works of James Lyon and William BILLINGS. In its typical form, a fuging tune begins with a section in chordal style, continues with an imitative section that is then repeated, and closes with a return to homophonic texture.

fugue—A French word (the German equivalent is *Fuge*, the Italian, *fuga*) for a contrapuntal composition based on a cumulative exposition of a theme in a definite number of parts, followed by an alternation of modulatory episodes and stable tonal entries of the subject. Fugue constitutes, therefore, a special kind of imitation, and traces its history back to the RICERCARE and the MOTET. The presence of two themes, either successively, simultaneously, or both, denotes a double fugue. The organ was a favorite instrument for fugue composers, and the church a favorite place of performance. Among its outstanding practitioners were FRESCOBALDI, BUXTEHUDE, HANDEL, and, above all, J. S. BACH. In his Fugue in C Minor (BWV 574), Bach begins with a theme derived from Legrenzi (example 16a), continues by introducing a second fugue on a contrasting subject (example 16b), and – before a brilliant closing cadenza – combines both themes in a masterful double fugue (example 16c).

Gabrieli, Giovanni (c.1556–1612) – Gabrieli was the culminating figure in the development of the Venetian polychoral style in the late Renaissance, a time when Venice had gained recognition as the most progressive musical center in Europe. The highly esteemed positions of choirmaster, first organist, and second organist at Saint Mark's had gradually passed from the Netherlanders into the hands of Italian musicians. Among the Italians was Giovanni's uncle Andrea, who served as one of the cathedral organists and almost certainly taught his nephew. After some years in Germany at the court of Duke Albrecht V of Bavaria,

EXAMPLE 16a. J. S. Bach, Fugue in C Minor, BWV 574 (meas. 1–7)

EXAMPLE 16b. (meas. 37–40)

Gabrieli returned to Venice and served as an organist at Saint Mark's and at the Scuola Grande di San Rocco for the remainder of his life. After his uncle died in 1586, Gabrieli composed the ceremonial music for the cathedral, and hired the extra singers and instrumentalists required. His enduring fame lies not only in the quality of his music, but also in its novelty. The composer was among the first to compose vocal works with independent instrumental parts, and to designate specific instruments as well as dynamics in his works.

Giovanni Gabrieli composed nearly one hundred MOTETS, a number of MASS sections (including perhaps one complete ORDINARY), many works for various instrumental ensembles, and some organ pieces. His major vocal works were gathered together and published in 1597 and (posthumously) in 1615, both times under the title *Sacrae symphoniae* (Sacred Symphonies). As opposed to the contrapuntal tradition of the Netherlands and to the even more austere Roman style of PALESTRINA, Gabrieli cultivated the art of contrast in his music, especially the art of contrasting sonorities. In his earlier works, such as "Magnam mysterium" and "O Domine Jesu Christe," he maintained the traditional Venetian preference for antiphonal choirs in a diatonic idiom. During this period he achieved greater expression by varying his thematic material as it passed from choir to choir and by increasing the use of dissonance. New traits included his greater reliance upon thematic conciseness—even brevity—and speech rhythms, both of which are emphasized by his prevailing homophonic textures.

EXAMPLE 16c. (meas. 71–76)

    The later vocal works found Gabrieli not only specifying his instrumental parts but also differentiating their style from the vocal parts and the style of the solo vocalists from choral singing. Contrasts of style and *tessitura* (vocal range) between and among choirs became of greater importance to the composer, as did the use of tone-painting through heightened use of dissonance and chromaticism (e.g., "Timor et tremor"). In the concertato-like motet entitled "In ecclesiis benedicite Domino" (In the Congregation, Praise the Lord), Gabrieli employs two soloists, two four-part choirs, and a six-part instrumental ensemble (violin, three cornetti, and trombones) to achieve maximum contrasts of thematic material, texture, meter, and above all, sonority, within a sectional formal plan unified by the use of a recurring Alleluia refrain and a strong tonal center. (See example 17.)

EXAMPLE 17. Giovanni Gabrieli, "In ecclesiis benedicite Domino," *Sacrae symphoniae* II (meas. 25–30)

Among the instrumental compositions by Gabrieli are many canzonas and sonatas for ensemble, and RICERCARI, INTONAZIONI, and CANZONAS for organ. The ensemble works rank among the finest of the period, especially the canzonas from the *Canzoni et sonate* of 1615. The sonatas generally remain rather conservative in style, but the canzonas reveal more truly idiomatic instrumental writing, particularly in the florid upper parts, and they require the harmonic support provided by keyboard realization of the basso continuo line.

Geisslerlied—A compound German word for a flagellant's song, a monophonic genre cultivated by Medieval penitents; it seems to have connections with the earlier Italian LAUDA and the later CHORALE tune.

German Mass—See DEUTSCHE MESSE.

Gibbons, Orlando (1583–1625)—Although he was a gifted organist and harpsichordist, it was through his sacred vocal music that Gibbons became the outstanding English composer of his generation. Even before he took his degree at Cambridge in 1606, the composer had begun his impressive and well-rewarded musical career at court. In addition to his long-held post as first organist of the CHAPEL ROYAL, Gibbons served as virginalist to the king and, from 1623, organist of Westminster Abbey.

Two Anglican SERVICES and approximately forty ANTHEMS constitute the bulk of Gibbons's church music, none of it published during his lifetime. The liturgical music offers a marked contrast between the beautifully expressive Second Service, written for solo voices and full choir, and the modest four-voice chordal texture of the Short Service. Both works are basically throughcomposed, and repetition of text is avoided, but Gibbons reveals in the former one his mastery of harmony, expressive melismas, counterpoint, and contrasting timbres. The greater textual variety of the anthems seems to have inspired the composer to his greatest heights. The majority of them are composed for full choir in as many as eight voice-parts, as in "O Clap Your Hands"; in them, Gibbons amply demonstrates the Renaissance tradition of imitative counterpoint. In the fifteen verse anthems, on the other hand, soloists are once again used in contrast with the full choir to create a more forward-looking texture. Although a consort of viols is normally employed in his verse anthems, substituting the organ for the viols brings many of the anthems within the scope of modern choirs. One of the best known verse anthems, "This Is the Record of John," requires only an alto soloist, a choir in five voice-parts (SAATB), and a consort of viols. Gibbons composed this anthem for the president of one of the colleges at Oxford, the university from which he received his doctoral degree in music in 1622. (For a description and an example of a verse anthem by Gibbons, see example 1.)

Gloria — Sung on festal occasions in the Latin Mass directly after the "Kyrie," the "Gloria in excelsis Deo" is a hymn of praise that begins with the song heard by the shepherds, in which the angels herald the birth of Christ (Luke 2:14). Part of the Ordinary of the MASS, the "Gloria" in its present textual version dates from ninth-century manuscripts, while its earliest plainchant melodies come from the tenth century. The problem presented by the length of the text has been given various solutions by composers, including syllabic settings and sectional structure.

Gloria in excelsis Deo,	Glory to God in the highest,
Et in terra pax	And on earth peace
hominibus bonae voluntatis.	to men of good will.
Laudamus te, benedicimus te,	We praise you, we bless you,
Adoramus te, glorificamus te,	We worship you, we glorify you,
Gratias agimus tibi	We give thanks to you
propter magnam gloriam tuam.	because of your great glory.
Domine Deus, rex caelestis,	Lord God, heavenly king,
Deus Pater omnipotens,	God the Father almighty,
Domine Fili unigenite,	Son of the Father,
	only-begotten,
Jesu Christe.	Jesus Christ.
Domine Deus, Agnus Dei,	Lord God, Lamb of God,
Filius Patris,	Son of the Father, you who
qui tollis peccata mundi,	take away the sins of the world,
miserere nobis.	have mercy upon us.
Qui tollis peccata mundi,	You who take away the sins of
suscipe deprecationem nostram.	the world, receive our prayer.
Qui sedes ad dexteram Patris,	You who sit at the right hand
	of God the Father,
miserere nobis.	have mercy upon us.
Quoniam tu solus sanctus,	For you only are holy,
tu solus Dominus,	you only are the Lord,
tu solus altissimus,	you only are most high,
Jesu Christe, cum Sancto	Jesus Christ, with the Holy
Spiritu,	Spirit,
in gloria Dei Patris,	in the glory of God the Father,
Amen.	Amen.

Gloria Patri—The opening words (Glory Be to the Father) of a song of praise to the Holy Trinity that is sung at the end of various sections of the liturgy. Also known as the Lesser DOXOLOGY.

Gospel—A reading from one of the four Biblical Gospels (by Matthew, Mark, Luke, and John) which, in the Roman Catholic church, may be spoken or chanted.

Gospel motet—A MOTET on a text from one of the four Gospels: Matthew, Mark, Luke, or John. Since the Gospel reading was the chief of the lessons for each day of the LITURGICAL YEAR, entire cycles of Gospel motets were collected to correspond to the assigned readings. Among the best of the historical Protestant publications of Gospel motet cycles are those by Melchior Vulpius (1612–1614) and Melchior Franck (1623). The Gospel motet was one of the traditional genres revived in twentieth-century Germany. (See example 24.)

Gospel music—Religious music that seeks to express the personal and emotional religious experience of evangelical Protestants. Unlike the Negro spiritual, the gospel song has a composer (either white or black) and communicates in a popular, not a folk-song, idiom. Perhaps the best measure of gospel music's popularity has been the assimilation of a significant body of favorite songs into the hymnals of Baptists, Methodists, and other Protestant denominations.

The history of gospel music begins with the early nineteenth-century popular HYMNODY that was sung in the CAMP MEETING and published in collections for use in Sunday schools and domestic settings. Songs in the same simple melodic and harmonic manner, often in strophic form with use of a refrain, played a large role in the evangelistic revivals of the later nineteenth century. The revival meetings led by the evangelist Dwight L. Moody and the musician Ira D. Sankey seem to have made the gospel song a common term, while the immensely popular collections published by Sankey and P. P. Bliss placed gospel songs in churches and homes all over the country.

As gospel songs and gospel singing won wider acceptance, musicians introduced more and more popular elements into revival music. The informal manner and joviality of Charlie Alexander not only spread the gospel message, it also reflected an increasing degree of commercialism: Alexander's collections of gospel hymns brought him considerable personal wealth. The gospel musican Homer Rodeheaver, famous for his long association with the evangelist Billy Sunday, established a highly successful publishing house for gospel music and his own record company. He also introduced into his revival services the use of large choirs and orchestral instruments, a practice that was to be followed by many in the new era of radio evangelism.

The modern era of gospel music coincides with radio evangelism on the one hand, and with the growth of the fundamentalist denominations spawned by revivalism on the other. The director of the Moody Bible Institute's radio station from its beginning in 1926 was Wendell Loveless, who composed many popular gospel choruses that reflected the more sophisticated language of early twentieth-century popular song: occasional chromatic harmonies, dance-like rhythms, and catchy sentimental melodies. Another modern trend is for people to listen to performances of gospel music by others, whether by choirs, one soloist, or such favorite ensembles as male quartets. Consider the status of the gospel song in the ministry of Billy Graham: it is sung mainly by soloist and/or chorus; it is a relatively small part of the revival proceedings; and it is usually an old favorite that is well known to the audience. Although many gospel songs are still being written, it is in general only familiar repertory that is heard in the context of white radio and television evangelism.

Alongside the white tradition of gospel music, and sharing in its heritage, there arose a distinctive and distinguished black gospel music tradition. Its roots lay in the same fertile soil that produced the Negro spiritual and the blues. Even when songs were drawn from the white gospel tradition, the manner of performance was distinctively black, especially in its reliance upon improvisation. Black gospel music grew as an integral part of black church services. As in the case of white gospel music, it was, in general, at its most emotional and powerful among the congregations lowest on the social scale. Gospel quartets and gospel choirs flourished in black churches, leading highly responsive congregations. Among the most characteristic musical features of black gospel music were its unique vocal timbres, the important place of improvised ornamentation, and the use of call and response between leader and chorus or congregation. The simplicity of the structure and reliance upon repetition in black gospel songs are related to their suitability for individual improvisation.

After World War II, when recordings and radio stations made black gospel music widely known, its popularity and influence grew tremendously. Composers such as Thomas A. Dorsey ("Precious Lord, Take My Hand") and performers such as Mahalia Jackson reached many thousands with their gospel message. Although gospel music at first drew upon popular styles like the blues and, in the 1950s, rhythm and blues, to increase its expressive possibilities and attract a wider audience, by the 1970s popular music styles such as "soul music" had reversed the direction of influence and were relying in large part on the style of gospel music for their appeal. Among the best of present-day popular musicians are many who, like Ray Charles and Aretha Franklin, came from the ranks of gospel singers.

The current popularity of gospel music—now completely secularized—may be estimated by the results of a survey made in 1980 by Warner Communications, which ranked "Christian Music" as the fifth-highest selling category of long-playing discs. Among the subcategories that make up this body of Christian music are: Southern quartet-singing, usually by whites; contemporary gospel music performed by black musicians; traditional gospel music, which refers to the earlier black style of Mahalia Jackson, among others; and contemporary Christian music. The term "contemporary Christian music" refers mainly to recent styles cultivated largely by white musicians. After the fairly conservative gospel idiom of the early 1960s, when harmonies were for the most part traditional and the religious message was neutral, came a change to a more sophisticated chord vocabulary, to contemporary instruments (like electric guitar), and to a bolder message, as in the highly popular songs of the Bill Gaither Trio. The rebellious state of youth in the later sixties and seventies found even more emphatic expression in the heavier beat, more complex rhythms, and "heavy metal" sound of Christian rock music as heard in groups such as Servant and The Resurrection Band.

Gospel music, most of it somewhat traditional in nature, is undoubtedly a significant factor in the religious movement in which approximately twenty-five percent of Americans regard themselves as "born-again Christians," according to a Gallup poll of the early 1980s. It seems likely to remain an important means of musico-religious expression and a potent commercial force in the music and entertainment business for years to come.

Gradual (Latin, *graduale*)—The liturgical book that contains the chants for the Roman Catholic Mass. The term also refers to an item of the Mass Proper that is sung after the reading of the Epistle. As a chant, therefore, a Gradual is usually based on a text from the psalms; its music is frequently melismatic (having several notes per syllable of text) and is sung in a RESPONSORIAL manner.

Great Service—See SERVICE.

Gregorian chant—The official liturgical music of the Roman Catholic church. (See CHANT.)

Grigny, Nicolas de (1672–1703)—An outstanding French organist and composer of organ music, Grigny was briefly (1693–1695) organist of Saint Denis in Paris, and then returned to his birthplace to serve for the rest of his life as organist of the Cathedral of Rheims. Like his great contemporary François COUPERIN, the composer came from a musical family, of which several members had been organists in Rheims.

Grigny's reputation rests firmly upon just one collection of organ music, a volume that J. S. BACH himself saw fit to copy in 1703. The *Premier livre d'orgue* (First Book for the Organ) of 1699 contains an ORGAN MASS, five hymn settings, and four miscellaneous church pieces. Listed among the contents of the Mass are five VERSETS for the KYRIE, nine for the GLORIA, an OFFERTORY, three versets for the SANCTUS, an Elevation, two versets for the AGNUS DEI, and a COMMUNION. For the sections of the Mass ORDINARY and for each of the five hymns, the composer offers first a polyphonic setting of the appropriate Gregorian CANTUS FIRMUS, and then a fugal movement based on themes drawn from the plainchant. The other movements are set more freely, usually without reference to chant. According to Almonte Howell (*The New Grove Dictionary*, vol. 7, p. 731), Grigny excelled in his use of the organ pedals and of contrasting timbres: "In other respects, too, Grigny's work is more distinguished than that of his predecessors and contemporaries: in richness of texture, complexity of counterpoint, expressiveness of melodic embellishment, seriousness of purpose and intensity of feeling."

hallelujah—See ALLELUIA.

handbells—A set of hand-held bells encompassing from two to five chromatic octaves. Originally, handbells were rung in sequence as a means of practice by ringers of church bells. They came to be used for civic occasions in the eighteenth century, especially at Christmas season. In the twentieth century, they have become a popular part of the church music program, a community activity for amateur musicians, and an alternative ensemble for college students.

Handel, George Frideric (1685–1759)—The founder and greatest composer of oratorio in the English language, Handel was also the leading composer of Italian opera in the late Baroque period. Born in Germany, he served briefly as an organist at the Calvinist cathedral in Halle, then chose to make his career principally as an opera composer, first at Hamburg (1703–1706), then in Italy (1706–1710), and eventually in London (1710–1737). Only after 1737, when the cause of opera in England faltered, did he focus his attention on the composition of oratorios. During intervals in oratorio performances he displayed his ability as an organ virtuoso with a wonderful gift for improvisation.

Handel wrote very little church music. An enthusiastic and renowned organist, he nevertheless did not compose any organ music for use in the church service. Although he composed a PASSION (now at least doubtful in provenance) and later a Passion oratorio in his native language, his departure from Germany clearly indicated that he did not wish to be a church musician. In Italy, his few Latin MOTETS on Psalm texts, a SALVE REGINA, and two oratorios in Italian were but a part of his learning experience. In his adopted country of England he composed fewer than twenty ANTHEMS and twenty-six English ORATORIOS, none of which was designed as church music or performed regularly in churches during his lifetime. Perhaps his greatest contributions of that kind were the three hymn tunes he composed for the Methodist Wesleys, now known as "Fitzwilliam," "Gopsall," and "Cannons." During the eighteenth century, conditions forced creative musicians to seek their careers elsewhere, and church music fell into decline. Although he was certainly a believer, Handel's lifelong Lutheranism was shaped during the Enlightenment as a nondogmatic faith enriched by humanism and marked by well-documented generosity towards the needy. The Founding Hospital was a favorite charity, and one of his finest anthems, "Blessed Are They That Consider the Poor," was composed for it. The anthem is one of few distinguished by the presence of a chorale melody ("Aus tiefer Not").

Handel's anthems are basically of a ceremonial rather than a religious nature. All of them require an orchestra, which was no longer common in regular religious observances, even in the CHAPEL ROYAL. Eleven of them were composed between 1716 and 1720 for devotions at the estate of the Duke of Chandos, who was much concerned with displaying his lavish patronage. Composed almost entirely on texts drawn from the Psalms, the Chandos anthems represent the wide scope of Handel's art, ranging from the grand manner of "The Lord Is My Light" (No. 10) to the penitential character of "Have Mercy on Me, O God" (No. 3). His mastery of choral writing and of fugue are particularly striking for an opera composer. Not only did these anthems establish patterns for many of his later works, they also contain many sections that he later used again. Among the occasional anthems by Handel, who served more or less as composer laureate of England at this time, are four for the coronation of 1727 (among them the magnificent "Zadok, the Priest"), two for royal weddings, and one for a funeral (the exceptionally moving "The Ways of Zion Do Mourn"); the famous Dettingen anthem and his TE DEUM were composed in 1743 to celebrate a military victory.

The English oratorios of Handel were conceived as popular, semi-religious entertainments for the concert hall, and not as acts of worship. The genre underwent some years of evolution between his first efforts in 1718 and his wholehearted adoption of it after the success of *Saul* in 1739. Although the composer was often impeded by weak libretti, he found that the genre offered advantages not found in opera. Chief among them was the use of a true chorus, the usual size (about twenty) and makeup (boy sopranos and men) of which may surprise some modern choir directors. Choruses in the oratorios could be patterned after the motet and compositions in concertato style, or they could be written in fugue or for double chorus. This wider variety of styles contributed in part to the greater artistic and popular success of the genre, but its major attraction seems to have been its Old Testament subjects and the English public's presumed identification with the chosen people of God. There are five basic types of Handelian oratorios, only three of them biblical in substance: the dramatic-heroic (e.g., *Belshazzar*), the narrative-heroic (*Jephtha*), and the choral epic (*Israel in Egypt*). The nonbiblical types are either mythological (*Hercules*) or allegorical (*Alexander's Feast*). In both its theme and its reliance upon the chorus, *Messiah* belongs to the choral or anthem type of oratorio. Its popularity was not immediate; there was opposition in particular to the presentation of a sacred subject in the theater.

Handel's music had an enormous and lasting effect upon English musical life and, by extension, upon music in America; it elevated the taste of the public and contributed significantly to the founding of societies for choral singing. The imitations of his style, however, and the posthumous adaptations of his works for use as anthems, cantatas, psalms, and hymns in the church proved injurious not only to native creative efforts, but also to Handel's reputation, since they diminished and obscured the magnitude of his achievement.

harmonium—A keyboard instrument whose reeds are set in vibration by bellows operated by pedals or by electricity. Invented in the nineteenth century and popular as a substitute in America for the church organ, it was widely used for domestic and theatrical music-making.

Haydn, Franz Josef (1732-1809)—The major contributor to the establishment and evolution of Classical style, Haydn was largely responsible for bringing the symphony and the string quartet to artistic maturity; he was also the principal Classical master of both the MASS and the ORATORIO. His experience with church music began when his beautiful singing voice earned him a place at the age of eight as a choirboy at Saint Stephen's Cathedral in Vienna. It continued even after his voice changed, since playing the organ and the violin, as well as singing in church services, helped him to earn his living during the difficult period between the ages of seventeen and twenty-seven, when he applied himself to mastering music theory and composition. After a brief period as music director to Count Morzin, Haydn became in 1761 vice-Kapellmeister to Prince Nikolaus Esterhazy, whose family he was to serve for the rest of his life. His responsibility for supplying sacred music for the court chapel did not begin until 1766, however, when he succeeded Gregor Werner as KAPELLMEISTER after Werner's death.

Haydn was a devout Catholic all his life. "In nomine Domine" (In the Name of God) appears at the beginning of each of his major works, sacred or secular, and "Laus Deo" (Praise God) usually appears at the end. When composition became difficult for him, it was his practice, whatever the task at hand, to kneel and pray or say several *Aves* from his rosary. Nevertheless, he was very much a man of the Enlightenment, unaffected by the cult of PALESTRINA that would soon attempt to restrict church music to an archaic style. For Haydn, the most expressive contemporary styles — from folk-like to operatic — could find expression in his sacred music. A joyous or lighthearted attitude often prevails, as in his important *Missa brevis* in F major from about 1750. In order to abbreviate the length of the Mass, which calls for just two sopranos, a four-voice chorus, and a small orchestra of two violin parts, organ, and string bass, the composer employs a homophonic texture; he also shortens the longer movements by adopting the custom of having each of the four voice-parts sing different lines of the Mass text simultaneously. The sacred works from Haydn's youth were essentially Italianate in style, since Vienna had long been a musical satellite of Italy. The Neapolitan influence of Porpora, an important teacher for Haydn, can be heard in his *Salve Regina* in E major (c.1756), for soprano solo, four-voice chorus, two violin parts, and basso continuo. Among the liturgical works of this period, many of them of questionable authorship, the one which most clearly reflects the hand of a promising composer may be the *Te Deum* in C (c.1762–1765); it has also been attributed to Haydn's younger brother Michael, who enjoyed a successful career as a church composer in Salzburg.

Part of Haydn's duties as Kapellmeister at Esterhazy was to provide sacred music for the court chapel. He composed six Masses and numerous smaller liturgical settings between 1766 and 1783, when edicts against elaborate music as well as instrumental music in the church caused him to shift his interests away from church music. The Masses, three of which are composed on a very large scale, all require orchestra, four-voice chorus, and (with the exception of the *Little Organ Mass*) four vocal soloists. They reveal a gradual synthesis of Italianate traits with various Austro-German Baroque and Classical features to create a style of the composer's own. Of particular significance for the future is his adoption of the symphonic sonata-allegro form in the Kyrie of *Missa Cellensis* (Mariazeller Messe) of 1782. Among the other liturgical works from this period are a "Salve Regina" (1766) and a large "Stabat Mater" (1767). The composer's growing reputation led, in 1770, to a new contract as Kapellmeister in which the Prince yielded rights of ownership over Haydn's compositions to the composer. Outside commissions now became more common, and one of them resulted in a grand oratorio entitled *Il ritorno di Tobia* (The Return of Tobias). Composed on an Italian libretto, it was performed with great success in Vienna in 1775 and contains some of Haydn's finest music in the Italian manner, as well as some excellent choruses (several of them added in a later revision). Another commission led to the composition of *The Seven Last Words*, which began its life in about 1785 as a series of orchestral pieces for Lenten performance at the Cathedral of Cadiz in Spain.

When Haydn turned once again in earnest to the composition of sacred music, the new level of symphonic writing he had attained in the London symphonies was to be reflected in all of his remaining compositions for orchestra. After 1790, restrictions on church music had been eased under a new emperor, and the accession of a new Prince Esterhazy in 1794 gave Haydn the obligation to compose a new Mass each year to celebrate the name day of Princess Maria. From 1796 to 1802 six Masses were composed, each among the great masterpieces of Haydn's last period.

The *Missa in angustiis* (also known as the *Lord Nelson Mass*), composed for performance in 1798, reveals many features common to the group: a purely Classical style rooted in large-scale symphonic structures; more independent and more varied use of the orchestra; greater variety in the use of the chorus combined with a reduced role for the vocal soloists; greater concern for expressing the text; an increased use of third-relationships; emphasis upon a simpler melodic idiom; and an increased use of contrapuntal writing and of fugue. An exceptional degree of intensity characterizes the *Missa in angustiis*, deriving partly from its beginning in minor mode and partly from Haydn's unusual use of an orchestra that has three parts for trumpets and none for woodwinds. Also noteworthy are the antiphonal writing in the Kyrie and the Gloria, the composer's use of canon to open the Credo, the beauty of the slow movement for solo soprano at "Et incarnatus," the dramatic return of the opening fanfare of the Kyrie during the "Crucifixus," the recurrence of D minor for the "Benedictus," and the powerful fugue that closes the Agnus Dei.

The small-scale sacred pieces from Haydn's last years also deserve mention, among them six English psalms for two sopranos and bass; an Offertory in *stile antico* entitled "Non nobis Domine," for four singers and basso continuo; and especially a powerful *Te Deum* in C composed for the Empress Marie Therese. The *Te Deum*, composed for a four-voice chorus and large orchestra, opens by quoting the eighth Gregorian psalm tone and closes with a magnificent double fugue.

Perhaps Haydn's most stimulating musical experiences during his two visits to London were the performances he heard of Handel's *Messiah* and *Israel in Egypt* in 1791. His attraction to the genre of oratorio as shaped by Handel was immediate and was to result in the composition in 1798 of the oratorios that culminate his long career. First, almost as an exercise, Haydn adapted *The Seven Last Words* into a Passion oratorio in 1796 by (1) adding text, four vocal soloists, and a four-voice chorus to the somewhat modified orchestral interludes of the original composition, (2) inserting *a cappella* chanting by the chorus of each sacred word before its corresponding movement, and (3) composing a striking new instrumental movement to open the second part of the composition.

Die Schoepfung (The Creation) was composed by Haydn from 1796 to 1798 on an English text inspired by the Bible and John Milton's *Paradise Lost*. It was translated into German by Baron Gottfried van Swieten, who had also adapted the words for the vocal version of *The Seven Last Words*. Van Swieten, a noted connoisseur of music and an amateur composer, not only served as translator for *The Creation*; he also seems to have written some of the words, and he certainly made suggestions that Haydn usually followed as he composed. Narration and description of God's work takes place in the first two parts of the oratorio through the archangels Gabriel, Uriel, and Raphael; the last part introduces Adam and Eve among its four soloists. The oratorio unfolds in three large parts, the first beginning with a wonderful orchestral representation of Chaos, the second with the fifth day and the creation of animals, and the third with a pastoral scene of praise by the first human beings; each part unfolds in recitatives, arias, ensembles, and choruses that reveal Haydn at his most inventive. Everywhere the glories of the natural world are depicted by magical use of orchestral tone-painting, often preceding the explanatory text. Finally, each part closes with a powerful chorus, part 1 with the popular "The Heavens Are Telling," part 2 with "Achieved Is the Glorious Work," and part 3 with a double fugue.

In 1801, Haydn followed the enormous success of *The Creation* with *Die Jahreszeiten* (The Seasons), based on an English text by James Thomson. Once again van Swieten translated and adapted the text, this time not entirely to the Haydn's satisfaction. Nevertheless, the elderly composer summoned all his powers and succeeded in adapting the same musical means he had employed in *The Creation* to the humbler realm of humanity observing the passing of the four seasons.

In his late oratorios, free of liturgical demands and inspired by the words of the Bible, Haydn's imagination took wing and created the ultimate synthesis of all his hard-won musical skills: his mastery of the Classical symphonic ideal and of the orchestra, his Handel-inspired renewal of interest in choral writing, and his gift for vocal music of a dramatic kind. The oratorios constitute a tribute to a remarkable and decaying era, the Age of Enlightenment. Just as the Roman Catholic church intervened in 1783 in a belated attempt to keep secular elements from the Mass, so it objected immediately to *The Creation* and banned it from ecclesiastical edifices. Like the orchestral Masses, the oratorios of Haydn must be regarded primarily as religious music for the concert hall, even when that hall happens to be located in a church.

Historia—A Latin and Italian word (in English, "history") that was used during the the BAROQUE PERIOD to refer to a musical setting of a biblical story, most often the events of Christmas, the Passion, or the Resurrection. The word has often been used for the Latin oratorios of Giacomo CARISSIMI, but it remains unclear whether such titles as *Historia di Jephte* were supplied by the composer or by later copyists. Such works are usually treated by scholars as ORATORIOS. In France during the Baroque period the term *histoire sacrée* (sacred history) was used with reference to oratorio-like compositions by Marc-Antoine CHARPENTIER, a student of Carissimi. In Germany, Heinrich SCHUETZ used the word *historia* in the titles of several works, such as *Historia, der freuden- und gnadenreichen Geburth Gottes und Marien Sohnes, Jesu Christi* (History of the Joyful and Gracious Birth of God and Mary's Son Jesus Christ); in this instance, perhaps for obvious reasons, the composition is popularly known as *The Christmas Story* and it is usually discussed with the history of oratorio. Works on the Passion story that Schuetz entitled *Historia* are now called PASSIONS. When Hugo DISTLER and other twentieth-century German composers revived the historia after the acknowledged model of Schuetz, as in Distler's *Die Weihnachtsgeschichte* (The Christmas Story), they often used in their titles the German word *Geschichte*, which means "history" or "story".

Historicus—A Latin word that refers to the narrator in an oratorio. In Italy, the term used for the narrator was *testo*.

Holy Communion—In some Protestant services, in contrast to its central position in the Roman Catholic MASS, Holy Communion (partaking of the sanctified bread and wine) is often observed only on special occasions or at regular intervals. It is also known as the EUCHARIST.

hosanna—A Greek and Hebrew word of praise and beseeching that occurs most notably in the SANCTUS of the MASS Ordinary.

Hovhaness, Alan (1911–)—An American who has received acclaim for his success in creating a significant body of church music in a thoroughly modern idiom, Hovhaness has composed prolifically in a wide variety of mediums and genres. His choral works number more than sixty, approximately half of them featuring one or more soloists. Many of them, through the composer's use of modality and various non-Western characteristics, sound quite different from standard Western church music and yet, through his concern for their functional use, prove both performable and pleasing. In the *Thirtieth Ode of Solomon* (1948), a CANTATA for baritone, chorus, and string orchestra plus trumpet and trombone, the composer achieved a considerable success by employing both vocal and instrumental cantillations along with exotic timbres. Another of his many accompanied choral works rendered challenging but still singable by his use of complex rhythms and counterpoint is the ANTHEM entitled "From the End of the Earth" (1952). The use of the chorus is particularly noteworthy in the composer's *Magnificat* (1959), written for four soloists, chorus, and orchestra, in which the words are enhanced by powerful sections marked *senza misura* (without measure). Among the church compositions by Hovhaness that best capture his lyric gift are those requiring a solo vocalist, such as his revised setting from 1958 of "Out of the Depths." Hovhaness's abiding love for music of the RENAISSANCE period found expression in his many unaccompanied church works, including numerous MOTETS, while his concern for communicating with his audience led to the composition of a folk MASS, *The Way of Jesus* (1974).

Howells, Herbert (1892–1983) — An Englishman, Howells ranks among the best twentieth-century composers of church music in the English cathedral tradition. Like VAUGHAN WILLIAMS, a close friend, he studied composition with Charles STANFORD at the Royal College of Music, where, beginning in 1920, he taught composition for more than sixty years. From 1936 he also served for many years as music director at Saint Paul's Girls' School, where he succeeded Gustav Holst. As a young man, Howells established his name as a composer of keyboard pieces, chamber music, and orchestral works. His secular output also includes many choral pieces and, worthy of special emphasis, more than forty songs. His style represents an individual synthesis of elements drawn from such respected contemporaries as Vaughan Williams, Edward Elgar, and Frederick Delius.

Howells composed a significant and varied body of music for the church. Most of the organ works, among them two sonatas and six psalm-preludes, were written before World War II, while most of the sacred choral music was composed afterwards. Among the works on liturgical texts are a number of CANTICLES, *Hymn for St. Cecilia*, *Sequence for St. Michael*, a STABAT MATER, and several MASSES, some in English and some in Latin. Certain of these works, like the *Missa Sabrinensis*, are composed for soloists, chorus, and orchestra on the large scale traditional for the major English choral festivals and societies. Much smaller in scale and relatively few in number, the ANTHEMS and MOTETS also contribute to the composer's reputation; "Take Him, Earth, for Cherishing" is an unaccompanied motet written in 1964 on the death of President John F. Kennedy. Perhaps the finest of Howells's works is *Hymnus Paradisi*, composed in 1938 for soprano, tenor, chorus, and orchestra. Set to a variety of English and Latin texts, some drawn from the liturgy and some from the Bible, it is the composer's memorial for the death of his young son.

Humfrey, Pelham (1647–1674) — Humfrey was among the leading composers of the Restoration period in England, the time after 1660 when the musical traditions of the CHAPEL ROYAL were re-established along with the monarchy. Humfrey spent the years from 1660 to 1664 as a chorister in the Chapel Royal. A period of foreign travel followed, during which he became acquainted firsthand with contemporary French and Italian music. In 1667, Humfrey became a Gentleman of the Chapel Royal; it remained the focus of his efforts until his death. Church music stands foremost in the composer's relatively small output: eighteen extant ANTHEMS (and one written together with Blow and Turner), five sacred songs, one complete SERVICE (including Morning Prayer, Communion, and Evening Prayer), and one chant for the Anglican Service. The anthems are generally acknowledged to be his finest works. As verse anthems, they rely mostly upon solo and ensemble singing rather than the chorus; introductory instrumental movements and ritornellos are assigned to an ensemble of four-part strings. Italianate expression of emotion in response to a moving text, as in "By the Waters of Babylon," characterizes the best of his anthems.

hymn—In the ordinary application of the term, "hymn" refers to a strophic song that expresses a religious emotion; its metrical text is generally sung in the worship service by a group rather than an individual. The hymn had already found a place in the Divine OFFICE of the Roman Catholic church by the third century, principally in LAUDS and VESPERS. (See also HYMNODY.) It should also be noted that the word has been used in a special sense for almost any song of praise, as in Edmund Spenser's "Hymne in Honour of Love."

hymn-anthem—The transformation of a hymn, often one unknown to the congregation, into an ANTHEM for the use of a church choir became common in both England and the United States during the late nineteenth and twentieth centuries. Such distinguished composers as Gustav Holst and Healey WILLAN have contributed to the repertory, drawing upon some of the traditional techniques of the CHORALE in the process.

hymn meter—The meter of a hymn as expressed by the number of syllables in its lines and the placement of its poetic accent. The former falls most often into Common Meter (8.6.8.6), Short Meter (6.6.8.6), or Long Meter (8.8.8.8); the latter follows the patterns for iambic, trochaic, anapestic, or dactylic accents.

Hymn of the Week—See DE TEMPORE HYMN.

hymn tune—The melody of a hymn, as distinct from its harmony. Tunes that have a fixed text are termed "proper"; those used interchangeably with other tunes of the same meter are termed "common."

hymnal—A collection of hymns, usually those of a certain denomination. The various churches created by the Protestant Reformation generated a long series of hymnals designed to increase congregational participation in their services.

hymnody—The foundation of Christian hymnody lies in the Hebrew songs of praise contained in the Old Testament. They were used as hymns by the early Christians, who soon added songs of their own invention. The liturgical hymn was concisely defined as early as the sixth century by Saint Ambrose, who wrote that "a hymn. . .contains three elements: song, and praise, it being praise of God." Ambrose himself contributed a number of hymns to the repertory of the early Christian church, where they served as a model for succeeding poets. Saint Augustine enthusiastically accepted the Ambrosian model, adding to it the condition that Christ serve as one of the objects of praise, as in the New Testament references to hymns by Paul. Among the early Latin hymns that have served through the centuries is the Advent hymn entitled "O Come, O Come, Emmanuel" by its translator, John Mason Neale.

No single formula has ever been accepted for the style or the structure of hymns. Even the aspect of congregational participation has not always applied, particularly in the Roman Catholic church, which did not officially recognize the hymn as part of the service until the twelfth century. Emphasis upon the OFFICE in monastic life during the Medieval period provided many opportunities for hymn writers; one of the best known of them was the renowned Bernard of Clairvaux. It was also during this time that a special kind of hymn, the SEQUENCE, emerged; so prominent was its use in the service that action was taken during the COUNCIL OF TRENT to abolish all but four sequences from the liturgy.

The impact of a powerful congregational hymnody lay at the heart of the Protestant Reformation, a movement led by Martin LUTHER that split the church asunder in the sixteenth century. Among Luther's contributions to the German hymn (known as the CHORALE) are numerous translations of Latin hymns; many paraphrases from the Psalms (among them the famous "Ein' feste Burg ist unser Gott"); and a few original hymns (e.g., "Christ lag in Todesbanden," later the text of a chorale CANTATA by J. S. BACH). German hymnody of the subsequent period was less vigorous and more expressive of personal religious feelings, a trend that had considerable influence on English hymnody in the eighteenth century.

The outstanding figure in the rise of English hymnody was Isaac Watts (1674–1748), who was often called the "founder of English hymnody." The simplicity and clarity of expression he achieved in such well-loved poems as "When I Survey the Wondrous Cross" and "O God, Our Help in Ages Past" established a model for succeeding hymn writers and served as a link to the religious revival led by John and Charles WESLEY later in the century. The Wesleys' main contribution was the evangelical hymn, a spiritual call-to-arms during a period when the hymn played an insignificant role in the Church of England. In the nineteenth century, the single most important hymnist was John Mason Neale, who wrote numerous original hymns and translations that have never, since then, been absent from English-speaking churches. During the second half of the century, English hymnody was influenced by the Oxford Movement; with its publication of HYMNS ANCIENT AND MODERN (1861), the doors of the Anglican Church were at last open to the hymn.

As in England, the rise of the hymn in the United States occurred when the introduction of hymn collections by Isaac Watts and the Wesleys offered an alternative to traditional psalm singing. In addition, Mennonite and Moravian immigrants brought their hymns with them and eventually sang them in English translations. Noteworthy among those who forged a distinctive poetry for American hymnody were Timothy Dwight (a Presbyterian), George Washington Doane (Episcopalian), Samuel Longfellow (Unitarian), and Ray Palmer (Congregational). Lowell MASON stands foremost among composers of hymn tunes, not only for his approximately 1,200 original melodies (e.g., "Olivet," sung to the words "My faith looks up to thee"), but also for his hundreds of hymn adaptations from music by European composers. Two distinctively American sources also enriched church hymnody during the nineteenth century: the SPIRITUAL and GOSPEL MUSIC.

In the twentieth century, modern hymnals have brought together a wide range of hymns from the past and the present. While the renewed interest in church music by twentieth-century composers of substance has, in general, not included hymnody, the original hymn tunes and hymn arrangements by Ralph VAUGHAN WILLIAMS are outstanding exceptions. More significantly, hymnody has served as a focal point for introducing timely social issues and contemporary musical idioms into the church. Popular elements, such as jazz styles, are expressed in hymn tunes, while hymn texts reflect increasing concern for world brotherhood and social relevance. The interested reader is invited to pursue the subject of hymnody past and present in such books as Erik Routley's *Panorama of Christian Hymnody* (Liturgical Press, 1979), Austin Lovelace's *Anatomy of Hymnody* (Abingdon Press, 1965), and William Reynolds's *Survey of Christian Hymnody* (3rd ed., Hope Publishing, 1987).

hymnology—The study of all aspects of the HYMN constitutes the discipline of hymnology.

Hymns Ancient and Modern—One of the most significant collections of songs for congregational worship, this hymnal was published in 1861 by a committee representing more than two hundred Anglican clergymen. The major hymnological contribution of the Oxford Movement, a nineteenth-century attempt to deepen spirituality in the Church of England, it was designed to include both the old and the new, from Latin hymns with their plainsong melodies and favorite German hymns of the past to the best of contemporary hymns. Its popularity led to sales of sixty million copies by 1912, and to various revised editions dating from 1875 to the present; its influence extended to all English-speaking churches.

imitation—The term refers to the appearance of the same theme in different voice-parts, each entering in turn. Imitative COUNTERPOINT is one of the basic textures of church music; its relatively impersonal quality—as opposed to solo singing—is particularly suited for maintaining liturgical propriety, but its inherent demand for considerable compositional technique places it outside the grasp of most amateur composers.

Improperia—Latin for "reproaches," the term refers to God's disappointment with man. This is expressed in the Roman Catholic liturgy during a series of chants on Old Testament verses sung at the Veneration of the Cross on Good Friday. The verses have often been performed in the settings by PALESTRINA.

in nomine—An English tradition developed in the sixteenth and seventeenth centuries whereby John TAVERNER's setting of the Latin words *in nomine Domini* (found in the BENEDICTUS of the MASS and meaning "in the name of God") served as a CANTUS FIRMUS for many subsequent instrumental compositions, some of them bearing the title "Gloria tibi Trinitas," after the SARUM antiphon by that name.

Incarnation—The belief that a god can assume human form has been common to many of the world's religions. Central to the Christian religions is the belief in God's incarnation in human form in the person of Jesus.

intonazione—Italian for "intonation"; the short liturgical pieces composed for organ with this name were intended to establish the pitch and the mode of the liturgical CHANT that followed. Those by Giovanni GABRIELI preserve the genre's improvisatory character. (See also ORGAN MUSIC.)

intoning—Like the Roman Catholic use of reciting tones to convey psalms and other texts, the practice of intoning is common in Anglican and Lutheran churches for the singing of prayers and VERSICLES.

Introit—In the Roman Catholic liturgy, the Introit stands first among the chants of the Mass PROPER. It is sung during the procession of the celebrant to the altar in the following order: ANTIPHON, psalm verse, antiphon (sometimes omitted), GLORIA PATRI, and antiphon. Antiphon texts are usually drawn from the Bible, many of them from Psalms, and are related to the liturgical theme for the day. Verse texts are always from the Psalms. Introit antiphons vary widely in musical style; the verses and the Gloria Patri offer contrast by being chanted to the appropriate PSALM TONE. Historically, the Introit seems to have originated in the practice of antiphonal psalm singing by the congregation. Because each Sunday in the LITURGICAL YEAR has its own Introit, various lesser Sundays can be referred to by the first word of the Introit. The same practice is responsible for the name of the REQUIEM MASS.

During the Renaissance, instrumental settings of the antiphon for the Introit sometimes replaced part or all of the singing, the resulting compositions were also referred to as introits.

invitation hymn—A hymn used after the sermon in evangelical Protestant churches as an invitation to those in the congregation to declare or reaffirm their faith.

Invitatory—An ANTIPHON whose purpose is to invite the congregation to participate in the subsequent singing of the VENITE in the Anglican service. The antiphon also serves as a refrain between verses of the psalm.

invocation—The prayer which, in speech or in song, calls upon God at the beginning of the worship service.

Isaac, Heinrich (c.1450–1517)—One of the outstanding Franco-Flemish composers of his era, Isaac was greatly respected during the Renaissance and after for both the quality and the variety of his works. In addition to the Masses and motets expected of a Renaissance Netherlander, Isaac mastered the French chanson, the Italian frottola, and the German Lied, in each case respecting their native traditions. For much of his life, Isaac occupied two important court positions. From about 1485 to 1495, he served as a composer and singer at the court of Lorenzo the Magnificent and at the cathedral in Florence, a city with which he maintained close ties. In 1497 he became court composer to Emperor Maximilian I, in whose service he was to remain without the obligation of constant attendance. Through his example and the significance of his students, such as Ludwig SENFL, Isaac exercised considerable influence upon both secular and sacred music in Germany.

Isaac composed about forty settings of the MASS Ordinary, most of them for four voices. About half of them follow the practice in the Netherlands of using either CANTUS FIRMUS or PARODY technique. The remainder represent the custom that Isaac adopted at Maximilian's court of basing the Mass on appropriate Gregorian chants. In keeping with the German practice called ALTERNATIM, these works allow portions of the text to be performed in chant. There are also more than fifty MOTETS by Isaac for use in the church service, principally settings of psalm texts, hymns, RESPONSORIES, and ANTIPHONS. Perhaps Isaac's most noteworthy contribution to the repertory of church music lies in his settings of the parts of the Mass PROPER, a practice that he found customary in Germany. His settings, which are based upon cantus firmi drawn from Gregorian chant, were published after his death in three remarkable volumes entitled the *Choralis constantinus*.

Ite, missa est—The closing words of the Mass Ordinary, meaning "Go, (the congregation) is dismissed." The term MASS derives from this phrase.

jazz (ecclesiastical)—Serving the Word with popular musical idioms is not a new practice in the twentieth century; it has probably always been present to some degree, as in the Medieval use of the SEQUENCE and the Reformation use of the Lutheran CHORALE. Nevertheless, the contrast between the traditional style associated with church music and the secular origins of jazz has presented a greater obstacle than did the differences found in earlier periods of music history. Not until the second half of the twentieth century has jazz gained acceptance in some churches as an indigenous and artistic expression of American culture. Jazz elements in the *Folk Mass* composed in 1956 by Father Geoffrey Beaumont inspired a number of successors, among them a setting of the Methodist liturgy created by Edgar Summerlin in 1959, entitled *Liturgical Jazz: A Musical Setting for an Order of Morning Prayer,* and the *American Jazz Mass* composed by Frank Tirro in 1960. Since that time an increasing number of leading jazz musicians have expressed their faith through church music, including Duke Ellington and Dave Brubeck. Among church musicians, the most noteworthy use of jazz instruments and rhythms seems to have been made by Heinz Werner ZIMMERMAN, as in his *Psalmkonzert* of 1958.

Jewish music—Since religion permeates everyday life in traditional Jewish cultures, there is no clear separation of the sacred from the secular.

Sabbath observances in the home, for example, provide an occasion for religious but nonliturgical music, whereas the synagogue serves as the focus for liturgical singing. There are three major traditions of Jewish music, all of which are represented in modern Israel: (1) the Eastern tradition, influenced to some extent by Middle Eastern music; (2) the Sephardic tradition, which reveals mainly Arabic and Turkish influences; and (3) the Ashkenazic tradition, which is the most influenced by European music. Although all of the traditions sing the same biblical texts and some of the same nonbiblical ones, their liturgies differ significantly.

Jewish synagogue music is traditionally sung to Hebrew texts by men (and perhaps boys) without instrumental accompaniment. Cantillation is the name given to the practice of chanting biblical texts in free rhythm following notated accent marks and using stereotyped melodic formulas. A simple form of cantillation is used in PSALMODY, for which ANTIPHONAL or RESPONSORIAL realization is possible. Prayers are sung to biblical or nonbiblical texts from memory in a melodically and metrically free manner by a soloist, by a soloist along with the congregation, or by a soloist and the congregation in a responsorial fashion. Finally, HYMNS offer nonbiblical religious poetry; they are usually sung by a soloist, often with a great deal of improvisation.

Transmission of the Jewish musical heritage has been by oral tradition and a system of apprenticeship for those chosen to fulfill the leadership role of *chazzan*, or cantor. The traditional system of notation reveals neither pitch nor rhythm to the singer. To an as yet undetermined extent, the music of the early Christian church drew upon the great body of monophonic and modal Jewish chant.

Josquin des Prez (c.1440–1521)—Widely recognized by his contemporaries as the greatest composer of his time, Josquin is now generally ranked among the finest composers who have ever lived. Between his youth in northern France and his return there at the end of his long and distinguished career, he travelled widely and held a number of significant positions. Such was his fame and the quality of his works that publication of them took place not only during his lifetime, especially after 1500, but most remarkably, for many years after his death. Nevertheless, a full and accurate account of his life and of the chronology of his works remains to be written. What is certain is that the composer achieved in his music a new and closer relationship between words and music, a new balance between the linear element of melody and the vertical and structural power of harmony, and a new emphasis upon the texture of imitative counterpoint.

Josquin composed about one hundred MOTETS and twenty MASSES, as well as approximately seventy-five equally famous secular works, mostly chansons. Because of the variety of their texts and Josquin's creation of untraditional solutions to problems of structure, the motets illustrate best the remarkably inventive and expressive power of his music, whereas the Masses demonstrate his extraordinary craftsmanship on the largest scale known to Renaissance composers. In his music, more so than in the works of any other single composer, may be seen the transition from the world of sound of the Early Renaissance to that of the High Renaissance.

The early years of the composer's career found him employed (from 1459 to 1472) in Milan as a singer at Santa Maria Maggiore, and also active (until perhaps 1479) at the court of the Duke of Milan. The compositions of these years lie solidly in the Franco-Flemish tradition of OCKEGHEM, with whom Josquin may have studied. The five-voice motet "Illibata Dei virgo nutrix," for example, begins with a long two-voice passage of a melismatic kind common in the mid-fifteenth century; its structure is based, also traditionally, upon a CANTUS FIRMUS. As far as can be determined among works of such uncertain chronology, the composer's early Masses also demonstrate his interest in abstract structural devices. The *Missa Ad fugam*, which appears to be an early Mass, is unified by a consistent use of CANON between the superius and the tenor parts; in addition, as in the works of Dufay, a head motive opens each movement of the Mass Ordinary. Like so many of the composers in the Franco-Flemish tradition, Josquin seems to have thrived upon self-imposed compositional limitations.

The years from about 1480 to 1505 found Josquin still in Italy, at first possibly in the service of Cardinal Ascanio Sforza, then (from about 1486 to 1494) as a member of the papal chapel, and (perhaps until 1505) in Ferrara at the court of Duke Hercules d'Este I. The motets of these years display on occasion the use of a cantus firmus or of freely paraphrased plainchant, but more likely now is the systematic use of the technique of IMITATION; by its adoption the composer is better able to derive his melodic materials directly from his texts and to express the meaning of the words in a web of interdependent parts. In the motet "Ave Maria... virgo serena," for example, the prevailing texture of imitative counterpoint is masterfully varied by intervening passages for fewer voices and by sections of homophony; the rate of rhythmic flow, the weight of every cadence, and the pitch intervals and the lengths of the imitative entries are carefully arranged to create a greatly varied and yet unified whole. The same elements of style mark those Masses that can be placed with some assurance in the composer's middle years. In the *Missa "Malheur me bat,"* Josquin used various melodic lines from the chanson by Ockeghem in an original synthesis of such traditional procedures as cantus-firmus technique and canonic writing with the newly developed technique of systematic imitation; in drawing upon more than just the melody of the original chanson, the composer foreshadowed the later sixteenth-century technique of PARODY.

The last fifteen or so years of Josquin's life, during which he apparently enjoyed for some time the patronage of the French court, were spent near his birthplace in northern France. Notwithstanding his advanced age, he composed motets and Masses regarded as the greatest of an era noteworthy for its high musical achievement. Characteristic of the composer's later works are the subordination of his extraordinary technical skill to the formal and expressive ends appropriate for his texts. From this period came such magnificent motets as his five-voice "Salve, Regina" (Hail, Queen), which is based upon the repetition of a four-note motive drawn from plainchant, and the five-voice "De profundis" (Out of the Depths), distinguished by its symbolic and structural use of canon.

In his later years Josquin seems to have enjoyed responding to the musical challenge posed by settings of complete psalms without sacrificing the need to express the essence of his texts in a manner compatible with his humanistic ideals. The text of "Miserere mei, Deus" (Have Mercy upon Me, Lord), which is a moving plea for the remission of sins, is composed of the entire twenty verses of Psalm 50 in the Vulgate Bible. Josquin distributed the verses in such a fashion that the unusually terse cantus firmus, which consists of just two pitches, is sung twenty-one times, and serves as a full five-voice refrain in contrast to the variety of theme and texture given each new phrase of text. The structural plan involves, in part 1, the descent of the cantus firmus through an octave of the phrygian scale; in part 2, diminished by half in note values, the cantus firmus ascends through the same scale; finally, in part 3, the cantus firmus again descends by step, this time in a context expanded and made more expressive by the use of imitation and antiphonal repetition, to a final cadence on the fourth scale-degree of the mode. Not only did the composer render in music the basic theme of man's supplication (in the prominent motives of stepwise ascent of part 1) and God's mercy (in the descending motives of part 3), but he also found musical means to express the words on a smaller scale, as in his use of canon at an unusual duration in order that the music would "lack truth in its inward parts" ("ecce enim veritatem dilexisti"). (See example 18.)

In the Masses of his later years, Josquin also demonstrated fresh solutions to the problem of how to express the meaning of the words

EXAMPLE 18. Josquin des Prez, "Miserere mei, deus" (meas. 56–60)

while constructing a musical parallel to the syntax of the text. In his transcendent *Missa "Pange lingua,"* the composer achieved unparalleled
economy of means by not employing the Gregorian melody as a cantus
firmus in the traditional manner, but rather drawing upon it freely so
that it could inspire every line and every section of the work. In its original
form it can only be heard at the beginning of each section of the Mass
Ordinary. So clearly do the later motets and Masses of Josquin project
both the words and the spirit of his texts that they served as models for
succeeding composers for the remainder of the sixteenth century.

Jubilate—The opening word of Psalm 100 ("O Be Joyful in the Lord"), which may be sung in the Anglican SERVICE during MORNING PRAYER in place of the BENEDICTUS. Among those who have composed Services containing the "Jubilate Deo" are William BYRD and Henry PURCELL.

jubilus—A Latin word referring to the outpouring of jubilation that is permitted to take place musically by means of a highly melismatic passage sung to the final syllable of the Gregorian ALLELUIA. In keeping with its exceptional nature, the *jubilus* received a great variety of musical settings, some of them quite unlike most chant; frequently, the music of the *jubilus* recurs at the close of the verse that follows the Alleluia.

Kantional—See CANTIONALE.

Kapellmeister—A German term that means "master of the chapel," that is to say, of the singers and instrumentalists who make up the musical establishment of a church or, especially in the eighteenth century, a court.

Kyriale—A modern liturgical book of the Roman Catholic church, it contains the chants of the Mass ORDINARY.

Kyrie eleison—An invocation in Greek employed since at least the sixth century in the Roman Catholic MASS. Sung directly after the INTROIT, it constitutes the first item of the Mass ORDINARY. The earliest extant Kyrie chants come from the tenth century, by which time the nine-fold structure of the chant was already established. They frequently bear titles (e.g., "Kyrie Rex genitor") drawn from the Latin words and phrases (commonly called TROPES) that were added in early usage and later suppressed. Before the emergence of the musically unified Mass Ordinary, polyphonic settings of the Kyrie might have been independent or paired with the GLORIA. Because of its brief text, which encouraged melismatic musical treatment, and its clear tripartite structure, the Kyrie was especially favored by composers.

Kyrie eleison (thrice)	Lord, have mercy upon us.
Christe eleison (thrice)	Christ, have mercy upon us.
Kyrie eleison (thrice)	Lord, have mercy upon us.

Lamentations—The Lamentations of Jeremiah, which are found in the Old Testament, serve as the source of texts for liturgical music performed in the Roman Catholic church during Holy Week. Nine groups of verses are used, three each at MATINS on Maundy Thursday, Good Friday, and Holy Saturday. If they are sung in Gregorian CHANT, a special reciting formula is employed (the *tonus lamentationum*). Polyphonic settings appear before the end of the fifteenth century; composers of polyphonic settings in the Renaissance included PALESTRINA, LASSUS, and VICTORIA. Curiously, musical settings retain the Hebrew letters that precede the Biblical verses; the letters are often set in a more contrapuntal style than the Latin text. Settings of the Lamentations in the expressive manner of the Baroque were composed in Italy by CARISSIMI and Alessandro SCARLATTI, and in France—as *leçons de ténèbres*—by CHARPENTIER and François COUPERIN. Notable among the few settings composed during the nineteenth and twentieth centuries is Igor STRAVINSKY's *Threni*.

Langlais, Jean (1907–　)—An outstanding French organist and composer, Langlais has made a significant contribution to both twentieth-century organ music and vocal church music. His works also include orchestral and chamber music and songs. Blind from birth, he won first prize for organ (1930) and then for composition (1932) at the Paris Conservatory, where his teachers included Marcel Dupré, Charles Tournemire, and (for composition) Paul Dukas. In 1939, he succeeded Tournemire as organist at Sainte Clotilde, the church which César Franck had served so long and well. Langlais also taught composition and organ and conducted the choir at the Institution des Jeunes Aveugles. During his career as a concert organist he has made several tours in the United States and has also taught there. Worthy of special note is his extraordinary ability to improvise, a traditional skill among great French organists.
　　Nearly all of the composer's music has been an expression of his religious faith; a prominent aspect of it emerges in his imaginative use of Gregorian chant melodies and modes. The works for organ include three "Paraphrases grégoriennes" (1934), two organ symphonies, *Homage à Frescobaldi* (1952), eight "Pièces modales" (1956), an *Organ Book* (1956), *Office pour la Saint Trinité* (1958), *Livre oecumenique* (1958), *Trois Méditations sur la sainte Trinité* (1962), three voluntaries (1969), and five *Méditations sur l'apocalypse* (1974). Among the vocal works are four Masses, including *Missa in simplicitaté* for chorus and organ (1953) and *Missa Orbis factor* for chorus and organ (1969); three psalms; and a "Festival Alleluia" for chorus and organ (1971).

Lassus, Orlandus (1532–1594)—A master of all the styles and forms of the High Renaissance, Lassus represents the culmination of the great

Franco-Flemish tradition of composition. While still a boy he served the Viceroy of Sicily in a musical capacity and became acquainted firsthand with music in Italy. At twenty-one he was maestro di cappella at the Church of Saint John the Lateran in Rome. After some time in Antwerp, he joined the lavish musical establishment of Duke Albrecht V of Bavaria, where he remained for the rest of his life. At first appointed as a tenor, he became court Kapellmeister in 1563. So close were his ties to the royal family that he chose to stay there after the severe cutbacks that followed Albrecht's death in 1579. Among the duties of the court Kapellmeister were the provision of morning Mass, music for special occasions, and the music education of the choirboys. As a friend and companion of the Duke, Lassus was also called upon to do considerable travelling. A measure of his fame is the estimate made by Jerome Roche in his book entitled *Lassus* (Oxford University Press, 1982), that between 1555 and the composer's death, 530 musical publications (approximately half of all the music printed in the period) contained something composed by Lassus. Signal honors came to Lassus in 1570, when he was knighted by Maximilian II, and in 1574, when the pope made him a Knight of the Golden Spur.

Despite the considerable number and the magnificence of Lassus's own publications, it remains difficult to supply dates and estimated quantities for his enormous output. Widely recognized during his time and ever since as a peerless master of the MOTET, Lassus certainly composed more than five hundred of them, not including compositions on liturgical texts. About two-thirds of the motets are in five or six voices; the remainder range from two or three to as many as twelve voices. Some, to be sure, are not religious, but ceremonial, didactic, on classical texts, or humorous. His first book of motets (in five or six voices) from 1556 reveals Italianate influence as well as the influence of such Netherlanders as Gombert. As early as 1562, however, when the first motet publication (*Sacrae cantiones*) of his years in Germany appeared, his unique mastery is evident; among these works for major church occasions are some of his finest compositions in five voices, including "Videntes stellam" (Seeing the Star). In the well-known motet, "Tristis est anima mea" (My Soul Is Sorrowful), which was published in 1565 in Paris, may be heard his concern for a full triadic sonority, for a balance between contrapuntal and chordal textures, for freedom of imitative writing, and especially for his love for tone-painting. (See example 23.) From 1568 to 1573 no fewer than twenty-four collections of motets poured from his pen, among them the noteworthy Epistle motet entitled "Stabunt justi." In contrast to the expansiveness and elegance of PALESTRINA, the style of

Lassus became somewhat more terse and powerful in his later years, as in his "Ave verum" from a collection in six voices published in 1582.

Lassus composed thirty-four complete psalm settings in three to twelve parts during his career. Since they end before the DOXOLOGY, they are properly termed psalm-motets. The composer chose not to use the Gregorian PSALM TONES as pre-existing material, and he also went against tradition by setting all the verses, rather than leaving the alternate verses for plainsong performance. A special place must be given to his great cycle of seven penitential psalms (*Psalmi Davidis poenitentiales*), which was probably completed in about 1560. As in his other psalm-motets, all the verses are set; by way of exception to the composer's usual practice, the "De profundis" (Out of the Depths) is based upon the use of a Gregorian CANTUS FIRMUS. Yet another cycle of special motets reveals the young Lassus as a forerunner of the expressionistic madrigalists of late Renaissance; the *Prophetiae Sibyllarum* (Sibylline Prophecies) express their humanistic Latin texts in the most intense chromatic language the composer ever employed.

The number of liturgical works by Lassus is also very large, and includes settings of HYMNS, CANTICLES, and RESPONSORIES. Worthy to stand beside the best of his motets is his magnificent five-voice setting of the Lamentations of Jeremiah (*Hieremiae prophetae lamentationes*, 1585). The four PASSIONS, in particular the St. Matthew Passion *(Passio Domini nostri Jesu Christi secundum Mattheum*, 1575) also deserve mention. The composer sets the words of Peter and the others in two- or three-voice imitative counterpoint in contrast to the chordal declamation used for the crowd; the words of the Evangelist and of Christ are left to be sung in plainchant. PLAINCHANT also plays a role in most of the composer's more than one hundred MAGNIFICATS, since he generally set only the even verses of the text. Among the Magnificats are five cycles of settings for each of the eight psalm tones and approximately twenty-five parody settings, perhaps the first of their kind. Most of the composer's approximately sixty MASSES also employ the PARODY technique, which seems to indicate his freedom from the pressures of Tridentine reform felt in Italy. In at least seventeen instances (e.g., *Missa 'Locutus sum'*), he used his own motets as pre-existing material for a Mass. Even more often he used secular models, as in *Missa 'Quand'io pens'al martire'* (based on a madrigal by Arcadelt) and *Missa 'Triste départ'* (based on a chanson by Gombert). In style the composer ranged from simple Missae breves to elaborate polychoral settings, the greatest number of them in five or six voices. With their increasing availability in modern editions it has become clear that the best of the Masses do not lower the standing of this most versatile and prolific of Renaissance composers.

lauda—An Italian term for a song of praise, a nonliturgical genre that flourished in monophonic form during the thirteenth century and remained in use for centuries thereafter. The monophonic *lauda* is folk-like in character and anonymous in provenance. Although it consisted of alternate statements of verse and refrain, its overall musical structure varied. Interpretation of rhythm in monophonic *laude* remains uncertain. Polyphonic *laude* in two or three voices appeared in the fourteenth century; the genre eventually became rather popular in the late fifteenth and sixteenth centuries, as evidenced in the four-voice collections published by Ottaviano Petrucci in Venice in 1507 and 1508. The devotional movement that accompanied the Counter-Reformation brought renewed interest in the *lauda* in the later sixteenth century. Their simple chordal settings and frequent use of traditional tunes and texts often aided congregational worship in the oratories of Filippo Neri.

Lauds—Derived from *laudes* (the Latin word for "praise"), Lauds constitutes the second of the eight services of the OFFICE.

Leisen (or Kirleisen)—A term for German folk hymns (the singular would be *Leise* or *Kirleise*). It stems from use of the Greek words *Kyrie eleison* (Lord, have mercy) at the conclusion of each stanza of the hymn. Monophonic *Leisen* were sung in the early Middle Ages mainly by pilgrims for a variety of religious purposes; at times they were heard as nonliturgical additions to Mass. Certain *Leisen* came to be sung at particular festivals and played an important role in the development of congregational vernacular singing. "Christ ist erstanden" (Christ Has Risen), for example, was sung at Easter by German congregations in alternation with the choir's Latin verses of the sequence "Victimae paschali laudes" (Praises to the Paschal Victim). After the Reformation, the genre was often sung in the Lutheran church in polyphonic settings by such composers as Johann Walther and Michael Praetorius.

Leonin—A Frenchman active as a musician in Paris in the late twelfth century, Leonin is described by the thirteenth-century theorist known as Anonymous IV as the creator of the famous *Magnus liber organi (Great Book of Organa)*. In fact, the music of the manuscript is preserved only in later sources, and Leonin's exact role in its creation is unknown. He may have been the first significant composer of polyphony and the first great composer of church music. The *Magnus liber* contains GRADUALS,

EXAMPLE 19. Leonin, "Viderunt omnes," *Magnus liber* (meas. 31–36)

om _ _ _ _ _ _ _ _ _ _ _ _ _ _ _ _

ALLELUIAS, and RESPONSORIES for the enrichment of the entire church year, thirty-three works for the MASS, and thirteen works for the OFFICE. In these pieces, the various styles of two-voice ORGANUM are extended over the entire liturgical repertory and, apparently, the use of the rhythmic modes is established. (See example 19, an excerpt from the composer's famous "Viderunt omnes" (All the Ends of the Earth Have Seen) in which the closing measures of a passage in free, or sustained, organum is followed by a few measures in DISCANT style.) When *organa* were used in the service, they were sung by two soloists in alternation with plainchant sung by the choir.

Liber responsorialis—A modern liturgical book that gathers the Roman Catholic chants, in particular the RESPONSORIES, for MATINS.

Liber usualis—A modern liturgical book containing (with some exceptions) texts and chants for the most important feasts for both the Roman Catholic MASS and OFFICE.

Lied (plural, *Lieder*)—The German word for "song" of all types. During the MEDIEVAL period and the RENAISSANCE many German songs, whether monophonic or polyphonic, were set to religious but nonliturgical texts.

lining out—The process of leading congregational singing by having each line sung (or read, or both) by a leader before the worshippers sing it. It has frequently been used in English and American Protestant hymn singing since the seventeenth century, initially because of illiteracy.

litany—A liturgical prayer in which words of invocation by a leader alternate with words of petition from the congregation. The word "litany," which comes from the Greek language, may also refer to a procession during which the liturgical words are sung or recited. Litanies have played a significant role in Jewish ritual from an early period, and they have retained an important place in various Eastern Christian liturgies. In the Roman Catholic church, the Litany of the Saints (also known as the Greater or Major Litanies) was instituted in the fifth century, while the Lesser (or Minor) Litanies followed by several centuries. Other litanies also developed, the best known of them being one in honor of the Virgin Mary called the Litany of Loreto (Litania lauretana), for which Mozart composed two settings. Polyphonic settings of the litanies begin to appear in the sixteenth century and eventually include among their authors such major composers as VICTORIA, PALESTRINA, and LASSUS. In the Anglican liturgy a litany (or General Supplication) came to precede the communion service, but did not attract settings by major composers. In the Lutheran Vespers, a litany may be used in place of the MAGNIFICAT.

Liturgia horarum—See LITURGY OF THE HOURS.

liturgical books—See the entries for ANTIPHONAL, BOOK OF COMMON PRAYER, BREVIARY, EVANGELIARY, GRADUAL, KYRIALE, LIBER RESPONSORIALIS, LIBER USUALIS, MARTIROLOGIUM, MISSAL, ORDINAL, PONTIFICALE, PSALTER, RITUALE, SACRAMENTARY, TONARY, TROPER, VESPERALE.

liturgical drama—A dramatic presentation, with both action and music, of a biblical story, usually of Easter or Christmas. With some exceptions, the liturgical drama was sung in the church in Latin by the clergy. Since it flourished chiefly from the tenth to the thirteenth centuries, the music was monophonic in texture and was sometimes drawn directly from Gregorian chant; its rhythms were, in general, not notated in a manner that can be interpreted clearly. Although it has been the subject of considerable research, the liturgical drama remains a complex phenomenon that may not lend itself to a definitive study.

liturgical year—A clear understanding of the major divisions of the liturgical year will enable one to comprehend both the reasons for and the functions of specific forms and pieces of sacred music. Essentially, the Western church bases the Christian year on the week and on the festivals of Easter and Christmas. As a liturgical institution, the week derived from the Jewish observance of the Sabbath as set forth in Exodus (31:13–17) and Deuteronomy (5:14). Christians originally accepted the idea of a day of rest specifically dedicated to God, but transferred that to the first day of the week (Sunday) because the Resurrection occurred on that day. Further, Christians adapted the Jewish fasts of Tuesday and Thursday to Wednesday (the Betrayal) and Friday (the Crucifixion) during Easter. In addition, during the Middle Ages, Thursday became a time of rejoicing because of the Ascension and the institution of the Eucharist, while on Saturday, Christians dedicated themselves to the Blessed Virgin Mary.

The liturgical year begins on the first Sunday in Advent: in the Western church, this commences on the Sunday nearest Saint Andrew's Day (November 30), while the Eastern church places the occasion and its celebration in the middle of November. In the Roman Catholic church, the calendar of the liturgical year is composed of two cycles of feasts: the Proper of the Time (the *Temporale*) and the Proper of the Saints (the *Sanctorale*). The former consists of feasts commemorating events in the life of Christ, while the latter consists of feasts honoring the lives of the saints. Of primary importance in the Christian year is Easter, a movable feast celebrated on the Sunday following the first full moon of spring and lasting for fifty days, until Pentecost. For three centuries Easter was the only festival observed by the entire church. In time the forty days before Easter became known as Lent, a period of prayer and fasting for the entire congregation. In a similar manner, the four weeks before Christmas, a fixed feast adopted in the early fourth century on December 25 to counter a major pagan festival, became a period of preparation known as Advent. Following Christmas comes Epiphany, celebrated on January 6 to mark the visit of the Magi. Forty days after Easter comes the feast in honor of the Ascension, followed by Pentecost (or Whitsunday), which celebrates the Descent of the Holy Ghost on the Apostles. The remaining season of the church year has become a time of Christian education known as Trinity, the name of the Sunday on which Thomas à Becket became Archbishop of Canterbury in 1162. Trinity has itself been subdivided in some twentieth-century American Protestant churches into two seasons: Pentecost and Kingdomtide (which begins on the last Sunday of August). In 1969, the Roman Catholic church introduced a calendar whereby, after Epiphany, the Sundays of the liturgical year are numbered consecutively, excluding the period from the beginning of Lent to Whitsunday (Trinity Sunday). Finally, one may note the tripartite year established by the Eastern church: (1) triodian (the ten weeks before

Easter); (2) pentecostarion (the paschal season); and (3) octoechos (the remainder of the year).

Liturgy of the Hours—The name under which the Second Vatican Council carried out its extensive changes of the Divine OFFICE. Published in 1972, the *Liturgia horarum juxta ritum romanum* designated LAUDS and VESPERS (under the names Morning and Evening Prayer) as the most important hours, transformed MATINS into an Office of Readings that may be said at any time, eliminated PRIME, made it possible to choose among TERCE, SEXT, and NONE, and retained COMPLINE as Night Prayer. Although PSALMODY remains the substance of the Hours, the actual content of the services has been shortened and revised, and an increased role given to hymn singing. Although Gregorian CHANT should be given preference when Latin is used in the Liturgy of the Hours, liturgically suitable music in the vernacular is permitted.

Low Mass—A simplified form of the Roman Catholic MASS that is spoken by a single celebrant, and does not include singing.

Luther—The prime mover of the Protestant Reformation and founder of the Lutheran Church, Martin Luther (1483–1546) believed strongly that music could serve theology by proclaiming the Gospel. As a musician who knew firsthand the power of the medium, he enthusiastically supported not only congregational singing of a popular kind, such as the Lutheran CHORALE, but also the highest levels of the art in the service of God. Even secular music could serve the cause through a process of transformation called CONTRAFACTUM. Two orders of worship were published by Luther as suggestions for his reformed church: the FORMULA MISSAE (1523), which followed closely the Roman Catholic Mass, and the DEUTSCHE MESSE (1526), which translated the service into the vernacular and revised it significantly, particularly in providing for congregational participation. (See LUTHERAN CHURCH MUSIC.)

Lutheran church music—Because Martin LUTHER recognized music as a gift from God and assigned it an important role in his church, the Lutheran musical tradition has been an extraordinarily rich one, as noteworthy for its vast repertory of ORGAN MUSIC as for its choral music and church CANTATAS.

In 1517, Luther led a movement against the Roman Catholic church that ultimately resulted in the establishment of the Lutheran church. Since his Reformation was essentially doctrinal, the traditional forms of worship remained much the same until the formulation in 1523 of his first liturgy, the Latin *Formula missae*, and in 1526 of the vernacular *Deutsche Messe*. Both liturgies allowed considerable latitude for musical development. The most outstanding example of this was the wholehearted adoption of the German hymn, or CHORALE, which was to become the basis not only for the late Renaissance Lutheran MOTET, but also for the elaborate musical genres of the BAROQUE PERIOD, and for much Protestant music in the nineteenth and twentieth centuries as well. Among the important composers of Lutheran church music are such great names as SCHEIDT, SCHUETZ, BUXTEHUDE, and J. S. BACH.

In the seventeenth century, Lutherans began to settle in the New World. Their numbers increased greatly when Henry Melchior Muhlenberg came to Pennsylvania in the early eighteenth century and assumed a position of leadership in the church. By the middle of the nineteenth century, there were so many different Lutheran churches and hymnals that they began to turn to early Lutheran hymnody as a means of unification. The movement towards unifying the liturgical and musical practices of the Lutheran church continued in the twentieth century, aided considerably by the growth of colleges and universities that began to offer degrees in church music after World War I. In time, the three major groups of Lutherans in the United States established the Inter-Lutheran Commission on Worship, which has produced a number of significant joint publications. Perhaps the outstanding result of the modern effort towards uniformity has been the increased role of the congregation in the service, particularly in the chanting of the PSALTER. The Lutheran church has also taken a leading position in the ecumenical movement among Christian churches. (See, among others, the entries on LUTHER, CANTATA, CHORALE, HYMNODY, ORGAN MUSIC, PASSION.)

Machaut, Guillaume de (c.1300–1377) — Apparently the first to set the complete Mass ORDINARY in polyphony, Machaut was the outstanding French composer of the fourteenth century. Although he was an ordained priest, secular vocal music set to his own poetry and intended for the entertainment of his patrons dominated Machaut's output. Even his motets usually have French texts in the upper voices, making them unsuitable for church use. Much of the composer's life was spent as secretary to King John of Bohemia and in service to various high French nobles. Only after the death of his principal patron in 1346 was Machaut able to settle independently in Rheims, where he had been named canon by the pope.

Machaut's church music consists of his famous Notre Dame MASS, several Latin MOTETS, and one Latin piece based on the stylistic device known as hocket (by which a melody is distributed in short fragments

between two voices). The *Messe de Nostre Dame* has often been published
and recorded; it is composed for four voices which, after the practice
of the time, may be doubled by organ or other instruments. In addition
to the usual five movements of the Mass Ordinary, the composer set the
"ITE MISSA EST" (Go, You Are Dismissed). The shorter movements are
composed in isorhythmic fashion on Gregorian cantus firmi. The chief
difficulties in performance of the Mass stem from Machaut's linear
approach to the composing process, which results in complex aggregate
rhythms and a high level of incidental dissonance. (See example 20.)

EXAMPLE 20. Guillaume de Machaut, "Kyrie," *Messe de Nostre Dame* (meas. 1–7)

Of the Latin motets, one was composed for the election of an archbishop
in Rheims and another in honor of Saint Quentin, patron of the church
where the composer was a canon. Certain of them could have been
substituted for chant in appropriate places in the Office. The great double
hocket entitled *Hoquetus David* is based on a MELISMA from an Alleluia
verse. In all of his liturgical music, Machaut may be said to have created
a musical equivalent of the surrounding Gothic architecture through his
use of such rhythmic devices as isorhythm and hocket.

machicotage—A French term referring to the application of ornaments
to PLAINCHANT by singers called *machicots*.

madrigale spirituale — An Italian genre created by setting a nonstrophic religious text in the throughcomposed manner of the Renaissance madrigal or, in some cases, by simply replacing the secular text of an existing madrigal with a devotional one, the resulting composition being termed a CONTRAFACTUM. *Madrigali spirituali* were sung in nonliturgical contexts during the Counter-Reformation, frequently as Lenten entertainment in courts and oratories. They were composed by some of the finest church musicians of the period, among them WILLAERT, PALESTRINA, and Gesualdo.

maestro di cappella — Italian for "master of the chapel"; the term *cappella* refers not only to the place of performance, but also to the musical establishment (the singers and instrumentalists) maintained by an aristocratic patron. In German, the term becomes *Kapellmeister* (or Capellmeister); in French, *maître de chappelle*. By itself, the word *maestro* was, and is, used rather freely to refer not only to conductors, but also to composers, soloists, and teachers of performance. Obviously, there is considerable historical justification for its application to choir directors.

Magnificat — The first word of the CANTICLE of the Blessed Virgin Mary: "Magnificat anima mea Dominum" (My soul doth magnify the Lord; Luke 1:46–55). The Magnificat is sung during VESPERS in the Roman Catholic liturgy and at EVENING PRAYER in the Anglican service. In the early Christian church, the verses of the Magnificat and the succeeding Lesser DOXOLOGY were sung in plainchant to a suitable PSALM TONE. During the RENAISSANCE, it was set polyphonically by most of the great church composers, sometimes with and sometimes without reference to the psalm tone. Many of the settings preserved the customary practice of alternating verses between plainchant and polyphony. In the BAROQUE PERIOD the text was frequently divided into sections and set for soloists, chorus, and orchestra in the manner of a church CANTATA.

Marian antiphon — An ANTIPHON for the Blessed Virgin Mary. The most important ones are those sung, according to the season of the year, at the end of COMPLINE: "Alma Redemptoris Mater," "Ave Regina coelorum," "Regina caeli," and "Salve Regina." All of the Marian antiphons have been favorite sources for composers of polyphony. (See example 12.)

Martirologium — The Latin title (translated as *Martyrology*) of the Roman Catholic liturgical book containing the lives of the saints. It is read as part of the Divine OFFICE.

Mason, Lowell (1792–1872)—The single most influential figure in American music of the nineteenth century, Lowell Mason did much to raise the level of church music and the level of music education in the United States. Born to a musical New England family, Mason went into business as a young man in Savannah, Georgia, where he was able to study music with the German Frederick Abel. Several years of serving as an organist, of composing hymns and anthems, and of teaching in singing schools led him, in 1822, to publish his first collection of church music, *The Boston Handel and Haydn Society Collection of Church Music; Being a Selection of the Most Approved Psalm and Hymn Tunes; Together with Many Beautiful Extracts from the Works of Haydn, Mozart, Beethoven, and Other Eminent Modern Composers*. Its enormous success—twenty-two editions by 1858—prompted his return to Massachusetts in 1827 to become president and music director (until 1832) of the Handel and Haydn Society. He also served area churches as organist and choir director. In 1833, he aided in the founding of the Boston Academy of Music, where he took part in training music teachers. Then, as superintendent of music for the Boston public schools from 1837 to 1845, he oversaw the introduction of music instruction as a regular part of the curriculum for the first time in the United States. Following a trip to Europe in 1851, he centered his activities in New York City, enjoying the fruits of his success and receiving in 1855 the impressive accolade of an honorary doctorate from New York University.

Mason's unflagging efforts on behalf of music were highly successful; indeed, they were highly profitable because they pleased the majority of churchgoers. Through nearly fifty publications of religious music and of collections for children. Mason led a movement of reform that offered European music and musical style as models for American taste and education. Because he often did not indicate the composers of works that appeared in the collections he compiled, it can only be estimated that he composed as many as 1,200 hymn tunes. His "Missionary Hymn" (From Greenland's Icy Mountains), "Bethany" (Nearer, My God, to Thee), and "Olivet" (My Faith Looks Up to Thee) remain among the best-loved American hymns. In addition, he is said to have "adapted" as many as five hundred hymns and anthems from the music of various European composers. To contemporary scholars, however, Mason's efforts had their drawbacks: he failed to recognize the value of the roughhewn New England fuging tunes and anthems that constituted an indigenous American tradition, and he was biased against American folk idioms, including the folk-like nature of revival music. By the time of his death it was difficult for an American to have a significant musical career without European training, and perhaps American musical life has been formed as much in spite of as because of his endeavors.

Mass—The most important and principal public service of the Roman Catholic liturgy, the Mass recreates and commemorates the Last Supper (the Eucharist or the Communion) of the Lord Jesus. The term stands for the Latin word *missa*, as it is found in the closing words of the Mass ceremony: "Ite, missa est." (Go, the congregation is dismissed.) The texts of the Mass vary according to the day of the LITURGICAL YEAR (these texts comprising the Mass Proper), or they remain the same (these comprising the Mass Ordinary). The service may be celebrated either with singing (High Mass) or without (Low Mass), the former frequently resulting in the following three-fold division of texts:

PRAYERS/RECITATIONS	PROPERS	ORDINARY
	1–INTROIT	
		2–KYRIE
		3–GLORIA IN EXCELSIS
4–COLLECT		
5–EPISTLE		
	6–GRADUAL	
	7–ALLELUIA	
	(or TRACT)	
	8–SEQUENCE	
9–GOSPEL		
		10–CREDO

....

	11–OFFERTORY	
12–PREFACE		
		13–SANCTUS
CANON (spoken)		
14–PATER NOSTER		
		15–AGNUS DEI
	16–COMMUNION	
Prayers (spoken)		
17–Postcommunion		
18–ITE MISSA EST		
(or BENEDICAMUS)		

The portion of the Mass up to and including the Credo constitutes the first part of the service, also known as the Liturgy of the Word or the

Mass of the Catechumens (referring to the unbaptized still receiving religious instruction). The second part of the Mass (originally only for the baptized), beginning with the Offertory, comprises the Liturgy of the Eucharist.

As commonly employed by musicians and laypersons, the term *Mass* refers to the principal sung portions of the Mass Ordinary: Kyrie, Gloria, Credo, Sanctus (including the Benedictus), and Agnus Dei. These constitute neither a unified liturgical structure nor the essence of the Eucharistic ceremony. Musical settings of the Ordinary vary widely in style, ranging from CHANT to large-scale compositions for soloists, chorus, and orchestra. A complete service usually offers a mixture of various styles according to the means and taste of the church and the solemnity of the occasion. (See also ORGAN MASS and REQUIEM MASS.)

Plainchant Masses do not represent fixed artistic entities composed by one person. They were usually selected by choice or custom from various large compilations of chants on the same text and arranged in a complete service by church musicians as anonymous as those who composed the individual chants. With the gradual adoption of polyphony by church musicians, the Mass remained a piecemeal whole in which certain texts, generally those of the Mass Proper, were given the special significance accorded by polyphony, while the rest were sung in plainchant.

The earliest important collections of polyphonic church music extant are the eleventh-century manuscripts called the Winchester Tropers and the twelfth-century organa preserved at the monasteries of Santiago de Compostela in Spain and Saint Martial of Limoges in France. The principal genres of early sacred polyphony, especially that of ORGANUM (whose texts were usually drawn from the Mass Proper), are represented in the manuscripts of Medieval music from Notre Dame in Paris, where such great musicians as LEONIN and PEROTIN were active. Polyphonic settings of texts from the Mass Ordinary began in the fourteenth century, some of them comprising only two sections of the Ordinary and a very few constituting a musical whole. Foremost among extant Medieval Masses stands what is perhaps the first Mass Ordinary written by a single composer, the *Mass of Notre Dame* by Guillaume de MACHAUT (c.1300–1377). Machaut employs plainchant cantus firmi as well as isorhythmic technique. To consult the several scholarly editions of this Mass and to hear some of its modern performances on recording would be a highly instructive introduction to both Medieval church music and present-day realizations of it. To perform it (or a portion of it) would open up a new world of sound for those unfamiliar with Medieval music. (See example 20.)

The emergence of the Mass as a major genre of musical expression took place in the fifteenth century with the common adoption of
the cyclic Mass, whose movements shared the same musical theme or
unifying idea. The Renaissance period became the golden age of Mass
composition, with the contrapuntal texture of the genre suiting the solemnity of the text, and the enormous wealth and prestige of the church as
patron ensuring extensive cultivation. Among the numerous great Mass
composers of the time, all of whom are represented in modern editions,
were DUFAY, OCKEGHEM, and JOSQUIN in the fifteenth century, and PALES-
TRINA and LASSUS in the sixteenth century.

Guillaume Dufay (c.1400–1474) composed approximately thirty-
seven individual or paired movements from the Mass Ordinary and at
least eight complete Mass Ordinaries. He was prominent among those
who used a single melody (CANTUS FIRMUS) in the tenor voice as the basis
for a complete, musically unified Mass, thus establishing the leading
model for successive generations of composers well into the sixteenth
century. In addition, Dufay sometimes freely paraphrased his borrowed
cantus firmus (resulting in the so-called "paraphrase Mass") and occasionally used a very short unifying musical motive (the motto technique).
He may also have been the first to use a secular melody rather than a
chant as his unifying cantus firmus. With Johannes Ockeghem
(c.1420–1497), who composed thirteen cyclic Masses (three of them
incomplete), the Mass returns to a more austere, modal style and, on
three occasions, departs from custom by apparently being free of borrowed
material. In one extraordinary tour de force (the *Missa Prolationum*),
the composer concealed double mensuration canons in music of
surpassing beauty. (See example 26.)

The later Renaissance masters – Josquin des Prez (c.1440–1521),
Orlandus Lassus (1532–1594), and Giovanni da Palestrina (c.1532–1594),
to name just three among many great composers – continued to employ
the common types of Mass already established with ever more polyphonic
parts (ranging from the customary four parts of Josquin to the frequently
used six parts, the occasional eight, and up to twelve parts in the late
Renaissance). Each of them, however, turned with special interest to
a new technique, that of imitation or parody. In the so-called "parody"
Mass, the composer borrowed polyphonic material, not merely a melody,
from a pre-existing composition, in many instances from a secular composition of his own. While bringing to the Mass the new technique of
systematic imitation and the new humanistic attitude towards the text,
Josquin (eighteen Masses) also retained the Franco-Flemish interest in
technical ingenuity; his *Missa Hercules dux Ferrariae (Ercole, Duke of*

Ferrara), for example, derives its subject from the notes named by the vowel sounds in the patron's name. Of the late Renaissance masters, Lassus (approximately sixty Masses) carried on Josquin's penchant for dramatic expression of the words, whereas Palestrina (104 Masses) reestablished the classical balance and the modality of a more austere tradition. The time of Palestrina was also the time of the Council of Trent, which had profound impact on the Mass musically, through its desire for reform of church music, and liturgically, through the implementation of liturgical unity by revision of the BREVIARY (1568) and the MISSAL (1570). It was the wondrously smooth and refined style of Palestrina that the Church sanctioned as a model for succeeding composers, an action that would not prove fruitful for the further development of the polyphonic Mass as an important musical genre. (See example 21.)

Through misinterpreting the term *a cappella* as meaning choral polyphony unaccompanied by instruments, modern performances of Renaissance music often sacrifice not merely tone color but security of pitch and intonation. In fact, the term (meaning "in the chapel") was used for music without separate instrumental parts. The voices may have been unaccompanied by instruments in special circumstances or places, as in the Sistine Chapel, but the ordinary practice appears to have been to use instruments or organ to double the vocal parts; in early Renaissance music, realization of the cantus firmus or of lines accompanying a treble melody may well have been by instruments alone.

With the gradual decline in the Baroque period of the Church as patron and of the Mass as a rewarding musical challenge, the interests of leading composers were diverted to secular channels, and especially to the styles of monody and concertato and to the genres of opera, ORATORIO, and CANTATA. Even those who adhered to the tradition of Palestrina by writing in STILE ANTICO rarely followed the common Renaissance practice of relying on earlier polyphonic compositions. Among those who sought to reconcile the Mass with the new style (or, after Monteverdi, the SECONDA PRATTICA) were Giovanni GABRIELI (c.1556–1612) and Giacomo CARISSIMI (c.1600–1674), both of whom introduced separate instrumental parts into their Masses. Some composers carefully kept the two styles of composition separate: Alessandro SCARLATTI, for example, composed eight of his ten Masses in *stile antico* and saved his best "sacred" music for his oratorios. By the early eighteenth century, it had become customary in Masses composed in the modern style to divide the text into ever shorter sections and to set certain of them for soloists rather than for chorus. The influence of the Italian operatic style pervaded Mass composition across Europe. It may be heard

EXAMPLE 21. Giovanni da Palestrina, "Gloria," *Pope Marcellus Mass* (meas. 108–112)

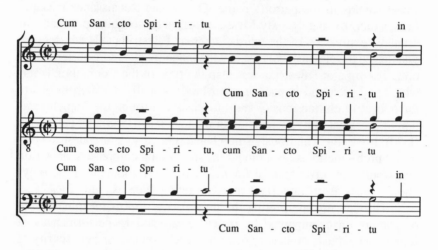

not only in the fourteen Masses of the great opera composer Johann Adolf
Hasse (1699–1783), but also in the outstanding example of the entire
Baroque period, the Mass in B Minor by Johann Sebastian BACH. Like
many other Lutheran Masses, the Mass in B Minor was conceived as
a setting of the Kyrie and the Gloria; only later was it expanded to include
Credo, Sanctus, and Agnus Dei.

In spite of the continuing decline of church patronage as an important factor in music history, the support and prestige accorded the Mass
as a musical form in Austria, particularly in Vienna, produced a very
high point in the history of the genre. The noteworthy early eighteenth-

century Viennese tradition begun by Johann Joseph Fux and Antonio Caldara culminated in the masterpieces by Franz Josef HAYDN (fourteen Masses) and Wolfgang MOZART. Not only did these great composers achieve a compelling synthesis of such disparate influences as Baroque counterpoint and Italian opera, they also introduced the dramatic, symphonic, and structural innovations of the sonata form and style. It should not be surprising that they tended to regard the liturgical text as more or less a vehicle for musical expression, an attitude carried to its Classical extreme in BEETHOVEN's *Missa Solemnis* (1823), which represents the culmination of the Viennese tradition and also points directly to the Romantic conception of the Mass as a genre composed for the concert hall.

Viewed from the standpoint of ecclesiastical function and liturgical sobriety, the Mass did not flourish in the Romantic period. Trends towards reviving older styles and accommodating the declining skills of church choirs or the limited abilities of amateur choral societies did not in general inspire either outstanding music-making or leading composers. The emergent individualism and resulting nonconformity of nineteenth-century composers of genius did, however, result in isolated masterpieces for the concert hall by Gioacchino Rossini (*Petite messe solennelle*, 1864) and Franz Liszt (*Coronation Mass*, 1867); and the Mass for the Dead (REQUIEM MASS) received inspired settings by Hector BERLIOZ, Giuseppe VERDI, and Gabriel Fauré. As in the Classical period, Vienna proved an exception to the general rule, providing a receptive setting for the Masses by Franz SCHUBERT (1797–1828) and Anton BRUCKNER (1824–1896). After several early Mass settings (four by Schubert and seven by Bruckner) distinguished principally by their lyricism and a Romantic concern for instrumental sonority, both composers achieved masterpieces in the genre of the symphonically accompanied Mass that are fully worthy of their Classical predecessors: the Masses in A-flat (1822) and E-flat (1828) by Schubert, and the Masses in D Minor (1864) and F Minor (1876) by Bruckner. In his Mass in E Minor, Bruckner reflected the concerns of the Cecilian movement by employing an eight-voice chorus with a small accompaniment of winds, and by invoking the modality and the contrapuntal techniques of the Renaissance.

Twentieth-century settings of the Mass text reveal both a continuation of the grand symphonic tradition and a reaction to it. The highly dramatic *Glagolitic Mass* (1926) by Leos Janacek, for example, offers both nationalist elements of style and exploration of the musical speech-values of a non-Latin text; three of its eight movements are purely instrumental. The Mass in G Minor (1922) by Ralph VAUGHAN WILLIAMS, on the other hand, adheres largely to the principles for suitable liturgical music laid down by Pope Pius X in his influential *Motu proprio* of 1903. Composed for four soloists and an eight-voice unaccompanied choir (with organ doubling if necessary), it frequently unfolds in choral declamation with little repetition of words. Still another trend—involving the congregation in the singing of the liturgy—is manifested somewhat later in the century, and is exemplified in the alternation of accompanied unison singing by the congregation with choral polyphony in the *Messe solennelle "Salve regina"* (1947) by Jean LANGLAIS.

The *Motu proprio* sought to restrict severely the use of instruments (including the piano) in church, to maintain the Latin text of the Mass without alteration or repetition of the words, and to forbid keeping the priest waiting at the altar during the service on account of the music. Subsequent interpretations of the document resulted in the banning of certain popular hymnals and of the Masses of Haydn, Mozart, Schubert, and Rossini for their liturgical unfitness. Among the outstanding works that reflect the new austerity of the genre is a Mass in G (1937) by Francis POULENC, which requires only an unaccompanied chorus in four to eight parts. (See example 33.) The same Neoclassical stance is found in the well-known Mass completed in 1948 by Igor STRAVINSKY. Composed for double wind quintet and a four-voice chorus (of which the sopranos and altos are children), it largely eschews both solo vocal writing and melismatic passages in favor of chantlike choral declamation. A return to styles of the past, in particular to the style of Bach, has also taken place among the leading composers of the Lutheran Mass, among them Johann Nepomuk DAVID and Ernst PEPPING.

The winds of liturgical change have blown strongly in the twentieth century, making a larger perspective on contemporary settings of the Mass difficult to achieve. One of the strongest tendencies in the Roman Catholic church—that towards increasing the involvement of the congregation in the service—seems to have been at the heart of the decrees promulgated in 1963 by the Second Vatican Council. The very structure of the Mass was also modified by changes in the MISSAL and the GRADUAL and by the adoption of a threefold division of the Mass: Introductory Rites, the Liturgy of the Word, and the Liturgy of the Eucharist. More important was the permission to translate the ceremony into the vernacular and encouragement for congregational singing during the service. Since the new freedoms came into effect in 1964, polyphonic settings of the traditional Latin Mass Ordinary have been few, while settings in various vernacular languages have appeared with folk, or folk-like, and popular styles of music, including jazz and rock. Perhaps the most eclectic as well as the most worthy Mass-related composition of the later twentieth century is *Mass: A Theater Piece for Singers, Players, and Dancers* (1971) by Leonard Bernstein. Composed for the opening of the John F. Kennedy Center for the Performing Arts in Washington, D.C., *Mass* draws from the styles of opera, rock, Broadway musical, and contemporary counterpoint in a dramatically compelling, but wholly nonliturgical, manner that would not seem to offer a viable avenue for further use. Whether or not the future brings simply another conservative reaction, the prognosis for music composed to the Latin Mass text does not appear at this time to be bright.

Recommended for further study of the Mass are, on a small scale, the article by Richard Sherr entitled "Mass" in *The New Harvard Dictionary of Music* and, on a large scale, the detailed historical account by seven authors in volume 12 of *The New Grove Dictionary of Music and Musicians*.

Mathias, William (1934–   ) – Born and educated in Wales, Mathias returned there after studying with Lennox Berkeley at the Royal Academy of Music and became in 1970 a professor of music at University College in Bangor. As a composer, he has achieved considerable distinction in music for orchestra, including three piano concertos, as well as in chamber music. Stylistically, his works reveal an eclectic approach less concerned with technical considerations than musical expression. Like Hindemith and Tippett, whose styles appear to have had significant impact on his early music, Mathias's harmonic language is basically one of expanded tonality, within which he reveals a special liking for modal inflections and cross-relations, and for vigorously contrapuntal textures. Rhythmic vitality stems from frequent use of cross-rhythms and syncopation.

Among the composer's considerable number of choral works are many on sacred texts. Psalm settings with organ accompaniment include "Make a Joyful Noise" (Psalm 100), "O Sing unto the Lord" (Psalms 96 and 98), and "Bless the Lord, O My Soul" (Psalm 104). There are also works on liturgical texts, among them the *Festival Te Deum* (1964), a Communion Service in C for unison voices and organ (1967), a Magnificat and Nunc Dimittis for chorus and organ (1970), a Missa Brevis for chorus and organ (1973), and a Communion for unison voices, optional chorus, and organ (1976). In addition, there are anthems, hymn tunes, and a number of organ works for the church service.

Matins – The first service of the Roman Catholic Divine OFFICE, Matins was usually held very early in the morning, before 3 a.m., and so was also referred to as the Night Office. Perhaps the earliest and liturgically the richest of the CANONICAL HOURS, it has been much altered in the

LITURGY OF THE HOURS. In the Lutheran church, Martin Luther retained Matins as part of the liturgy.

Maunder, John (1858–1920) — One of the best known composers of church music of his time, particularly among singers at English parish churches, Maunder spent his life as an organist and choirmaster at various churches just outside of London. So skillfully composed were his works for their generally somewhat modest purposes that the popularity of his ANTHEMS and church CANTATAS did not wane until well into the twentieth century. The most enduring of the anthems, such as "Praise the Lord, O Jerusalem," touch a responsive vein in both singers and congregation, while remaining safely within the vocal grasp of the volunteer choirs who sing them. The church cantatas, lacking the functional value of the anthems, have not maintained the place they once held in the repertory; nevertheless, such works as *The Martyrs* (1894) and his immensely popular *From Olivet to Calvary* (1904) probably represent their time and audience better than many a loftier and less accessible masterpiece.

Medieval period — The Middle Ages (sometimes called the "Dark Ages") were created when historians designated the supposed rebirth of culture in the fourteenth and fifteenth centuries as the RENAISSANCE, leaving a gap between that period and the ancient world of the Greeks and Romans. In fact, a considerable number of important musical developments took place between circa 500 and 1450 (dates commonly assigned to the Medieval period by music historians), among them the musical staff, the church modes, the organ, polyphony, cantus firmus technique, the rhythmic modes and mensural notation, and isorhythm. Significant genres of church music of the time included CHANT, ORGANUM, CONDUCTUS, MOTET, and MASS; their principal composers were LEONIN, PEROTIN, Guillaume de MACHAUT, and DUNSTABLE. It should be kept in mind that terms such as Medieval are merely pedagogical conveniences; cultural historians may, in fact, give them various meanings and use them in a confusing number of ways.

melisma — A Greek word, it refers to the practice of singing more than a few notes to one syllable of text, particularly as this occurs in Gregorian CHANT.

Mendelssohn(-Bartholdy), Felix (1809–1847) — Born in Germany of Jewish heritage, the composer was in several ways a product of the Enlightenment rather than a full-fledged Romantic. His family's conversion to Christianity (at which time they added Bartholdy to their name) reflects the ecumenicism of his philosopher-grandfather, and his own penchant for balance and reasoned argument in composition recalls the musical values of that earlier era. In no small measure the composer was a product of the eighteenth-century North German traditions inculcated by his teacher, Friedrich Zelter.

Even before he made his mark as a significant composer of religious music, Mendelssohn had contributed to the medium through his performances of Bach's *St. Matthew Passion* in 1829 and of several oratorios by Handel (e.g., *Israel in Egypt* in 1833). His compositions written on religious texts naturally vary according to the opportunities presented by his career moves from Roman Catholic Duesseldorf to Lutheran Leipzig (as conductor of the Gewandhaus Orchestra and then director of the Leipzig Conservatory), as well as on ten separate occasions to Anglican England. His works also vary in quality, becoming on occasion rather too predictable in their rhythmic and harmonic motion. There are Latin and German MOTETS, PSALM settings (some of them for liturgical use), CHORALE CANTATAS (e.g., *Jesu, meine Freude*), Anglican CANTICLES and ANTHEMS, and various compositions for organ, especially the Bach-inspired PRELUDES and FUGUES of Opus 37 and sonatas of Opus 65. Said to be particularly noteworthy among the choral works are Psalms 42, 98, and 114, as well as the six unaccompanied anthems for double chorus of 1848. Less fortunate, criticized in fact by the composer himself, was W. H. Cummings' arrangement of a chorus from Mendelssohn's *Festgesang* into "Hark, the Herald Angels Sing."

Above all the other religious works by Mendelssohn stand the two grand Handel-inspired ORATORIOS, *St. Paul* and *Elijah*. The former was first performed in 1836 as *Paulus* in Duesseldorf, then later in the same year (translated into English) in Liverpool. The love of the flourishing British choral societies for Mendelssohn's music was immediate and immense. His choruses and biblical texts were taken directly to English hearts. *Elijah*, based on the story of the Old Testament prophet (and originally conceived in German), was first performed in 1846 in Birmingham, England. Like its predecessor, it places emphasis upon choral movements and reveals a notable variety of forms and textures. (See example 28.) It should be mentioned that the composer's Symphony No. 2 (1840), subtitled "Lobgesang" (Song of Praise), constitutes in its fourth movement more or less an extended sacred cantata for vocal soloists, chorus, and orchestra. Yet another work that would certainly have been an oratorio, *Christus*, was left incomplete by the composer at his death.

Messiaen, Olivier (1908–)—A seminal composer and teacher of far-reaching influence, Messiaen may have been the outstanding twentieth-century contributor to the literature of the organ. Born in southeastern France, he was sent in 1919 to study at the Paris Conservatory, where his teachers included Paul Dukas for composition and Marcel Dupré for organ. Beginning in 1930, he served for more than forty years as organist at the Church of the Trinity. As a teacher, he was appointed in 1936 to the École Normale de Musique and the Schola Cantorum; in 1942 he became professor of harmony at the Paris Conservatory and, in 1966, he was named professor of composition. He has had enormous impact on the careers of many significant composers, among them Pierre Boulez, Karlheinz Stockhausen, Luigi Nono, and William ALBRIGHT.

In keeping with his view that art was the ideal manner in which to express religious belief, most of Messiaen's compositions express his personal faith as their most important aspect. (See example 22, "The Word," *The Birth of Our Lord*.) The unconventional music he places at the service of Roman Catholic dogma, however, naturally raises the

EXAMPLE 22. Olivier Messiaen, "Le Verbe," *La Nativité du Seigneur* (meas. 48–49)

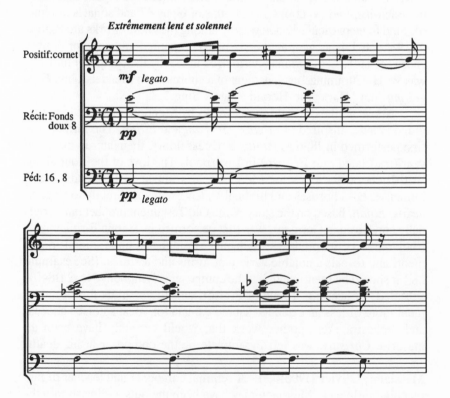

question of its suitability for general use in the church service. Has he succeeded in synthesizing such diverse elements as imitations of bird songs, chant-like melodies based on his own modes of limited transposition, nonfunctional harmonies, and rhythmic motion independent of tonality and simple meters, in forms based upon free use of variation? In extending the principle of serialization to parameters of style other than pitch, Messiaen anticipated a major development in contemporary music; and yet, in his way, he represents a culmination of the Romantic programmaticism found in the organ music of such earlier Frenchmen as Charles Tournemire and Jean LANGLAIS. The following list of Messiaen's organ works makes clear how frequently his subject appears in his title: *Le banquet céleste* (1928), *Apparition de l'église éternelle* (1932), *L'ascénsion* (an arrangement of an orchestral composition, 1934), *La nativité du Seigneur* (1935), *Les corps glorieux, sept visions brèves de la vie des réssuscités* (1939), *Messe de la Pentecôte* (1950), *Livre d'orgue* (1952), *Verset pour la fête de la dedicace* (1960), and *Méditations sur le mystére de la Sainte Trinité* (1969).

Methodist church music—In keeping with its roots as a popular movement led by JOHN WESLEY within the Church of England, the Methodist church (originally the Methodist Episcopal church) has long nurtured congregational singing of HYMNS. During the nineteenth century, although authorized hymnals remained largely traditional in style, the popularity of revival movements and CAMP MEETINGS, as well as the rise of Sunday schools, brought so-called GOSPEL MUSIC into such prominence that it has been well represented in twentieth-century hymnals. Few denominations can boast the variety and scope of the hymns in the *United Methodist Hymnal* (1989), which range from plainchant to traditional German hymns, and from camp-meeting songs to SPIRITUALS and folk songs. (See also the article on John WESLEY and HYMNODY.)

Miserere—"Miserere mei, Deus" (Have mercy upon me, O God) are the first words of Psalm 50 in the Latin Bible, which corresponds to Psalm 51 in the King James version. As one of the PENITENTIAL PSALMS, it is sung at the Lauds of Maundy Thursday, Good Friday, and Holy Saturday, as well as in the Office of the Dead and at other places in the liturgy. Polyphonic settings were composed during the Renaissance by such significant composers as JOSQUIN DES PREZ, PALESTRINA, and LASSUS.

Missa brevis—The so-called "short MASS," for which a composer generally sets just the KYRIE and the GLORIA, although sometimes the SANCTUS is included as well.

Missal (Latin, *missale*)—The liturgical book of the Roman Catholic rite that contains all of the texts, but not the music, for the MASS. See GRADUAL.

modes—See the article CHANT and the entry RHYTHMIC MODES.

monophonic—An adjective describing a single line of music, as in Gregorian CHANT or in Medieval religious songs such as the LAUDA.

Morales, Cristobal de (c.1500–1553)—Generally regarded as the first major Spanish composer, Morales achieved this reputation through a large body of church music that was widely distributed during his lifetime and for a generation afterwards. A volume of his Masses became the first polyphonic music copied for use in the New World. His career took him from Seville, where he was born, to the post of *maestro de capilla* at the cathedrals of Avila and Plasencia, and ultimately to Rome. With some interruption he served as a singer in the papal choir from 1535 until 1545, a time of high papal interest in music. Opportunities to perform his music before the leading rulers of the Western world must have helped disperse knowledge of his music widely. Upon his return to Spain, where he probably hoped to be well-rewarded, he served rather unhappily in several significant posts before his death.

Among the sacred works of Morales are twenty-three MASSES, two of them for the REQUIEM service, sixteen MAGNIFICATS, four LAMENTATIONS, and more than one hundred MOTETS. His style rests basically upon judicious use of imitative versus chordal textures in four to six voices, in a harmonic idiom noteworthy for its approach to tonality (rather than modality) and for its forward-looking treatment of dissonance in the expression of the words.

Moravian church music—Perhaps the most outstanding church music composed in the United States before the twentieth century was written for the Moravian church in America. Founded by missionaries from Saxony, the church was centered in cities like Bethlehem (from 1741) and Nazareth in Pennsylvania, and it flourished until the middle of the nineteenth century. Both vocal music, especially ANTHEMS with German texts for mixed chorus and a small instrumental ensemble, and instrumental chamber music were cultivated by a number of significant composers, the best known being Johann Friedrich Peter (1746–1813).

Morning Prayer—Also known as Matins, Morning Prayer is one of the chief liturgical events of the Anglican church. Elements for Morning

Prayer were drawn from the Catholic canonical hours known as MATINS, LAUDS, and PRIME.

motet—A term derived from *mot* (French for "word") and *motetus* (Latin for the voice-part to which French words had been set). From about 1200 through 1800, the motet was the major extraliturgical genre used in the church service. Although its precise meaning has changed through the centuries, it was defined during its most significant era—from about 1450 to 1600—as a polyphonic composition on a sacred but nonliturgical Latin text. In conventional usage the term is often used for settings of ANTI-PHONS and PSALMS, but not with regard to HYMNS, CANTICLES, and such special texts as LAMENTATIONS. It is not used for the ANTHEM, apparently because the anthem's texts are in English; nevertheless, it is used when religious texts are in German.

The motet originated as a TROPE, specifically a substitute *clausula* (a section in DISCANT style) written to replace a section of an existing ORGANUM. It was therefore a liturgical genre. In its earliest usage, the word *motetus* designated an upper part with words of its own set against a CANTUS FIRMUS. Soon the term came to be used for all works of this kind, even if one of the one to three added parts was secular in nature; by virtue of this expanded definition, the motet had become the main form of polyphonic composition by the end of the thirteenth century and an important locus for fundamental changes in the rhythmic notation of music. In the works of the great early fourteenth-century composer Guillaume de MACHAUT, motets with secular texts in the upper voices still outnumber those completely in Latin; nevertheless, some of the Latin motets were suitable for liturgical use in the Office. By the end of the fourteenth century, however, the motet had been superseded by the new secular styles of such genres as the chanson. It became once again a genre of sacred music, but its use was now generally limited to settings of Latin nonliturgical texts. Its principal distinction was that it served as the focal point for the development of the complex Medieval structural device called isorhythm.

The period of the Renaissance was the golden era of the motet. In the early fifteenth century it served as a principal genre for Guillaume DUFAY; by the end of his career, it had become the focus of a more freely expressive approach that produced some of his greatest works. (See the entry for Dufay and also example 12.) As composers came to value more and more the greater freedom of expression inherent in its texts, as opposed to the fixed liturgical texts of the Mass, they increasingly favored the genre. The motets of JOSQUIN des Prez called upon all the expressive resources of his genius specifically because of the varied challenges offered by their texts. (See the entry for Josquin and also example 18.) In a similar manner, the motets of the great sixteenth-century composers—among them, Adrian WILLAERT, Giovanni PALESTRINA, Orlandus LASSUS (see example 23), and William BYRD—represent a uniquely expressive body of church music that speaks as directly to twentieth-century churchgoers as do the masterpieces of painting, sculpture, and architecture of the Renaissance. (See the entry for Byrd and also example 5.)

In the BAROQUE PERIOD, the word "motet" underwent changes in usage. On the one hand, composers continued to write motets in

EXAMPLE 23. Orlandus Lassus, "Tristis est anima mea," *Penitential Psalms* (meas. 1–8)

Renaissance style—now referred to as STILE ANTICO—without independent instrumental parts; traditional motets of this kind were numerous
in both Italy and Germany. This traditional use of the term was broad-
ened in Protestant Germany to apply to sacred compositions in the
vernacular. On the other hand, composers of the Baroque period increasingly employed independent instrumental choirs and the concertato style
in their nonliturgical sacred compositions; what music historians
frequently refer to as concertato motets were often termed sacred concertos
(*geistliche Konzerte*) or sacred symphonies (*symphoniae sacrae*) by their
composers. Among the outstanding progresssive composers were
Giovanni GABRIELI (example 17) and Heinrich SCHUETZ; in the works of
the latter may be seen the formative stages of the German church
CANTATA (example 6). In France, the adoption of the new style elements
on a large scale led to the development by Lully and CHARPENTIER of
the *grand motet*, a genre distinguished by its use in the Royal Chapel.
In England, confusingly enough, sacred compositions in the vernacular
are referred to as ANTHEMS rather than motets.

After the Baroque period, the motet shared the gradual decline of
all church music brought about by the sanctification of tradition and the
increasing reluctance on the part of churches to offer patronage to significant contemporary composers and styles. To be successful in their art,
Classical composers had to master the great secular genres—the opera,
the symphony, and the concerto. Fortunately, some of these successful
composers, foremost among them HAYDN, occupied court positions that
called for occasional motets, Masses, and other sacred music. Unfortunately, as in the case of MOZART, the church was not able to retain
within an ecclesiastical setting precisely those composers who might have
maintained its glorious tradition. By the time of BEETHOVEN, much of
the truly significant music on religious and liturgical texts was composed
for the public concert hall, not the church. Nevertheless, as a more modest
genre than the Mass, the motet was still being cultivated as church music
during the ROMANTIC PERIOD, especially in France after the middle of
the century. Elsewhere, the CECILIAN MOVEMENT helped to inspire motets
by Liszt, BRUCKNER, and VERDI. (See example 39.) Toward the end of
the century, the Protestant motet found an adherent in Johannes BRAHMS.
(See example 3.)

During the twentieth century, relatively few major composers have
concerned themselves with the motet. Among the leading styles of the
era, however, the trend towards Neo-Classicism lent prestige to those
who wished to revive the styles and forms of earlier historical periods.
German composers found the motet a perfect form with which to express

their renewed appreciation for BACH, for the art of setting CHORALE melodies and other CANTUS FIRMI, and for a revival of so-called *a cappella* writing. Max REGER, Hugo DISTLER, and Ernst PEPPING (example 24) were among those who cultivated the Protestant motet, while Johann Nepomuk DAVID and Hermann Schroeder contributed Latin motets suitable for performance in the Catholic worship service. In France, a significant amount of church music in Neoclassical style was composed by Francis POULENC, including four motets on penitential texts and four Christmas motets. A detailed historical account of the motet (by six authors) may be found in volume 12 of *The New Grove Dictionary*.

EXAMPLE 24. Ernst Pepping, "Das Weltgericht" (meas. 1–7)

Motu proprio—A statement issued by the pope without the official advice of others. The most noteworthy *Motu proprio* regarding music in the Roman Catholic church was issued by Pope Pius X in 1903. It specified the music of PALESTRINA as the appropriate model for church music, demanded greater respect for liturgical texts, restricted the use of instruments, and on the whole set forth standards by which, among others, the MASSES of HAYDN, MOZART, BEETHOVEN, and SCHUBERT would be forbidden in the church.

Mozart, Wolfgang Amadeus (1756–1791) – One of the principal composers of the Classical period, Mozart was an Austrian Catholic whose chief patron from 1769 until 1781 was the Archbishop of Salzburg, who was also a secular prince of considerable power as the Count Palatine. Mozart's father, Leopold, had come at age twenty-four (in 1743) to the thirty-three-member court orchestra of the archbishop as fourth violinist; for the rest of his life he served the court in various musical capacities but could rise no higher than deputy Kapellmeister. His own advancement, however, took second place in his life to providing the training and life experiences he deemed necessary for, in his words, "the miracle that God let be born in Salzburg." As a prodigious young keyboardist and composer, Wolfgang was taken from court to court by Leopold: at age six to Munich and Vienna; at age seven to Munich, Mannheim, Paris, Versailles, London, and The Hague; at age eleven to Vienna; and at age fourteen to Verona, Mantua, Milan, Bologna, Florence, Venice, and Rome. In Rome, he received the Order of the Golden Spur from the pope on July 8, 1770. During his travels, in addition to demonstrating his genius, the young Mozart took the opportunity to assimilate the period's musical culture.

In March of 1772, soon after the Mozarts returned home from yet another trip to Italy (this one to fulfill commissions there), Hieronymous von Colloredo became Archbishop of Salzburg. Unlike his tolerant predecessor, Colloredo was a reformist churchman who encouraged composition only for the church. He also held strong views on what constituted proper church music. Wolfgang became an official member of the archbishop's court as a violinist in July of 1772, but Leopold, who could not attain the status that he desired, felt that opportunities for Wolfgang were limited in provincial Salzburg and that the archbishop was not, in any case, favorably inclined to the Mozarts. Attempts to find a suitable position for Wolfgang eventually led to his not entirely amicable release by the archbishop in 1777. Once again he travelled to Mannheim and Paris, now no longer a child. Still appreciated by genuine connoisseurs, he nevertheless did not receive worthwhile offers of employment or significant commissions. When Leopold wrote of a better position in Salzburg as court organist, Wolfgang had little choice but to return to Salzburg in 1779 into the service of the archbishop. His duties were to play in the cathedral, in the chapel, and at court, as well as to compose on request and to teach the choirboys. The situation was not a happy one for a person of Mozart's genius and lofty musical – especially operatic – ambitions. When his opera *Idomeneo* was performed with success in 1781 in Munich, Mozart simply could not return for long to his servile status, the limited artistic horizons of the Salzburg court, and the abuse of the stern Archbishop Colloredo. His forceful dismissal from the security of his post at

Salzburg came on June 9, 1781; it marked a decisive turning point in his life, after which church music was of very little significance to him.

Mozart composed approximately seventy-five works either for the church or on religious subjects; close to fifty are on liturgical or at least Latin texts, including seventeen MASSES and some individual sections from the ORDINARY or the PROPER of the Mass. Also intended for use in the Mass were the seventeen Epistle sonatas for organ with, usually, strings in three parts. In addition, the composer left an incomplete REQUIEM MASS, several LITANIES, and two settings of VESPERS. Among the nonliturgical works are an ORATORIO (*La Betulia liberata*), two masonic CANTATAS, and two church songs in German.

Approximately sixty of Mozart's church works were composed for use in Salzburg, nineteen of them from the period up to about 1772. A song-like "Kyrie" (K.33) from 1766 constitutes his first attempt at church music. At the age of twelve he created an imposing Missa Solemnis in C minor for 4 soloists, chorus, and large orchestra. Certain of the youthful works were modelled closely upon works by older composers, the *Te Deum* of 1769, for example, on a *Te Deum* by Michael Haydn. From the works of this period the Mozart scholar Alfred Einstein recommended a Litany to the Blessed Virgin Mary (K.109).

After his official appointment to the court in 1772, Mozart appears to have applied himself quite seriously to learning about church music. A notebook in his hand from about 1773 contains nineteen church compositions by the estimable Salzburg composers Michael Haydn and Ernst Eberlin. That a certain amount of application was required in the twenty-two or so church works composed between 1772 and 1776 is proved by a letter of September 4, 1776, in which Mozart describes to Padre Martini the need for brevity at Salzburg:

> Our church music is very different from that of Italy, since a Mass with the whole Kyrie, the Gloria, the Credo, the Epistle sonata, the Offertory or Motet, the Sanctus, and the Agnus Dei must not last longer than three quarters of an hour. This applies even to the most solemn Mass said by the Archbishop himself. So you see that a special study is required for this kind of composition. At the same time, the Mass must have all the instruments – trumpets, drums and so forth. [As translated by Arthur Mendel and Nathan Broder in the 1962 Oxford Univ. Press edition of Alfred Einstein, *Mozart: His Character His Word*, 331.]

The *Missa Brevis* in F (K.192) and the *Missa Brevis* in D (K.194) reveal how Mozart, in keeping with his patron's demands, used chordal textures and avoided repetition of words as well as complexity of style. Even his *Missa in honorem Sanctissimae Trinitatis* (K.167) of 1773, a solemn Mass apparently for a special occasion, finds the composer concerned with restraint as well as brilliance; here, he eliminates soloists and unifies movements in a symphonic manner through thematic relationships. Perhaps Mozart did not entirely succeed during this period in the difficult task of reconciling the traditional ecclesiastial "strict" style and the newer, aristocratic *style galant*. A noteworthy example of the fashionable concerto-like style he had recently learned from the Italians is the famous motet for soloist and orchestra entitled "Exsultate, jubilate" (Exult, Rejoice, K.165), which was performed in Milan in 1773.

During the last years of his service in Salzburg, from 1776 until 1781, Mozart appeared to Alfred Einstein to have reached a mature style of his own, more expressive and more lyrical than before. Fifteen church compositions come from this period, including seven Masses, two settings of the Psalms for Vespers, and a significant *Litaniae de venerabili altaris sacramento* (K.243). The *Missa Brevis* (K.259) of 1776, with its exceptional use of solo organ in the Benedictus, displays the more self-assured manner of this period, while *Missa Solemnis* in C (K.337) of 1780 contains as a Benedictus what Einstein called "the most striking and revolutionary movement in all of Mozart's Masses" (*Mozart*, p. 345). Its severe fugal style would most likely have irritated the Archbishop. Worthy of special note for its musical beauty is the motet "Sancta Maria, mater Dei" (Holy Mary, Mother of God, K.273), for four-part chorus, strings, and organ. (See example 25.)

Of the three masterpieces of church music that were composed during Mozart's last decade, none were commissioned by or for the church. Two lesser works on religious themes, both of them cantatas on Masonic themes, were composed for and performed at Mozart's lodge. Even when Mozart finally received the long-awaited imperial appointment as chamber composer in 1787, he was not asked to compose for either the palace chapel or for Saint Stephen's Cathedral. Tragically, two of the three late church works — compositions that would rank among his best — were left unfinished. The great Mass in C Minor (K.427) consists of just Kyrie, Gloria, Sanctus, and Benedictus. It resulted from Mozart's vow to have a newly composed Mass performed on the occasion of bringing his new bride to Salzburg in 1783. In June of 1791, the composer completed for a friend who was a choirmaster the justly popular short funeral motet entitled "Ave verum corpus" (K.618), for four-part chorus, strings, and organ. Finally, just six months before his death, Mozart was commissioned by a stranger to compose a Requiem Mass. Apparently Mozart did not know that the stranger was a nobleman who,

EXAMPLE 25. Wolfgang Mozart, "Sancta Maria, mater Dei," K.273 (meas. 1–2)

in his own chapel, liked to perform the works of others as his own. In any case, Mozart completed only the Requiem and the Kyrie. Franz Suessmayr, a student, completed the rest of the movements, some of them (the eight sections from the "Dies irae" through the "Hostias") sketched by Mozart, and some (the Sanctus, Benedictus, and Agnus Dei) apparently not.

During his career, Mozart composed a significant amount of church music for his archiepiscopal patron. Some of it reached, at least intermittently, the level of his secular masterpieces, despite the fact that church music was at odds with the mood of the Enlightenment. It seems clear, however, that Mozart could not have remained in Salzburg and still have become the great universal genius of Western music, from whose pen flowed operas, symphonies, concertos, sonatas, chamber music, and dance music of inimitable quality.

Nativity—The birth of Jesus, or a reference to the day of his birth.

Negro spiritual—See SPIRITUAL.

Neo-Baroque—See NEOCLASSICAL.

Neo-Classical—A term originally used in music to refer to the revival of certain elements of style and structure from earlier periods in music history by twentieth-century composers reacting negatively to the emotional and stylistic excesses of Romanticism. In fact, music that draws freely upon the style of BACH ought to be termed Neo-Baroque, and that which draws on PALESTRINA's style, Neo-Renaissance, with the term Neo-Classical being reserved for imitation, transformation, and parody (in the musical sense) of the music of HAYDN and MOZART. Many post-Baroque composers have been influenced by the extraordinary sacred keyboard style of Bach, among them Mozart, MENDELSSOHN, Schumann, Liszt, BRAHMS, and REGER. Among major twentieth-century composers, Neo-classicism in its broader usage applies to several religious compositions of STRAVINSKY, including his *Symphony of Psalms* (example 37), as well as to those by POULENC (example 33).

noel—A French term for a Christmas song, often of a popular kind. It is much like the English CAROL, and some are sung like carols. The words of a noel were written in French instead of Latin, the structure was strophic, and the texture of the early ones was nearly always monophonic. So popular was the genre that French organists of the later seventeenth century, among them Dandrieu and Daquin, composed sets of variations on the tunes.

None—The sixth of the CANONICAL HOURS of the Divine OFFICE.

Nunc Dimittis—Latin for "Now lettest thou thy servant depart in peace," the opening phrase of the Canticle of Simeon (Luke 2:29–32). It is sung at COMPLINE in the Roman Catholic OFFICE and at EVENSONG in the ANGLICAN LITURGY.

obbligato—An Italian word that is used by musicians to designate an accompanying instrumental part that may not be omitted, as in many arias found in BACH church CANTATAS. In keyboard music, the reference is to a part that is written out rather than left to be improvised by the performer.

Ockeghem, Johannes (c.1410–1497)—Recognized as the finest composer of his generation, Ockeghem ranks among the greatest of all composers of sacred music. Such was his skill with the Mass that it became the principal musical genre of the time, and his motets are no less inventive. Franco-Flemish by birth, he made his early career as a singer; the theorist Tinctoris writes of him as having one of the best bass voices he had ever heard. The composer's activities during the early part of his career remain largely in the realm of conjecture. Only in 1443, which he spent as a chorister at the Church of Notre Dame in Antwerp, can he be surely located. In about 1445 he went to France, where he spent the rest of his life, at first in Moulins as a singer in the chapel of Charles I, Duke of Bourbon, and then—from about 1450—for many years at the royal court of three successive French kings. Among the rewards that came to the king's first chaplain and court composer were his appointment in 1459 as treasurer of Saint Martin-de-Tour, the wealthiest monastery in France, and his assignment from 1463 to 1470 as canon at Notre Dame Cathedral in Paris. His death was widely mourned by fellow musicians.

By the standards of the time, Ockeghem composed relatively little music. There are thirteen settings of the MASS Ordinary, three of them incomplete, and one separate Credo. Also incomplete is his setting of the REQUIEM MASS, which ends with the Offertory; perhaps the remainder was left to be sung in plainchant. Among the Masses are three groups: works based on a sacred CANTUS FIRMUS (e.g., *Missa "Ecce ancilla Domini"*); works based on a secular cantus firmus (Missa "De plus en plus," which uses a well-known chanson by Binchois); and works that apparently do not use a pre-existing cantus firmus (among them, *Missa "Mi-mi"*). A wide variety of techniques is employed, such as placing the cantus firmus in the bass (*Missa "Caput"*), paraphrasing the borrowed melody (*Missa "De plus en plus"*), and foreshadowing the later parody technique (*Missa "Fors seulement"*). In the so-called "free" Masses, Ockeghem composes with such extraordinary skill that the listener may well be unable to discern his technical devices, such as his use of double mensuration canons at various intervals in every movement of the *Missa prolationum (Prolation Mass)*; only two lines are notated in the original, and each of them is realized in two different prolations (meter signatures) by the performers. (See example 26.) Although he mainly followed tradition in the Masses with his use of cantus firmi, head motives, and passages of homophonic declamation, he was a leader in extending the range of the lowest voice downwards, in truly equalizing all the voices in four-part counterpoint, and perhaps in his occasional use of tone-painting. Within sections, the voices generally proceed in free modal counterpoint, avoiding cadences and sequence, and often launching a closing drive to the final cadence. Two of the Masses are in three parts and one (*Missa "Fors seulement"*) in five.

Some of the composer's eight or nine MOTETS, such as "Alma

EXAMPLE 26. Johannes Ockeghem, "Kyrie," *Missa prolationum* (opening meas.)

Redemptoris mater" (Mother Beloved of the Savior), employ the appropriate plainchant cantus firmus; its appearance in a paraphrased version in an inner voice is not distinguished in any way rhythmically from the other parts. In other motets, such as "Intemerata Dei mater" (Undefiled Mother of God), there is apparently no borrowed cantus firmus; set for five voice-parts, this motet reveals the composer's love for contrasting the sonorities of the highest and lowest voices and for generating increased motion before the final cadence. Because they do not bear so much weight from tradition, Ockeghem's motets may be in some ways even more striking than his Masses.

Offertory—From the Latin word *offertorium*, referring originally to the presentation of the elements for Communion. Soon the word came to refer to the offerings brought to the service by the congregation. Part of the Mass PROPER of the Roman Catholic liturgy, the Offertory apparently originated as ANTIPHONAL PSALMODY, but then developed an ornate character unlike that of other ANTIPHONS, as well as an unusually wide melodic range. The place in the service for the Offertory has often been used for nonliturgical but religious vocal music, or for instrumental compositions of various kinds. In denominations without a complex liturgy, the word "offertory" refers to the music sung or played during the process of collecting money from the faithful.

Offertory sentences—Passages of Holy Scripture that are said in the Anglican service during the collection of the congregation's gifts and during the presentation of the elements for Communion. These passages have often been set to music as offertory ANTHEMS.

Office—Historically, the eight CANONICAL HOURS have constituted the daily series of services that make up the Roman Catholic Divine Office, a custom retained from Jewish practice and observed somewhat differently in monasteries than in churches. The recitation of all the psalms in the course of a week lay at the heart of the Office as established by the Rule of Saint Benedict, along with various ANTIPHONS, RESPONSORIES, CANTICLES, and HYMNS. Office texts are found in the BREVIARY, Office chants in the ANTIPHONAL. Until the major revision known as the LITURGY OF THE HOURS, the parts of the Office were: MATINS, LAUDS, PRIME, TERCE, SEXT, NONE, VESPERS, and COMPLINE.

Office hymn—A hymn that constitutes part of the prescribed liturgy for the Roman Catholic OFFICE.

Old Hundredth—This is the familiar name given to the tune used for singing the popular Protestant doxology that begins, "Praise God from whom all blessings flow." The name comes from the fact that the same tune was used in Sternhold and Hopkins's important PSALTER of 1562 as a setting for Psalm 100.

Oratorio—A religious or moral drama performed entirely in song without the aid of scenery, costumes, or action. As in opera, solo singers (accompanied by orchestra) personify the characters of the story. Although its poetic and musical forms and styles derive largely from opera, oratorio was distinguished during much of its history by an emphasis upon choral singing; in addition, its smaller amount of RECITATIVE and its two-part, large-scale structure (as opposed to the three acts of an opera) contribute to its shorter duration. Not a liturgical genre, oratorio originated in the time of the Counter-Reformation, when even the arts were pressed into service in the search for effective ways to hold the faithful and to attract and convert nonbelievers.

Through the years, the word "oratorio" has had three distinct meanings. (1) During the Counter-Reformation, oratorio meant primarily an oratory—a prayer hall or chapel—in which spiritual exercises were held by religious societies such as the Congregation of the Oratory (also known as the Philippine Order after its founder, Filippo Neri). (2) The spiritual exercises that took place in an oratory eventually received the name of the hall in which they were held, and were also referred to as oratorio. Prayers, sermons in simple and familiar style, exhortations to Christian virtue and the like, as well as music, were usually included in the devotions. Although Filippo Neri did not established a musical form or found the new genre of oratorio, his oratory served as a model with considerable importance for the history of oratorio. (3) When used with reference to a musical form, oratorio came to refer to a setting, without dramatic representation, of a text based upon the Bible, the lives of the saints, or church doctrine. An oratorio is usually accompanied by instruments; it may or may not employ a chorus and a narrator. Essential for the creation of the genre was the adoption of monody (expressive accompanied solo singing), since recitatives and arias were indispensable for achieving its dramatic and subjective appeal.

When the independent, unified musical genre that came to be known as oratorio emerged in Italy towards the middle of the seventeenth century, two separate kinds could be clearly distinguished—oratorio in Italian (*oratorio volgare*) and oratorio in Latin (*oratorio latino*). The beginnings of oratorio in the vernacular language appear to lie partly in the LAUDA, which clearly suggested the textual form of the mature oratorio. Forms other than the lauda also offered models for textual form, and some, like the DIALOGO SPIRITUALE (in which passages of dialogue were assigned to individual singers), provided musical models. Although *dialoghi spirituali* might be preferred on festive occasions in the oratories, more casual gatherings often saw the performance of dramatic madrigals in spiritual guise. Both forms are found in Giovanni Francesco Anerio's *Teatro armonico spirituale di madrigale* (Rome, 1619), which was directly connected with the order of Filippo Neri. Dramatic elements may also have come from the SACRA RAPPRESENTAZIONE, the vernacular, staged mystery play of the Renaissance. *Oratorio volgare* won widespread popularity through its use of the vernacular language and its adoption of current musical styles. It soon became a regular part of the celebration of church feasts. Oratorios were sung during Lent, on Christmas and Easter, and for major feasts in the calendar of saints. During Lent, an entire oratorio might be given each Sunday and each day of Holy Week, or the parts of an oratorio might be given over two days. Oratorios in Italian were also performed on such occasions as receptions for important people, victory celebrations, consecrations of altars, and the taking of vows by candidates for religious orders. They also served as private devotions or entertainments in the palaces of nobles.

Like oratorio in the vernacular, oratorio in Latin also originated in Rome. It evolved from the Latin motets performed before and after the sermon in the Oratory of the Archiconfraternita del Santissimo

Crocifisso, located in the Church of San Marcello. Among its antecedents were motets with narrative and dramatic elements, the Latin *dialogus* (which evolved from the motet), and the traditional musical setting of the Passion, with its evangelist corresponding in function to the *historicus* of Latin oratorio. Unlike oratorio in Italian, early *oratorio latino* featured prose texts (most of them biblical). Although Latin oratorio was supported to the highest degree by the popes and by the clerical and lay aristocracy, it remained largely isolated at the Church of San Marcello, and was heard there only during Lent.

Simplicity and directness constitute the chief characteristics of the first major composer of oratorios, Giacomo CARISSIMI. Both his Italian and Latin works unfold in narrative form within a homophonic idiom carefully circumscribed in harmonic vocabulary and range of modulation. The use of a narrator, one of oratorio's distinguishing features, came under attack as early as 1656, when the influential librettist Archangelo Spagna justified the narrator's elimination by pointing to the need for writing on such new subjects as the lives of the saints. A corresponding musical change towards opera is clearly seen in the next generation in the Italian oratorios of Alessandro Stradella: he differentiates much more precisely between recitative, arioso, and aria than did Carissimi, and he emphasizes the aria rather than the recitative and chorus. Furthermore, his introduction of a concerted instrumental style helps to expand both the size and the breadth of his arias. Since it lacks a narrator, an oratorio by Stradella qualifies as a *melodramma sacro*, a term used by Spagna to describe the change of oratorio from an objective account of a sacred subject to a subjective, spiritual counterpart of opera. Records in the oratories document the increasing importance of prominent professional composers, singers, and instrumentalists; in addition, they reveal among the names of prominent librettists such aristocratic church patrons as Cardinal Benedetto Pamphili (approximately sixty libretti) and Cardinal Pietro Ottoboni.

Outstanding among composers who set texts by the two Roman cardinals was Alessandro SCARLATTI, whose approximately twenty-five extant oratorios (two of them in Latin) represent the high point of the genre in Italy. The later works find the composer transforming the nature of oratorio by adopting almost exclusively a fuller instrumental accompaniment with much use of OBBLIGATO instruments; a simpler, melody-dominated texture with the bass as harmonic support; and the musically dominant *da capo* aria (a ternary aria in which the return to the first section is signaled by the words *da capo*, "from the beginning"). (See example 27.)

EXAMPLE 27. Alessandro Scarlatti, "Ami, e amando," *San Filippo Neri* (meas. 6–9)

The changes that transform oratorio in the realm of style reflect the momentous and far-reaching religious and social changes that led oratorio from the prayer halls into the galleries of wealthy nobles. So successful was the genre in Italy that it gradually dispensed with its narrator and chorus and became more or less a Lenten substitute for opera. Like opera, oratorio soon spread across Europe, but outside of Italy—apparently because of its religious purpose—vernacular languages and a more conservative approach were preserved, and native composers played a larger role in its history. In France, oratorio was cultivated (in Latin) under the term *histoire sacrée* by Marc-Antoine CHARPENTIER, after the model of his teacher, Carissimi. Many German Protestant oratorios also achieved a nonoperatic spirit, partly through the retention of the narrator and the chorus, partly through the use of CHORALE melodies, and partly through the heavier German contrapuntal manner.

Many German oratorios were composed on the Death of Christ, making them PASSION oratorios.

By far the greatest Baroque composer of oratorios was George Frideric Handel, who created the English oratorio. Although he embraced a wider range of subjects and types than did the Italians, Handel reflects a truly Italian dramatic character in his oratorios; they constitute religious or simply moral entertainments and were not designed for performance in church. Handel's complete mastery of Italian opera and his acquaintance with the English masque as well as the German Protestant oratorio, his enhanced choral and orchestral resources and contrapuntal skill, and his remarkable musical and dramatic gifts enable his oratorios to represent perhaps even better than opera the quintessential values of Baroque sung drama. (See the article on HANDEL.)

Despite the continuance of the oratorio tradition and function, and notwithstanding the appearance of isolated masterpieces, composition and performance of oratorios declined markedly after the Baroque period. In Italy, the third decade of the eighteenth century brought far-reaching changes in oratorio texts. The leading librettists, Apostolo Zeno (1668–1750) and Pietro Metastasio (1698–1782), both turned away from hagiography and allegory as source material, preferring to range over a wide variety of subjects, some of them hardly religious. By 1786, oratorios appeared regularly on the stage with scenic representation, thus obliterating the last vestiges of distinction between oratorio and opera in Italy. During this time, Italian oratorio may have been more significant outside of Italy, in such nations as England, Spain, and Russia. Among the composers who wrote Italian oratorio for Vienna was Franz Joseph HAYDN (*Il ritorna di Tobia*, 1775), while Johann Adolph Hasse composed many of his Italian oratorios for Dresden.

Composition of oratorios in languages other than Italian took place in France, Germany, England, Spain, Denmark, and the United States. Oratorios were performed in France from 1758 to 1761 and from 1774 to 1790 at Lenten religious concerts known as the *concerts spirituels*. Most of these oratorios had French texts, including four highly original, so-called "Mass-oratorios" by Jean Francois LeSueur. German oratorios of the Classical period offer a greater variety of types and more flexibility of style than the heavily conventional, international Italian oratorio. The essentially dramatic type of oratorio found in Germany, which was composed on a biblical or hagiographical text, shared a certain number of traits with Italian oratorio, but the nondramatic, essentially contemplative type stood closer to the German church cantata. Indeed, some confusion now begins with the use of the terms "oratorio" and CANTATA.

A German oratorio can substitute for the liturgically proper Lutheran cantata during the worship service. In contrast to its Italian counterpart, a German oratorio offers less vocal display in arias—some arias can be folk-like—and there is usually much use of the chorus. The culmination of the genre in German occurs in the famous examples by Haydn entitled *The Creation* and *The Seasons*.

Towards the end of the eighteenth century, many performances of selections from Handel's oratorios were given in England and the United States, but relatively few oratorios were composed. In both countries, the inception of music festivals and singing societies laid the foundation for a significant and highly characteristic emphasis upon oratorio performances in the nineteenth century. For the most part, however, Handel and such foreign Romantic masters as Mendelssohn, Gounod, and Franck were the composers favored; musical taste became firmly conservative, and Romantic developments in style inevitably bypassed oratorio. Decline and conservativism continued in Italian oratorio; the popular form had become sacred opera, as in Rossini's *Mosè in Egitto (Moses in Egypt)*. French oratorio, which was performed largely in concert halls, attracted the best French composers, among them Hector BERLIOZ, César FRANCK, and Jules Massenet. The genre is noteworthy in France for its devotional and mystical Roman Catholic character.

Emphasis upon the popular Romantic themes of death, the supernatural, and ancient religious legends gave German oratorio a certain vitality in the ninetenth century; it also made especially welcome the new style traits of Romanticism, including intense cultivation of harmonic and orchestral color, achievement of unity through the use of leitmotifs and the cyclic principle, and introduction of programmaticism in instrumental numbers. Outstanding among the progressive composers was Franz Liszt, among the conservatives, Felix Mendelssohn. Mendelssohn's *Elijah* and *St. Paul* served as models for untold numbers of English oratorios. (See example 28 and the article on MENDELSSOHN.)

In the twentieth-century, the movement that led composers back to the principles and genres of Bach and Handel yielded oratorios by William Walton and other English composers; the same nation produced works in a rich post-Romantic vein by Edward Elgar and Ralph VAUGHAN WILLIAMS. New styles are represented in various isolated examples for concert performance by such outstanding composers as Arthur Honegger and Frank Martin (on French texts), Arnold Schoenberg and Franz Schmidt (on German texts), and Igor STRAVINSKY (on a Latin text). With Stravinsky and especially with the doctrine-conscious Russians, secular subjects continue to invade the genre and to belie its heritage. Finally,

EXAMPLE 28. Felix Mendelssohn, "Ye People, Rend Your Hearts," *Elijah* (meas. 1–3)

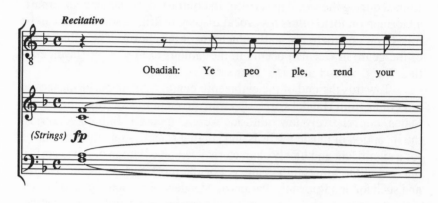

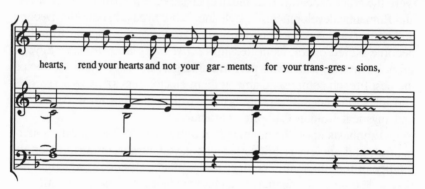

avant-garde composers have also taken up the oratorio, among them Olivier MESSIAEN, Hans Werner Henze, and Krzysztof PENDERECKI. On the one hand, the flexible format of oratorio has kept the genre alive in quite different circumstances than those which formed it; on the other hand, its versatility seems to have altered its character and function almost beyond recognition.

For those seeking more detailed knowledge about the oratorio, the standard source is the monumental *History of the Oratorio* (University of North Carolina Press, 1977–87), in three volumes, by Howard E. Smither. Highly recommended is the same author's overview of the subject that appears in *The New Grove Dictionary of Music and Musicians*.

Ordinal—An early liturgical book that described the order of Roman Catholic services in specific localities.

Ordinary—The term used for the parts of the Roman Catholic MASS and OFFICE for which the texts remain the same during the entire LITURGICAL YEAR. The melodies, found in the KYRIALE, need not remain the same. When composers set the Mass, they generally include only the following parts of the Mass Ordinary: KYRIE, GLORIA, CREDO, SANCTUS (and Benedictus), and AGNUS DEI.

organ—The pre-eminent church instrument since at least the tenth century, the organ consists of one or more sets of pipes through which wind passes and is controlled by one or more keyboards, and perhaps by a pedal-board. Each set of pipes is traditionally called a stop (in German, *Register*; in French, *jeu*). Organ registration is the art of selecting and combining organ stops in the performance of a specific composition, an art the composer often left entirely to the organist until well into the nineteenth century.

There have been many different kinds of organs through the centuries, reflecting the preferences and styles of the various Western nations. For a detailed historical account, the reader is referred to *A New History of the Organ: From the Greeks to the Present Day* (1980), by Peter Williams. After its invention during, or perhaps even before, the third century B.C., the organ was developed by the Romans into the hydraulis—a secular instrument in which the wind pressure was regulated by water. The use of the organ spread to the Byzantine empire and to Arabia. By the sixth or seventh century A.D., water had been replaced by a bellows, and it was this form of the instrument that eventually reached Western Europe. During the eighth century the organ was found in churches, but little is known about its use. Not until some time after the tenth century does it begin its rise to dominance in the church.

During the Medieval period the organ acquired an expanded range, chromatic pitches, and finally a pedalboard. Smaller organs, among them the positive (German, *Positiv*), also developed at this time and contributed much to the usefulness of the instrument. By the end of the Renaissance many churches had one large organ and several smaller ones. Variety of timbre had become possible through the use of separate stops, and separate keyboards served to control the greater tonal resources. Developments in the Baroque period, the organ's golden age, began to follow national or regional lines, as manifested in the large German instruments (with as many as four manual divisions and an independent pedalboard), the smaller and simpler French organs (distinguished by their powerful reeds), and the fairly rudimentary one-manual Italian organs without an independent pedal-board. Organ-building in England alternately waxed and waned with the vagaries of political and religious change, the low point coming with the destruction of most organs during the Commonwealth period. As in Italy and Spain, instruments in England did not have independent pedalboards.

The Romantic period brought a dynamic approach to musical style that was not suitable for the traditional organ. Major composers had already turned away from the instrument during the Classical period. The new Romantic instruments (and, unfortunately, many reconstructed old ones) attempted with varying degrees of success to emulate the kaleidoscopic dynamic and timbral aspects of the orchestra. The number of noteworthy organ-builders, so large in the Baroque period, dwindled to a handful, among whom the Frenchman Cavaille-Coll stands foremost. In the United States, the availability of electricity in the twentieth century led to its use in working the bellows of the pipe organ, and subsequently to the adoption of an electromagnetic valve action that permits the organist to use various adjustable pistons underneath the keyboards (and near the pedalboard) to control and change the selection of the organ stops. The next step in this direction was the development of the modern electronic organ, which did away with pipes altogether and employed fixed-pitch oscillators, electronic amplification, and loudspeakers to simulate the sound of the acoustic organ. In reaction to these modern trends, there has been a strong revival in the twentieth century of traditional organ types, many based upon either German Baroque specifications or a combination of German and so-called "classical" French characteristics. For an account of the development of music composed for the organ, see the article ORGAN MUSIC.

Organ Mass—A collection of VERSETS for the organ that replace alternate parts (usually the odd-numbered verses) of the items of the Mass ORDINARY and sometimes of the Mass PROPER, leaving the other parts to be sung. When the remaining verses are sung by a choir, usually in Gregorian CHANT, the practice is described by the term "in ALTERNATIM." The organ Mass began in about 1400, reached its peak during the seventeenth century, and ended with the banning of the practice by Pope Pius X in his MOTU PROPRIO of 1903.

From its inception, the organ Mass was essentially an improvisatory practice, exercised in a more or less traditional manner by countless organists all over Europe. The custom until the middle of the seventeenth century was to improvise on the plainchant that was not being sung, or at least to improvise in the same mode. Of the few organ Masses that were notated, most consist of versets for only the Mass ORDINARY. Among the various movements published by FRESCOBALDI in *Fiori musicali* (1635), however, the Kyrie is the only portion of the Ordinary that is set. Many organ Masses were published in France during the Baroque period, among them outstanding examples by Nicolas de GRIGNY and Francois COUPERIN. In several polyphonic Masses by Marc-Antoine CHARPENTIER, organ versets are played in alternation with choral polyphony rather than with Gregorian chant. The tradition of the organ Mass—which was still usually improvised—continued in France through the Classical and Romantic periods, and the genre remains in use, despite its ban, in the twentieth century, as in the *Messe de la Pentecôte* (1951) by Olivier MESSIAEN.

Organ music—When and how the organ was used in church services between the tenth and the thirteenth centuries, the time during which it became the principal, even the exclusive, instrument used in the church, remains largely unknown. Perhaps it was used only on feast days. Possibly the practice of performing verses of CHANT in alternation between choir and organ began as early as the eleventh century, but it can only be documented three centuries later. (See ORGAN MASS.) Compositions for the organ from these early centuries would undoubtedly help in dealing with historical uncertainties, but organ music does not appear in extant manuscripts until the fourteenth century, apparently because of a strong tradition of improvisation and because the use of familiar plainchant as a basis for composition was firmly established.

From the Medieval period until the present day, organ music composed on pre-existing vocal models, whether plainchant melodies, chorales, or polyphonic compositions, has remained among the most important music in the various genres. The most comprehensive of the fifteenth-century collections of organ music, the *Buxheim Organbook*, contains a significant number of compositions based on plainchant in which the CANTUS FIRMUS is usually stated in large note-values, but is sometimes ornamented or paraphrased. More than half of the approximately 250 compositions in the manuscript are based upon chansons or MOTETS, either by the use of a borrowed tenor voice as a foundation for a new piece, or by the incorporation of the entire original texture with one of the voices embellished. In both of the preceding categories, the texture of the music is usually created by one principal melody accompanied by two more or less equal lower voices. With the exception of some pieces written on *basse-danse* melodies, the last of the principal types of organ music in the *Buxheim Organbook* can best be described as preludes, although some of them offer contrasting sections fore-shadowing the toccata.

Most of the early manuscripts of organ music and most of the organ treatises are German in provenance. Their illustrations of how to improvise can be particularly helpful to modern performers. A special system of notation for the organ, called organ tablature, is used in the original sources. More significant for the history of the medium are the presence of organ compositions not based on vocal models and, of special importance, the appearance from about 1320 of works that require the use of organ pedals.

Modern church musicians often do not realize that there exists an abundant and varied repertory of unjustly neglected keyboard music for the church that does not require the use of an organ pedalboard. The pedal parts in most German and some Franco-Flemish organ music constitute an exceptional practice not followed until the nineteenth century in the church music of Spain, England, Italy, and, for the most part, France. A considerable amount of printed church music for keyboard neither specifies the organ as the exclusive instrument for performance nor reveals style traits that would confine it to the organ.

The earliest printed editions of organ music appeared in the sixteenth century; the principal ones — as with manuscripts — were German in origin. Among the earliest is a collection published in Mainz in 1512 by Arnolt Schlick. In addition to the expected plainchant and chorale-like compositions are examples of two genres derived from sectional vocal models that are destined for noteworthy careers — the canzona and the ricercare. Among the purely instrumental types of music are preludes, toccatas, and variations. Pointing towards the future of German organ music are the fourteen pieces composed for organ with pedals, some of which are in three and some in four parts.

Organ music also flowered outside of Germany during the Renaissance. From early in the sixteenth century comes the music of the great Spanish organist to the royal court, Antonio de Cabezon, whose church music includes *tientos* (ricercare-like compositions built on several themes) and plainchant settings. Two outstanding English composers of organ music in the sixteenth century were John Redford and Thomas Preston. Writing for instruments with manuals only (that is, without pedalboard), the English were among the leaders in developing passagework idiomatic for the keyboard and compositional techniques such as the use of the OSTINATO. Finally, organ music flourished in the later sixteenth century in Italy, especially in Venice. Serving as organists at the Cathedral of St. Mark were such eminent composers as Andrea Gabrieli, his nephew

Giovanni GABRIELI, and Claudio Merulo. Among the genres they cultivated were the RICERCARE and the CANZONA, the TOCCATA, and the intonation (INTONAZIONE), a short preludial or interludial piece composed
in one or another of the church modes and selected to knit the service
together smoothly.

In the seventeenth century, the achievement and reputation of
Girolamo FRESCOBALDI (1583-1643) as an organist, composer, and
teacher brought Rome to the forefront as a center for organ music. The
church music genres he performed with great acclaim in Saint Peter's — and
published with such success that J. S. Bach owned a copy of his liturgical collection, *Fiori musicali* (1635) — included principally the toccata
and the ricercare, compositions based on Gregorian chant, and three organ
Masses. Frescobaldi remained faithful to the genres of the Renaissance,
but his mature style reveals its Baroque orientation in its greater use of
textural and rhythmic contrast, and in its exploration of the middle ground
between modality and tonality. Since his occasional pedal parts double
the bass part played by the left hand, much of Frescobaldi's music can
be played equally well on organ or harpsichord. (See example 15.)

Spanish organist-composers carried on the tradition of Cabezon
in the seventeenth century, among them Sebastian Aguilera de Heredia
(c. 1565-1627), Manuel Rodrigues de Coelho (1555-1635), Francisco
Correa de Arauxo (c. 1576-1654), and, perhaps the finest, Juan Cabanilles
(1644-1712). In addition to short liturgical versets, mostly based on plainchant, they composed some toccatas, some variations, and many
TIENTOS. The imitative counterpoint found in the tiento has a significant
place in the early history of the fugue, especially in the monothematic
version of that genre. Like the ricercare, the tiento was more often
composed on several themes. The Spanish also wrote a special kind of
tiento full of the false relations and affective treatment of intervals and
dissonance characteristic of the early Baroque period.

First among significant French composers of organ music in the
seventeenth century was Jehan TITELOUZE (c.1562-1633), who published
several volumes of liturgical music for the Catholic church based upon
plainchant and designed to be played in alternation with the choir during
the service. In a style of modal counterpoint not far removed from choral
music, the plainchant either appears in the bass part as a cantus firmus
or, paraphrased, serves as a theme for a point of imitation. The second
half of the century brought many publications of organ music, which
reveal a gradual change from an optional to a fully independent pedal
part. The organbooks of Guillaume Nivers (c.1632-1714) established the
extraordinary mixture of elements that characterized French Baroque

organ compositions through the eighteenth century. They were drawn from liturgical music (mostly short versets for use in the service), from the unique structure of the French Baroque organ, and from secular (often dance-like) music. Other composers of special note include Louis Couperin (c.1626–1661), Nicolas-Antoine Lebègue (1631–1702) and his distinguished pupil, Nicolas de GRIGNY (1672–1703), and François COUPERIN (1668–1733). Among the most remarkable of the organ genres are duets and trios whose special character derives from their registration, which was generally specified by the composers in the titles of these compositions. (See example 10.)

The organ music of the Baroque remains unsurpassed by that of any other historical period in its abundance, variety, and quality. Far from standing alone, the church music of J. S. BACH is the culmination of a long and glorious tradition. With the growth of Lutheranism and the resurgence of Catholicism during the Counter-Reformation, there were two major Germanic traditions, corresponding geographically with the spheres of power established by the rival Christian faiths.

In the southern part of the Germanic territories, and especially in Vienna, organ music was composed mainly for the Catholic church. Its great master, Johann Jacob Froberger (1616–1667), studied in Rome with Frescobaldi and served as court organist to the Catholic emperor. Most worthy of note among his church music are the toccatas, in which dramatic improvisatory passages and imitative sections are linked in a manner that leads to the later Baroque toccata and fugue. In the second half of the century, the leading South German composer was J. C. F. Fischer (c.1670–1746). Among his organ music, *Ariadne musica* (1702) seems in its small-scale preludes and fugues to have served as inspiration and model for J. S. Bach's *Well-Tempered Clavier*, while *Blumen-Strauss* (1732) carries on Catholic tradition in the arrangement of its preludes and fugues according to the eight church modes.

In northern Germany, where the Lutheran church had its stronghold, organ music had as its great teacher and inspiration the Dutchman Jan Pieterszoon SWEELINCK (1562–1621). From the traditional Netherlands' art of counterpoint and the new keyboard techniques of the Renaissance, especially those derived from the English, Sweelinck composed a body of organ music most noteworthy for its variations on Lutheran chorales, FANTASIAS, and toccatas. (See example 13.) Foremost among his students, and the leading German organist-composer of the early seventeenth century, was Samuel SCHEIDT (1587–1654), Scheidt composed in the same genres as his teacher, as well as composing fugues and various parts of the liturgy. Most of his many settings of Lutheran chorales are

EXAMPLE 29. Samuel Scheidt, "Da Jesus an dem Kreuze stund," *Tabulatura nova* (Versus 6: meas. 1–6)

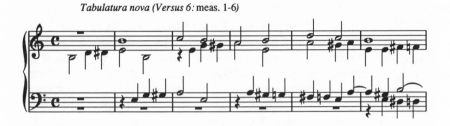

Tabulatura nova (Versus 6: meas. 1-6)

in simple four-part harmony for organ, but some (like example 29) reveal his mastery of counterpoint. The great organ composer of North Germany during the later seventeenth century emigrated to Germany from Denmark in 1668. Dietrich BUXTEHUDE (c.1637–1707) often composed traditional variations, short preludes, and virtuosic fantasias on chorale melodies. The freely conceived works are less easily described, since toccata-like or prelude-like sections alternate with fugal sections in an improvisatory fashion. In keeping with the contrapuntal North German approach, Buxtehude entrusted an important and fully independent part to the organ pedals. (See example 4.) Another leading figure of this period was Johann PACHELBEL (1653–1706), who is noteworthy especially for his liturgical music for the Lutheran service.

From the freely composed prelude, fantasia, toccata, ostinato forms, and FUGUE (with its predecessors, the ricercare and the tiento), to the chorale-based PRELUDE, PARTITA, and fantasia—each of the genres that contributed to the remarkable flowering of organ music in the Baroque period found its culmination in the more than 250 organ compositions by Johann Sebastian BACH (1685–1750). His works are grander in size and scope than those of his predecessors, and his fusion of the art of counterpoint with that of functional harmony is more expressive and perhaps more true. Like his contemporaries, Bach often combined different genres in a unified composition of larger dimension, as in the prelude and fugue, and he also gathered them in collections for publication. He seems systematically to bring every variety of each genre to its fulfillment, as in the chorale preludes (which constitute more than two-thirds of all the organ works). There are also trio sonatas for organ as well as arrangements of works not originally for organ, particularly concertos by Vivaldi. There are some works for manuals only as well.

Although many of the organ works were intended for church use, some are virtually concert pieces and some seem primarily didactic in design (e.g., the late keyboard fugues in *The Art of the Fugue*). Building a technique that will enable a player to perform the music of Bach remains the goal of every serious student of the organ. (See example 38.)

The time and the Germany of J. S. Bach also produced two composers widely regarded by Bach's contemporaries as the greatest of the age. Although neither contributed greatly to organ music, their progressive attitudes helped to break down traditional barriers between church music and secular concerts. Georg Philipp TELEMANN (1681–1767) usually avoided technical difficulties and appealed to a wider public in his church music, while George Frideric HANDEL (1685–1759) made his mark in England not simply through his choral and orchestral works, but in part through largely improvised performances at the organ. Handel's fourteen or fifteen organ concertos represent a new genre with a new public, since they were performed by the composer in a more or less secular setting between the parts of his oratorios.

The Classical period (c.1725–1825), which coincides in part with the Age of Enlightenment, represents an inevitable decline from the peak represented by Baroque organ music. Organists often found themselves having to earn part of their living outside of the church and having to please increasingly secular tastes. The period's multitude of short and technically easy pieces reveals that many organists were relatively untrained musicians with a preference in their preludes, toccatas, and fugues for the simpler textures and phrases of Classical music. Nevertheless, some noteworthy organist-composers were active, especially the Germans J. L. Krebs, J. C. Kittel, and J. P. Kirnberger—all pupils for a time of J. S. Bach—as well as J. G. Albrechtsberger, a teacher of Beethoven.

In an attempt to create a symphonic sound, the Romantic period brought changes in the nature of the organ. Recital instruments were built, and a concert repertory was developed that exhibited little connection with the church in its programmatic compositions. Eventually a reaction to secularization took place, as in the CECILIAN MOVEMENT and, in the United States, in the formation of the American Guild of Organists, with a view to raising the standards of both organ and church music. Several major composers, among them MENDELSSOHN, Schumann, Liszt, and BRAHMS, wrote a few organ pieces, most of them sonatas and fugues, but including some chorale preludes. More representative among the Germans were the sonatas of such organist-composers as Joseph Rheinberger (1839–1901), who kept alive a polyphonic approach to the instrument. A special niche was carved by Max REGER (1873–1916), a devout Catholic who nevertheless revered Bach, and composed fantasias on chorale melodies as well as variations, preludes, and fugues for the organ, which he regarded as a pre-eminent concert instrument.

In France, the study of the organ at the Paris Conservatory, the exceptional instruments of the great organ-builder Cavaille-Coll, and a thorough knowledge of and respect for Bach served as seeds for Romantic organ music that bore fruit in the works of the Belgian Cesar FRANCK (1822–1890) and the organ symphonies of Charles-Marie Widor (1844–1937), among others. The renewal in France continued well into the twentieth century in the works of Charles Tournemire (1870–1939), Jean LANGLAIS (1907–   ), Jehan Alain (1911–1940), and Olivier MESSIAEN (1908–   ). (See example 22.)

Organ music was propelled to the forefront of twentieth-century music through the innovative organ techniques and avant-garde musical language of Messiaen, with its emphasis upon asymmetrical rhythms, idiosyncratic harmonies, and a unique approach to timbre. His enormous influence, however, owes far less to his compositions than to his teaching position and his students at the Paris Conservatory, one of whom was the outstanding composer and organist William ALBRIGHT. All of the various progressive techniques of twentieth-century composition can be found in organ music, including serialism, aleatory methods, and electronic alterations or additions. Most listeners – at least in the United States – have probably experienced the organ as an electronic medium, regardless of repertory.

In reaction to modern trends, there has been a significant return to the structure of the organ of Bach's time (the "classical" organ), to contrapuntal principles, and to traditional liturgical genres, in a movement that began in the nineteenth century and remains strong in the 1990s. This coincides precisely with one of the most influential trends of the century, generally referred to as NEO-CLASSICISM, although its leading international figures did not compose organ music. Among the leading composers of both organ and church music whose works reflect the return of the organ to its traditional church function were Hugo DISTLER (1908–1942), Johann Nepomuk DAVID (1895–1977) and Flor PEETERS (1903–   ). (See examples 30 and 32.)

From the standpoint of the past, perhaps the greatest threat to both the traditional organ and to its historical repertory lies not in the fairly predictable assimilation of twentieth-century styles and techniques, but

EXAMPLE 30. Johann Nepomuk David, "Nun komm, der Heiden Heiland," Kleine Chaconne fuer Orgel (meas. 1–9)

©Breitkopf & Härtel, Wiesbaden

in the contemporary evangelistic movement, with its emphasis upon gospel music and the popular electronic media.

The fact that the history of organ music is inextricably linked in its early years with the history of keyboard music is evident in the article by several authors entitled "Keyboard Music," and in its accompanying bibliography found in volume 10 of *The New Grove Dictionary.* Perhaps the best survey of the organ music of J. S. Bach is *The Organ Music of Bach* (Cambridge University Press, 1980) by Peter Williams.

organum—A Latin word originally referring to any instrument, then specifically to the organ, and then to what has become its primary meaning: early vocal polyphony based on Gregorian CHANT. Polyphony began when a second line of music was added to chant, which created the need for a more specific system of notation for both pitch and rhythm, as well as for theories of consonance and dissonance. These changes constitute the "other path" that has characterized Western music. The development of organum proceeded from motion almost entirely in parallel fourths or fifths to a freer genre that offered an alternation between sustained-note organum (in which a melody unfolded freely over sustained notes in the CANTUS FIRMUS) and passages of organum in discant style (in which both voices moved in the RHYTHMIC MODES). The greatest composer of organum is said to be LEONIN. (See example 19.)

Orgel-Buechlein—German for *The Little Organ-Book*, the title of an unfinished collection of chorale preludes by J. S. BACH. Many later composers, emulating Bach, have subsequently published collections of organ pieces under the title (in various languages) "Organbook".

ostinato—An Italian word (meaning "obstinate") for a short musical theme or motive that is repeated persistently, often in the same voice.

Pachelbel, Johann (1653–1706)—One of the most significant and productive of German Baroque organist-composers, Pachelbel was by training and nature well-suited for bringing together style elements from different traditions and offering clear models for his successors through his compositions and his teaching. With the exception of two short court appointments—at Eisenach and Stuttgart—the composer's career was spent almost entirely as a church musician. A Lutheran by birth and training, he seized the opportunity in 1673 to assimilate the Italian Catholic church's music tradition by serving as deputy organist at Saint Stephen's in Vienna. His two most significant church positions were as organist at Lutheran churches in Erfurt (from 1678 to 1690) and in Nuremberg (from 1695 until his death). His influence was also felt as a teacher; Johann Christoph Bach, the teacher of the great Johann Sebastian, studied with Pachelbel, and Carl Theodor Pachelbel brought his father's training to the British colonies in America.

Pachelbel composed a great deal of functional church music. The majority of the organ works were composed for the Lutheran liturgy, including approximately seventy CHORALE PRELUDES for the service at Erfurt and ninety-five FUGUES for use in the MAGNIFICAT at Nuremberg. The chorale preludes display a wide variety of types, one of which appears to have been uniquely his—a short fugue on the opening phrase of the chorale melody followed by cantus firmus treatment of the remaining phrases in three or four parts. The fugues are short movements for performance *in* ALTERNATIM with sung verses of the Magnificat; they are in general unrelated thematically to the liturgical melodies. Although they do not offer contrasting episodes, Pachelbel's fugues seem to have been important in establishing the technical and tonal properties of fugal exposition that helped make possible the great organ fugues of the late Baroque. As for the nonliturgical organ music, most of the TOCCATAS, PRELUDES, FANTASIAS, FUGUES, and chorale variations are clearly intended for use in the church; many, however, do not require use of the organ pedals. In keeping with the functional nature of his organ music, the style of Pachelbel is noteworthy for its objective character and for working out modest technical problems of process and form on a small scale, as opposed to the display of virtuoso music-making or the expression of subjective states of emotion.

Recent research has enhanced Pachelbel's reputation by revealing that, in addition to his recognized importance as a composer of organ music, he produced a significant number of sacred vocal works. Among the liturgical works are thirteen MAGNIFICATS and twelve settings of the *ingressus*, both of which formed part of VESPERS at Saint Sebald's in Nuremberg. The settings of the *ingressus* begin with the versicle "Deus in adjutorium," continue with its response ("Domine, ad adjuvandum"), and close with the GLORIA PATRI followed by an Alleluia. The Magnificat settings represent Pachelbel at his best, introducing Italianate concertato features and employing a wide variety of structures, textures, and musical resources. About half of the Magnificats are written for five-voice chorus and call for wind instruments as well as strings and basso continuo. Eleven other cantata-like compositions, most of them written on chorale melodies, are extant; according to Ewald V. Nolte (*The New Grove Dictionary*, vol. 14, p. 51); the "most ambitious" of these is *Jauchzet dem Herrn, alle Welt*, while "in *Kommt her zu mir* he came closest to the later form of the church cantata." More conservative but equally well composed are Pachelbel's eleven double-chorus MOTETS, which were probably accompanied by continuo. There are also approximately twenty instrumentally accompanied arias intended for various special occasions in the church, such as weddings and funerals. Finally, of less importance, there are two MASSES, one of them a MISSA BREVIS.

Palestrina, Giovanni Pierluigi da (c.1525–1594)—Alone among his great predecessors and contemporaries in the Renaissance, Palestrina earned a reputation that endured through all the subsequent vicissitudes of music history. Upheld as a model for composers of sacred polyphony during his lifetime and by succeeding generations, Palestrina's style received the official sanction of the Roman Catholic Church and ultimately became the pedagogical focus for study and emulation of sixteenth-century counterpoint. An Italian church musician whose career was spent almost entirely in Counter-Reformation Rome, Palestrina created a wonderfully refined and thoroughly consistent style by suppressing the subjective and humanistic aspects of late Renaissance Netherlands counterpoint and stressing smoothness, euphony, balance, and restraint.

Palestrina received his early training as a choirboy at the church of Saint Maria Maggiore in Rome. From 1544 until 1551 he served as organist and singer at the cathedral in the nearby town of Palestrina and mastered the craft of composition. He was summoned back to Rome in 1551 by Pope Julius III (formerly the Bishop of Palestrina) as maestro di cappella of Saint Peter's, and after that time he was seldom out of the employ of one or another of the great Roman cathedrals: the Sistine

Chapel (1555), Saint John Lateran (1555–1560), Saint Maria Maggiore (1561–1566), and finally at Saint Peter's for the rest of his life (1571–1594). Personal tragedy touched his life particularly between 1572 and 1580, when his brother, two of his sons, and his wife all died of the plague. Although he took some steps towards the priesthood at that time, a second marriage with a wealthy widow took place in 1581, rendering his later years both secure and musically productive; his practicality had already been demonstrated during the years he spent in service to Cardinal Ippolito d'Este (1564–1571), for whom many of his madrigals were composed, and in his relations with other distinguished patrons.

Among Palestrina's compositions are 104 MASSES (the greatest number of the period by one composer), more than 375 MOTETS, and 65 HYMNS as well as 68 OFFERTORIES, 35 MAGNIFICATS, and four or five sets of LAMENTATIONS; of the 140 madrigals, somewhat less than half of them have spiritual texts. The Masses are composed for four, five, six, or eight voice-parts in all the standard arrangements of the period. Forty-one were published in six books during his lifetime, and 38 more had been printed in seven more books by 1601. In more than 50 Masses, the composer based his music on pre-existing polyphonic works (a technique usually referred to as parody), often on compositions of his own, but seldom on secular pieces. Melodies alone supply the basis for 35 more Masses (the technique being termed paraphrase), some of them deriving from a single plainchant or secular melody and some of them drawing upon the cycle of plainchants found in a Mass. There remain a smaller number of old-fashioned cantus firmus Masses, a few Masses that use canonic technique, and some freely composed Masses that do not employ traditional devices; one (*Missa Laudate Dominum*) reveals the influence of Venetian writing for double chorus. The well-known *Pope Marcellus Mass* exemplifies the composer's concern for the intelligibility of the text, a matter of some importance during the years during and after the Council of Trent. Published in book 2 (Rome, 1567) of Palestrina's Masses, it was probably composed in about 1562. It is apparently based on a new and original theme, an unusual practice for the composer, who preferred to use pre-existing themes. Although there are six voice-parts, with a seventh added for the second Agnus Dei, contrapuntal complexity is limited throughout to selected sections. It is replaced in importance in the Gloria and Credo by a structural use of contrasting sonorities, in which less than full voice groups alternate until the most effective moment for a full texture is reached. (See example 21.)

The motets are written in from four to eight voices or twelve voices; most are freely composed, but some use paraphrase or canonic techniques, and tone-painting is more evident than in the Masses. Those wishing to perform Palestrina should not overlook his hymns or, in particular, his OFFERTORIES, both of which were published in cycles for the entire liturgical year. It is not always necessary to perform Palestrina's music without instrumental doubling (a manner misleadingly termed *a cappella*), since the practice was certainly not universal in the sixteenth century.

Palestrina's fame was reflected in his lifetime by his significant church positions, his many publications, his assignment by the church to revise Gregorian CHANT—a project he did not complete—and in historical perspective by the nineteenth-century publication of all his works, the first corpus of Renaissance music to receive a complete edition.

paraphrase Mass—The technique of altering a pre-existing melody, perhaps simply by giving a Gregorian CHANT melody clearly notated rhythms and a few ornaments, became significant during the RENAISSANCE. When this technique was applied to a melody that served as the basis for a cyclic MASS, as in Palestrina's *Missa L'Homme armé* (his earlier setting), the resulting composition is a paraphrase Mass.

Parker, Horatio (1863–1919)—An American, Parker studied composition with George Chadwick in Boston, and then with Josef Rheinberger in Germany. Foreign training created opportunities for him in the United States, and successful compositions enabled him to become one of the country's most highly respected musicians. His career was spent as an organist and choirmaster in various New York and Boston churches, as a music teacher in cathedral schools and, briefly, in the National Conservatory of Music, and as a professor of music theory, then dean of the School of Music at Yale University. Parker devoted considerable effort to organizing and conducting the New Haven Symphony Orchestra and that city's Oratorio Society. Basically a traditionalist and somewhat of a late German Romantic in style, he composed a varied body of secular works, including (mostly from his early years) orchestral and chamber music and a considerable number of songs and choral pieces. His best-known composition is the ORATORIO *Hora novissima* (The Latest Hour), with a text drawn from a twelfth-century Latin poem by Bernard of Cluny entitled "On Contempt of the World." Written for the Church Choral Society of New York in 1893, its success in the United States led to performances at the great choral festivals in England and to the receipt of an honorary doctorate in music from Cambridge University in 1902. The climax of his career was probably the performance of his opera *Mona* at the Metropolitan Opera in 1912.

Parker is commonly regarded as the outstanding American composer of church music of his time, and fully an equal to the best of church composers abroad. Among his liturgical works are *The Morning and Evening Service in E, Together with the Office for the Holy Communion* (1890), another Office for the Holy Communion (1904), two settings of the MAGNIFICAT and NUNC DIMITTIS, and a TE DEUM (1893). For Christmas the composer wrote two cantatas, *The Holy Child* (1893) and *The Shepherds' Vision* (1906). There are also approximately twenty-five ANTHEMS, a MOTET in eight voices that reveals the influence of Renaissance polyphony ("Adstant angelorum chori"), and numerous hymn settings (in particular, a hymnal edited with H. B. Jepson entitled *University Hymns for Use in Battell Chapel at Yale with Tunes Arranged for Male Voices*). Although his more ambitious works, both sacred and secular, fell into disuse soon after his death, certain of Parker's hymns and anthems continue to be performed in church services.

parody Mass—A MASS that is based on a pre-existing polyphonic piece, usually a MOTET or a chanson. The resulting composition is then given the name of the composition parodied, as in Palestrina's *Missa "Assumpta est maria,"* which is based on one of the composer's own motets. Parody became one of the favorite techniques of the later RENAISSANCE.

partita—An Italian word used at first to refer to variations. A chorale partita thus becomes a set of variations on a CHORALE melody. In the Baroque period, however, partita also was used as a name for a suite.

passacaglia—Put simply, a passacaglia is a type of variation based upon a reiterated theme (an OSTINATO) that is usually heard in the bass line, as in J. S. Bach's monumental *Passacaglia in C Minor* (BWV 582) for organ. The term is one of many upon whose meaning composers have chosen to disagree.

Passion—A musical setting of events in the life of Jesus Christ from the Last Supper to the Crucifixion, usually as told in one of the four Gospels: Matthew, Mark, Luke, or John. The Passion texts are liturgically proper in Roman Catholic usage as Gospel recitations during Mass on Palm Sunday (Matthew), on Holy Tuesday (Mark), on Holy Wednesday (Luke), and on Good Friday (John).

In the Medieval period the Passion was sung, originally by one singer, in special reciting tones and in a manner which differentiated between the characters of the story. From at least the thirteenth century different singers had come to be used for the different characters, while the use of a chorus (singing in monophony) for the crowd can be documented as early as the fourteenth century. The plainsong CHANTS for the Passion texts are found in the *Cantorinus Vaticanus* and, for Good Friday, in the *Officium et Missa ultimi tridui*.

With the Renaissance came polyphonic settings of the Passion story. In the RESPONSORIAL Passion the words of the narrator (or Evangelist) remained in plainchant; in the "throughcomposed" Passion, all of the text, including that of the narrator, was set polyphonically. When the Reformation brought translation of the Passion text into German, both kinds of polyphonic setting continued to attract composers. The first German Passion, composed in about 1525 on the Gospel of Saint Matthew by Johann Walther, constitutes a responsorial setting in which a four-part chorus sings the words of the crowd, a tenor those of the Evangelist (or narrator), a bass those of Jesus, and an alto those of the other characters. Among the noteworthy Catholic responsorial Passions of the period are settings in Latin by Orlandus LASSUS, Tomas Luis de VICTORIA, and William BYRD.

An outstanding example of the Passion composed throughout in polyphony—including the part of the Evangelist—is the Passion according to Saint John (1631) by Johann Christoph Demantius. Its structure as a succession of polyphonic pieces has resulted in works of this kind being called motet-Passions. In addition to the traditional use of one Gospel text, motet-Passions could also be based on a shortened version of one of the Gospels or, in the case of the so-called *summa Passionis*, they could be set to a composite version pieced together from all four Gospels.

During the early Baroque period, the most influential model proved to be the responsorial Passion of Walther, but Heinrich SCHUETZ (1585–1672), the major seventeenth-century composer of the Passion, chose not to emulate either traditional model. In the three Passions which he composed in his eighties, the story unfolds in a uniquely conceived, unaccompanied kind of recitative for the Evangelist, Jesus, and the other characters, interspersed with short unaccompanied choral passages for the soldiers and the other groups.

The Passions of Schuetz could not stop the Baroque transformation of the Passion into more or less an ORATORIO based on a special subject. As long as the text remained faithfully biblical, this genre could be termed an oratorio-Passion, as in a *Saint Matthew Passion* (1642) by Thomas Selle. When the text was a libretto in which the Gospel words were freely embellished and rhymed in operatic fashion, and the musical structure was a succession of RECITATIVES, ARIAS, and choruses, then the genre was generally referred to as a Passion oratorio. In Italy and in areas of Germany under Italian musical influence, the purpose of the genre shifted perceptibly towards a form of spiritual entertainment. One of the most influential of Passion oratorios was composed in 1704 by Reinhard

Keiser under the title *Der blutige und sterbende Jesus* (The Bleeding
and Dying Jesus).

Because it adhered closely to one of the Gospel texts and thereby
met the devotional requirements of the Lutheran church, the genre of
Passion oratorio received the contributions of the major German
composers of the late Baroque, principally those of Georg Philip
TELEMANN (1681–1767) and Johann Sebastian BACH (1685-1750). As
director of music for Hamburg, where he served from 1721 until he died,
Telemann was responsible for composing a Passion every year. Apparently he set each of the four Gospels in alternation, beginning with Saint
Matthew in 1722 and ending with Saint Mark in 1767. In the approximately twenty Passions that survive, the composer retained the traditional use of recitative for the narrative, but shifted the focus from the
events of the Passion to lyrical arias and meditative choruses, including
chorale settings. Two complete Passions by Bach remain, one (according
to Saint John) from 1723 or 1724, and one (according to Saint Matthew)
from 1729. The former is a highly dramatic setting in sixty-eight separate
numbers, with additional passages of text drawn from Matthew and
nonbiblical sources, while the latter — which is considerably larger both
in size and in its use of vocal and instrumental resources — employs greater
restraint of style and a more devotional spirit to balance the dramatic
aspect of the Passion story.

The history of the Passion after Bach does not demand a lengthy
discussion. The advent of public concerts, amateur choral societies,
and grand music festivals brought untold performances of the masterpieces of Bach as repertory pieces, but most new settings of the Passion
story, such as BEETHOVEN's *Christus am Oelberge* (Christ on the Mount
of Olives, 1803) belong to the history of the oratorio. In the revival of
the genre that is taking place in the twentieth century, there remains a
clear distinction between works suitable for liturgical use and works
intended primarily for the concert hall. Among the former may be cited
the *Choral-Passion* by Hugo DISTLER (1933) and the *Saint Mark Passion*
(1965) by Daniel PINKHAM, an American; the latter group includes an
outstanding *Saint Luke Passion* (1967) in Latin by Krzysztof PENDERECKI.
During the Penderecki work, a panoply of avant-garde expressive
devices is heard, including both vocal and orchestral tone clusters and
glissandi, as well as such vocal effects as shouting and sighing from the
singers, and some striking dissonance of a conventional kind. (See
example 31.)

The best short survey of the history of the Passion is by Kurt von
Fischer and Werner Braun in volume 14 of *The New Grove Dictionary*.

EXAMPLE 31. Krzysztof Penderecki, "Te fons salutis," *St. Luke Passion* (Part I)

Passiontide—The season of the Christian year beginning with Ash Monday and ending on the eve of Easter; also known as Lent.

pastorale—Either a French or an Italian word for an instrumental composition evocative of the countryside. In the BAROQUE PERIOD such musical traits as dotted rhythms, drone basses, and meter signatures of 6/8 or 12/8 come to characterize a pastorale, and movements by that name turn up in connection with the Christmas story. By extension, instrumental works with a movement entitled "Pastorale," such as Arcangelo Corelli's Op. 6, No. 8, are sometimes connected with Christmas.

Pater noster—Latin for "Our Father," the first two words of the Lord's Prayer. It has a place in the Roman Catholic MASS and in two of the Canonical Hours, LAUDS and VESPERS.

Peeters, Flor (1903–   )—A noteworthy Belgian organist and teacher, Peeters may be the most prolific twentieth-century composer of organ music. He has also been active as a recitalist, teacher, and scholar. After studying the organ with Depuydt at the Lemmens Institute in Malines, he served as professor of organ there from 1925 until 1952. In 1948 he assumed the same position at the Royal Flemish Conservatory in Antwerp, where he became director in 1952 and acted in both capacities until 1968. In 1973, he celebrated his fiftieth year as organist of the Metropolitan Cathedral of Saint Rombaut in Malines. During these years, he also found time to teach organ elsewhere in Europe and in the United States, to give numerous recitals, and to make many commercial recordings. His teaching methods are summarized in the three volumes entitled *Ars Organi* (1952–1954); in addition, he published a *Little Organ Book* (1957) for beginners and a valuable book on the accompaniment of Gregorian chant (*Praktische methode voor gregorianische begleiding*, 1943). He also served as an editor of early organ music. As an organist, one of his greatest skills was that of improvisation.

The approximately five hundred organ compositions by Peeters reveal above all his love for Gregorian CHANT. Other influences include Flemish folk tunes and an intimate knowledge of RENAISSANCE works by Franco-Flemish composers. He has also acknowledged the influence of Charles Tournemire and Marcel Dupré, two great French organist-composers he met in Paris. Although Peeters experimented on occasion with polyrhythms and polytonality, his harmonic language remained tonal, however expanded by contemporary dissonance, chromaticism, and modality. In his "Paraphrase on 'Salve Regina' for Organ" (1973), for example, he surrounds the phrases of the Gregorian melody with unmistakably twentieth-century harmonies and rhythms within a thoroughly contrapuntal setting. (See example 32.) Rich contrapuntal textures are characteristic of the composer, who considered his "Passacaglia e Fuga," Op. 42 (1938), to be one of his most important compositions. Peeters preferred the traditional forms of fugue, toccata, partita and, especially, the chorale prelude. Despite his own virtuosity as an organist and composer, he composed many CHORALE and hymn settings for organists of modest technical ability, among them *30 Short Chorale-Preludes* (1959) and *213 Hymn Preludes for the Liturgical Year* (1959–1964).

Although they remain firmly in the shadow of his organ works, there are also a significant number of sacred choral works by Peeters, including many MOTETS, several psalm-settings, MASSES, a TE DEUM, and a MAGNIFICAT (1962).

Penderecki, Krzysztof (1933–) — Perhaps no other avant-garde composer has so consistently, directly, and successfully expressed in music his religious and ethical beliefs than Penderecki. Inspiration for his works has often come from liturgical ritual, either that of the Roman Catholic or the Orthodox church. Influence from music of the past, such as the

EXAMPLE 32. Flor Peeters, "Paraphrase on 'Salve Regina' for Organ" (meas. 21–24)

church music of J. S. BACH, is heard in his work after about 1964. A Polish Catholic, the composer began his career just as his countrymen were being granted greater artistic freedom. He soon found it not only artistically satisfying but also financially rewarding to set powerful subjects in an eclectic but intensely dramatic — even expressionistic — manner that draws upon pitched, unpitched, microtonal and, occasionally, electronic sounds, in an atonal, serial, or expanded tonal idiom. Special dramatic effects include tone clusters, instrumental and vocal glissandi, percussive devices, and the use of such instrumental techniques as *sul ponticello* (bowing a stringed instrument near the bridge); in addition, a chorus of voices may speak or shout in an unconventional manner, as well as sing. When notating his music required it, the composer turned to graphic use of time-fields expressed in seconds.

Among the outstanding sacred works by Penderecki are *Psalmy Dawida* (The Psalms of David, 1958), for chorus and percussion; *Psalmus* (1961), which requires electronic sounds; *The St. Luke Passion* (1965), for soloists, chorus, and orchestra; *Utrenia* (1971), in which two choruses and an orchestra unfold the story of the burial and the resurrection of Christ; *Magnificat* (1974), for soloist, boys' voices, mixed chorus, and orchestra; and *Te Deum* (1979), for soloists, chorus, and orchestra. When honored with a commission from the Lyric Opera of Chicago to compose an opera for the bicentennial celebration of the United States, he responded with a SACRA RAPPRESENTAZIONE on the subject of Milton's *Paradise Lost* (1978). The work was subsequently performed for the pope in Rome. A highly moving religious subject, *The Devils of Loudun*, served for Penderecki's 1969 opera. Nonsectarian humane impulses lay behind many of his works, including perhaps his best-known composition, *Threnody for the Victims of Hiroshima* (1960), written for fifty-two string instruments; another such work is his *Dies Irae* (1967), written on the subject of Auschwitz. Several of the composer's works have entered the international repertory, enabling him to receive significant commissions, to travel freely, to conduct his own works or to give lectures, and to live as he wishes. (See example 31.)

Penitential Psalms—The following seven psalms are designated as penitential (numbered as in the King James Bible): 6, 32, 38, 51, 102, 130, and 143. Many composers have set one or more of them; some have set them all, the most noteworthy example being Orlandus LASSUS. (See example 23.)

Pentecost—An important feast in the LITURGICAL YEAR for both Jews and Christians. Derived from the Greek word meaning "fiftieth," Pentecost is celebrated in the Christian church fifty days after Easter to mark the Descent of the Holy Ghost upon the Apostles. An English name for Pentecost is Whitsunday, called thus because people being baptized on this day in earlier times wore white garments. Two great Latin HYMNS are sung at Pentecost: in the OFFICE, "Veni Creator Spiritus" (Come, Creator Spirit), and as a SEQUENCE in the MASS, "Veni Sancte Spiritus" (Come, Holy Spirit). Palestrina set the latter twice in eight voices and used the Gregorian CHANT version of the former as the basis for a MASS. In the twentieth century, certain Protestant churches in the United States have divided the season of Trinity (which begins with Pentecost Sunday) into two parts called Pentecost and Kingdomtide.

Pepping, Ernst (1901–1981) —Widely regarded as the leading representative of twentieth-century choral writing in Germany, Pepping was among the first to revive the traditional importance of the Lutheran CHORALE. The favorable reaction in 1929 to a performance of several movements from his *Choralsuite*, a collection of seven unaccompanied chorale MOTETS for large and small chorus, signalled the beginning of a career that was to be spent largely in the service of church music. In 1931, Pepping published a cycle of six motets (*Deutsche Choralmesse*) that brought him still closer to functional liturgical music, a body of music that became a lifelong concern in 1934 with his acceptance of a position at the Spandau Church Music School in Berlin. Over the next several years, he composed more than 250 settings in two to six voices of melodies contained in the *Evangelisches Gesangbuch* of 1931 for his *Spandauer Chorbuch* (1934–1941), the largest collection of functional chorale settings since the CANTIONALE published by Johann Hermann Schein in 1627. About half of Pepping's chorale settings require just three voices, with the melody usually placed in the highest voice. Arranged according to liturgical function, they are in the same keys as in the hymnal so as to encourage congregational participation. In an appendix, the composer writes that available instruments may double or replace vocal parts, and that expansion of a cantata-like kind may be achieved by strophic variation. Another functional collection of chorale settings by Pepping appeared in 1959 as *Neues Choralbuch*, which is based on hymns from the *Evangelisches Kirchengesangbuch* of 1951, arranged according to the church year.

Compositions based on original melodies also occupy an important place among Pepping's works, and they provide greater challenges both technically and stylistically for performers. The composer asserted his independence from pre-existing melodies and from the aesthetic confines of the worship service in 1934 in an unaccompanied six-part setting of Psalm 90 ("Herr Gott, du bist unsere Zuflucht fuer und fuer"), and showed his independence even more forcefully in 1937 in one of his finest works, the *Prediger-Motette* (Ein jegliches hat seine Zeit) for unaccompanied chorus in four voices, on a text from Ecclesiastes. There are also liturgical settings of biblical texts, among them the Christmas motet "Uns ist ein Kind geboren" (1936). In his later years Pepping achieved a synthesis between the contrapuntal nature of his style and his desire to express the meaning of his texts. Especially noteworthy in this regard, as well as for his expanded harmonic language, are his *Passionsbericht des Matthaeus* (1950) for *a cappella* chorus, and the large-scale Gospel motet "Das Weltgericht" (1958), also for unaccompanied chorus in four parts. (See example 24.)

In addition to his choral works, Pepping composed a considerable amount of organ music, most of it for the church (e.g., *Preludes and Postludes to 18 Chorales*, 1969). Like many of his contemporaries, he did not restrict himself to church music, but also wrote secular choral works, songs, and symphonies.

Perotin—The outstanding church music composer of the late twelfth and the early thirteenth centuries, Perotin was a French musician active in Paris, perhaps at the Notre Dame Cathedral or its predecessor, the Cathedral of the Beatae Mariae Virginis. He is described by the thirteenth-century theorist known as Anonymous IV as optimus discantor, the greatest composer of DISCANT. Perotin revised the *Magnus liber* attributed to LEONIN, adding a third and sometimes a fourth voice-part. In his *organa,* the principle of modal rhythm is further developed and the groundwork is laid for mensural notation. In addition to his justly famous "Viderunt omnes" (All the Ends of the Earth Have Seen), a GRADUAL set in four voices for the Feast of the Circumcision, and "Sederunt principes" (The Mighty Took Their Seats), another gradual set in four voices for Saint Stephen's Day, Perotin was also noted for his *conducti*. (See CONDUCTUS.) His style is marked by two (or three) voices moving over a sustained tenor, or by all three (or four) voices flowing in the RHYTHMIC MODES. Short, reiterated patterns occur frequently, foreshadowing the important fourteenth-century technique of isorhythm. Perotin retained the customary alternation of polyphony sung by soloists with unison chant sung by the choir.

Pinkham, Daniel (1923-)—A leading contemporary American composer of choral music, Pinkham has served as music director of King's Chapel in Boston and, for many years, as chairperson of the Department of Early Music at the New England Conservatory of Music. By training and by inclination he was drawn to Neo-Classicism. Among his teachers at Harvard University were Walter Piston and Aaron Copland; in addition, like so many young American composers, he studied with Nadia Boulanger. After about 1950, however, the style of his music reveals the influence of serial procedures, at first within a tonal framework. Among his works are many significant contributions to the repertory of contemporary church music. There are four CANTATAS for chorus and orchestra, among them one for Christmas (1957), one for Easter (1961), and one for Ascension (1970). The liturgical works include a REQUIEM and a festival MAGNIFICAT (1963), a Stabat Mater (1964), and a PASSION according to Saint Mark (1965). Other compositions on religious themes include *Daniel in the Lion's Den* (1973), *The Passion of Judas* (1976),

When God Arose (1979), and *The Conversion of Saul* (1981). There are also many sacred choral works and solo works that do not require orchestra.

As an organist, Pinkham has also found occasion to enrich the contemporary repertoire of organ music with a Concertante for organ, celesta and percussion (1963), *Organ Concerto* (1970), and *Psalms* (1983) for organ and trumpet; collections for solo organ include *Blessings* (1977), *Epiphanies* (1978), and *Proverbs* (1980). Since 1970, the composer has explored the world of electronic sounds, which he frequently uses in conjunction with voices or traditional instruments, as in *Toccatas for the Vault of Heaven* (1972), for organ and tape.

plainchant, plainsong—See CHANT.

plainsong Mass—A MASS in which the composer has based each section of the ORDINARY upon the liturgically appropriate Gregorian CHANT for that section. Far more popular with composers was the cantus firmus Mass. (See CANTUS FIRMUS.)

plenary Mass—A setting of the full MASS, including the items from both the PROPER and the ORDINARY.

pointing—A method that assists singers in fitting the words of Anglican chant to its melodic formulas by marking the texts in appropriate places. The first publication of a marked PSALTER was that of Robert Janes in 1837; many have followed. (See ANGLICAN LITURGY.)

polychoral—Music composed for two or more choirs, as in much Venetian music of the late sixteenth and early seventeenth centuries. The Italian term is *cori spezzati*. (See WILLAERT and GABRIELI.)

polyphony—The word describes music composed in more than one voice-part. When the parts all move more or less together, the resulting texture is more properly called homophony. When the parts demonstrate a fair amount of independence, the texture is more properly called COUNTER-POINT. Unfortunately, some authors use the word polyphonic to mean contrapuntal.

Pontificale—The Latin name for the *Pontifical*, the Roman Catholic liturgical book containing the texts for ceremonies performed by a bishop, among them confirmation, ordination, and the consecration of a church.

portative organ (in German, *Portativ*) – Often used in the MEDIEVAL and RENAISSANCE periods, a portative was an organ small enough to be moved around or carried in procession. It could require the assistance of a second person to pump the bellows.

positive organ (in German, *Positiv*) – In the MEDIEVAL and RENAISSANCE periods, an organ with one keyboard and usually no independent pedalboard, but larger and less mobile than a portative organ.

postlude – The term is traditionally used as a title for the organ piece played (frequently improvised) at the close of a worship service; it is often employed in a generic sense for the closing piece of any ceremony.

Poulenc, Francis (1899–1963) – A self-confessed apostle of the Parisian popular song, Poulenc nevertheless created as many outstanding religious compositions as any twentieth-century composer. Able through his family's wealth to study music and live as he pleased, he quickly established himself as one of the most promising of the young French composers referred to as "Les Six." Piano music, chamber music, and music for the stage were his principal occupations until the accidental death of a friend in 1935 led to a renewal of his Roman Catholic faith and to his first setting of a religious text, *Litanies à la viérge noire* (Litanies to the Black Virgin of Rocamadour, 1936), for women's voices and organ. For the remainder of his career, he displayed a special affinity for vocal music. In addition to achieving general recognition as the finest French composer of art songs (*mélodies*) of his time, he wrote several highly successful works for the stage. His most compelling masterpiece may well be *Dialogues of the Carmélites* (1956), an opera in three acts about the martyrdom of a group of nuns executed during the French Revolution for refusing to abjure their vows.

The first of Poulenc's liturgical compositions is his MASS in G (1937), for unaccompanied mixed chorus in four to eight parts. Its dissonant but basically triadic tonality and its constantly changing meters bring to mind the NEO-CLASSICAL style of STRAVINSKY. (See example 33.) Other unaccompanied choral works for the church include four penitential MOTETS ("Timor et tremor," "Vinea mea electa," "Tenebrae factae sunt," and "Tristis est anima mea"), an "Exultate Deo" and a "Salve Regina" (1941), and four Christmas motets ("O magnum mysterium," "Quem vidistis pastores," "Videntes stellam," and "Hodie Christus natus est"). The emotional restraint characteristic of the unaccompanied works is

EXAMPLE 33. Francis Poulenc, "Benedictus," *Mass in G Major* (meas. 36–39) mitigated by the orchestra in Poulenc's large-scale sacred compositions: *Stabat Mater* (1950), *Gloria* (1959), and *Sept répons des ténèbres* (Office for Holy Saturday, 1961).

praeambulum—A Latin word used by some composers in preference to *praeludium*, meaning PRELUDE.

praeludium—The Latin word for PRELUDE.

precentor—Latin for "one who sings first." The name is given to the director of music of a cathedral, as well as to a CANTOR. (See also CANTORIS.)

Preces—Latin for "prayers." Prayers may be said or sung, and ordinarily consist of a series of versicles and responses.

Preface—In the Roman Catholic liturgy, the Preface is part of the MASS PROPER; together with the SANCTUS, which follows it immediately, it serves to introduce the CANON of the Mass.

prelude—With regard to church music, the term is used to refer to a composition, often an organ piece, performed before the service. It may well be based upon a CHORALE melody or, in the Roman Catholic service, upon a Gregorian CHANT that is proper for the occasion in the LITURGICAL YEAR. Composers have frequently paired a prelude with a contrasting second movement such as a FUGUE or TOCCATA. (See example 4.)

Prime—The third of the CANONICAL HOURS.

Proper—Liturgical items, constituting the Proper of the MASS, whose texts (and CHANT melodies) vary according to the LITURGICAL YEAR. (See also INTROIT, GRADUAL, ALLELUIA, SEQUENCE, OFFERTORY, and COMMUNION.)

proper tune—When a melody, especially a Lutheran CHORALE, is traditionally associated with the words of one hymn or psalm text, it is said to be a proper tune.

psalm—One of the sacred poems contained in the Bible in the Book of Psalms. Psalm singing forms an important part of worship in many religions. In the Roman Catholic church, the singing of all of the psalms over the course of a week traditionally formed a large portion of the Divine OFFICE. The numbering of the psalms in most Protestant versions of the Bible, including the King James Version, differs from that of the Latin Bible (known as the Vulgate Bible) as shown in the following table:

AUTHORIZED VERSION	LATIN BIBLE
1–8	1–8
9–10	9
11–113	10–112
114–115	113
116	114–115
117–146	116–145
147	146–147
148–150	148–150

psalm-motet—A setting of a psalm text in the polyphonic manner of the MOTET.

psalm tone—A melody used for chanting the psalms. In the Roman Catholic church, there is a psalm tone, or reciting tone, for each of the church modes, plus a special irregular tone called the *tonus peregrinus.* Each psalm tone begins with a formula called the *initium,* proceeds to the reciting pitch, and pauses in the middle at a half-cadence (the mediation); a return to the reciting pitch is made for further chanting, followed by a closing formula (the termination). (See example 9b.)

psalmody—The Old Testament Book of Psalms provided the primary source of devotions for the early Christians. Its songs of praise, of religious instruction, and of confession have remained important throughout the succeeding centuries. In the early Christian church, the practice of chanting the psalms led to the adoption of nine PSALM TONES for that purpose. But chanting of the psalms in the formal language and style of the Roman Catholic liturgy had to give way to metrical paraphrases in the vernacular languages before the common people could take the psalms to their hearts. The term "psalmody" is often applied to the music of the metrical psalms sung in English and American Protestant churches between the seventeenth and nineteenth centuries.

The metrical psalm formed one of the foundations for change in the religious life of the Western world. Just as German HYMNODY emerged to assist Martin LUTHER in his movement of Reformation, so metrical psalmody proved to be a mighty weapon in the hands of Jean CALVIN (1509–1564). Opposed to elaborate liturgy and suspicious of the power of nonscriptural hymns, Calvin adopted the psalms as virtually the only source for singing in the Reformed Church. The highly significant Geneva (or "Huguenot," or "French") PSALTER that was published in 1562 stood second in the Reformed Church only to the Bible; its metrical poetry was written by Clément Marot and Théodore de Beze, its music composed or edited by Louis Bourgeois. Influenced by the Geneva Psalter, the succeeding age cultivated metrical psalmody by way of translation in France, Germany, and England.

The first psalm translations in English were published before the Protestant Reformation. The most significant early English psalter was published in 1562, with metrical translations by Thomas Sternhold and John Hopkins. Sanctioned by the king and bound along with the Authorized Version of the Bible, the *Sternhold and Hopkins Psalter* maintained its influence for more than a century. Music was provided for this psalter when John Day published his four-voice settings in 1563. Among the many English psalters that followed, perhaps the one published by Henry Ainsworth in 1612 most deserves mention, since it dates from the time of the King James Bible and accompanied the Pilgrims to America in 1620; about half of the psalm tunes provided in the *Ainsworth Psalter* had appeared in the earlier *Geneva Psalter*.

English psalmody grew in significance with the rise of the parish choir and the practice of teaching the common people to sing the psalms. Psalm singing soon took a place alongside dance music and folk song as a fundamental musical outlet of the English populace. In time it became a focal point for Baptists, Methodists, and other dissenting congregations. Among these groups the trend was towards free paraphrase of the psalms in the popular manner established in 1719 by Isaac Watts in *The Psalms of David*. In fact, psalmody became simply another inspiration for the rising tide of evangelical HYMNODY. Among the elite of the church, literal translation of the psalms was superseded by a demand for greater poetic quality, a quest that included an incomplete version of the psalms by John Milton in 1648. The mantle of literary distinction seems to rest upon *A New Version of the Psalms of David*, published in 1696 by Nahum Tate and Nicholas Brady.

In the American colonies, a number of psalters were used in addition to the *Ainsworth Psalter*, among them the *Geneva Psalter* and the *Ravenscroft Psalter* of 1621. In contrast to collections with texts and tunes only, the *Whole Booke of Psalmes*, by Thomas Ravenscroft, offered four-voice settings from the English repertory of psalm tunes, while it retained vestiges of the Renaissance contrapuntal tradition. In time the first American psalter was printed, the *Bay Psalm Book* of 1640. The revision of 1651, known as *The New England Psalm Book*, dominated the American scene for many years. Eventually, as in England, metrical psalmody lost its attraction for the common people, who favored the HYMN and the GOSPEL SONG. With few exceptions, psalm singing gradually disappeared in American churches, and would not to be revived until the recognition of its historical significance in the later twentieth century. The interested reader may pursue the subject in William Reynolds and Milburn Price's *A Joyful Sound: Christian Hymnody* (3rd ed.; Hope Publishing Co., 1987).

psalter—The term "psalter" refers to the Old Testament Book of Psalms as translated into a particular language and adapted for use in the worship service. The Hebrew Psalter contains the poetry of various authors and covers a period from about 400 to 100 B.C. The Hebrew PSALM praises Jehovah as a holy and personal God whose power and mercy pervade every aspect of His relationship with man. The psalter became the primary source of liturgical and devotional literature for the earliest Christians, and it furnished models for the Christian hymns that emerged at the time of the apostles. As the structure of Christian worship became outwardly eucharistic, the celebration of Holy Communion leaned heavily upon the psalter as the devotional vehicle of Christ's spiritual existence as God made man. After the Reformation, the psalter—in the form of metrical psalmody—became the center of the Protestant spiritual revival. Lists of psalters published in the Western world up to the turn of the twentieth century are contained in John Julian's *Dictionary of Hymnology* (rev. ed., John Murray, 1925) under such titles as "English Psalters" and "German Psalters."

Purcell, Henry (1659–1695)—The leading English composer of the Baroque period, Purcell excelled in both vocal and instrumental genres. His stage music, songs, instrumental fantasias, and trio sonatas rank him among the best English composers of any period. As a chorister in the CHAPEL ROYAL of King Charles II, he became acquainted with the sacred music of BYRD, GIBBONS and Pelham HUMFREY. He also studied with John Blow, whom he succeeded in 1679 as organist at Westminster Abbey. Without relinquishing that position, he served the Chapel Royal from 1682 until his early death, as an organist, countertenor, and its foremost composer.

Purcell's church music includes nearly seventy ANTHEMS and, among a relatively small amount of liturgical music, one complete setting of the Anglican SERVICE. There are also a few organ VOLUNTARIES, some psalms and other works apparently for private devotions, and some excellent sacred songs for one or two soloists and basso continuo. The service in B-flat Major contains music in four (and occasionally six) voices for each of the usual six sections as well as for each of the four alternative CANTICLES: BENEDICITE, JUBILATE, CANTATE DOMINO, and Deus miserator. Basically syllabic and homophonic, it nevertheless offers numerous sections for less than full texture and also demonstrates the young composer's skill in canon. Other liturgical pieces include an Evening Service (MAGNIFICAT and NUNC DIMITTIS) in G Minor, and a festive TE DEUM and Jubilate in D Major for Saint Cecilia's Day of 1694.

The majority of the composer's anthems appear to have been written between 1680 and 1685, the year in which King Charles II died. Most of them are verse anthems, since that was the king's preference on the Sundays and holy days when he was present. Just one year after the monarchy was restored in 1660, the Chapel Royal was expanded to include a group of twenty-four violins, which could introduce and complement a select group of soloists (and a less active full choir) in performing verse anthems. Purcell's full anthems, most of them early works, generally contain verses for the soloists; they do not, however, have independent instrumental parts, except for organ continuo. In such full anthems as "O God, Thou Hast Cast Us Out" and "O God, Thou Art My God," the composer balances traditional contrapuntal style with homophonic passages, or with entire sections in homophony; in places he disregards conventional rules of part-writing and heightens expression through the use of chromaticism and unusual cadences. (See example 34.)

Purcell's verse anthems usually unfold in a number of sections, beginning with an instrumental overture or ritornello, continuing with solos or duets (generally for countertenor, tenor, and bass), and closing with a simple, usually joyous chorus. But some anthems are accompanied by organ alone, such as "Lord, How Long Wilt Thou Be Angry"; a setting of words from Psalm 79, it calls for three soloists (alto, tenor, and bass) and a chorus in five voices (SSATB). The shorter anthems remain in the same key, with the exception of an occasional phrase, but the longer ones offer sections in contrasting keys and come close in some cases to being CANTATAS in the German Protestant sense. "It Is a Good Thing to Give Thanks," for example, unfolds in an arch-like form, with a bass solo in the center, three verse sections on either side (verse 4 being like verse 3, and verse 6 like 1), several ritornellos dispersed somewhat asymmetrically, and a closing choral Alleluia to balance the opening French overture. With the exception of parts for sopranos (which were

EXAMPLE 34. Henry Purcell, "Man That Is Born of Woman" (meas. 90–94)

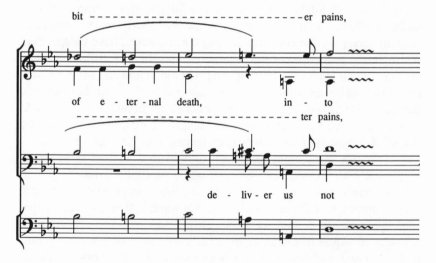

sung by boys), Purcell usually wrote in a florid and technically demanding way for the soloists and in a simple chordal style for the choir. In the most Italianate of the verse anthems, "O Sing unto the Lord," the broad melodic manner over a harmonically conceived bass line and the forceful chordal writing for chorus foreshadow the oratorio style of Handel more than a generation later. Some of the Purcell's anthems were composed for special occasions and are very large indeed. "My Heart Is Inditing," written in 1685 for the coronation of King James II, features choral writing on a grand scale, including antiphonal sections for double chorus and a powerful closing Alleluia. The death of Charles II and the consequent decline in the Chapel Royal, however, caused Purcell's interest to turn away from church music towards music for the stage.

Quempas—A Medieval Christmas carol that was popular in sixteenth-century Germany. Its name is derived from the Latin words "Quem pastores laudavere" (He whom the shepherds praised). By extension, the term came to refer to any Christmas CAROL.

Quicumque vult (Latin for "whosoever will be saved")—The opening words of the Athanasian Creed, which is used in the Anglican SERVICE during Morning Prayer on feast days in place of the Apostles' Creed.

rappresentazione sacra—See SACRA RAPPRESENTAZIONE.

recitative—A manner of setting words to music so that the rhythms and accents of speech take precedence over melodic concerns. Traditionally, passages of recitative are written in common meter, with many repeated pitches and an absence of regular motion and balanced phrases; in compensation, they may offer considerable harmonic interest through the use of modulation. Recitative came into being with the emergence of dramatic music and has always played an important role in opera, ORATORIO, and CANTATA. In these large-scale genres, the characters converse and declaim in loosely structured passages of recitative, and formal expression of emotions takes place in a subsequent AREA. In a well-known example of the use of recitative in an oratorio, Mendelssohn precedes the aria, "If with All Your Hearts" from *Elijah,* with a recitative beginning "Ye People, Rend Your Hearts." (See example 28.)

reciting tone—See PSALM TONE.

refrain—A section of a composition (usually including both words and music) that is repeated after intervening material, as in an alternation of verses and reiterated refrains.

Reger, Max (1873–1916)—Perhaps the most important German composer of music for organ since J. S. Bach, Reger was a prolific composer noted particularly for his instrumental music. Born in Bavaria, he learned music from his father and from the church organist Adalbert Lindner, for whom he soon deputized. In the course of becoming a schoolteacher, Reger became a pupil of Hugo Riemann, an eminent theorist. His career took him to a succession of German cities: Munich, where he functioned from 1901 to 1907 largely as a concert pianist and composer; Leipzig (1907–1911), as professor of composition and director of music at the university; Meiningen (1911–1914), as conductor of the court orchestra of Duke Georg II of Saxe-Meiningen; and Jena (1915–1916), for a period devoted to composing and concertizing. Reger's artistic mission appears to have been to seek a synthesis between the traditional German counterpoint of Bach, Beethoven, and Brahms, and the expanded harmonic vocabulary of the post-Wagnerian period. His embodiment of such essentially Germanic ideals and the virtuosity required to perform his music make it difficult to assess the degree of his success at his untimely death, and have contributed to the continuing unfamiliarity of his music outside of Germany.

Reger regarded the organ as, above all, a concert instrument *par excellence*. Freed from its traditional role in the worship service, it served him as a medium for great fantasias in the tradition of Liszt. Nevertheless, and in spite of the composer's strict observance of Roman Catholicism, he was so moved by his love for the Lutheran chorale that he joined with Arnold Mendelssohn as a leader in the late Romantic revival of Protestant church music. Many of his fantasias were composed on Protestant CHORALE melodies, among them Chorale Fantasia on "Ein' feste Burg" (Op. 27); Chorale Fantasia on "Wie schoen leucht't uns der Morgenstern" (Op. 40, No. 1); and Chorale Fantasia on "Wachet auf, ruft uns die Stimme" (Op. 52, No. 2). Of far more interest to the church organist (who should not be misled by the word "easy" in the titles) are the smaller organ works from later in Reger's career, including *Five Easy Preludes and Fugues* (Op. 56), *Fifty-two Easy Chorale Preludes* (Op. 67), and *Thirty Little Chorale Preludes* (Op. 135a).

Reger's organ music was at the heart of his progress as a composer before 1900; after this time, he concentrated his efforts on chamber music (e.g., Clarinet Quintet in A Major), piano music (Variations and Fugue on a Theme of J. S. Bach), and orchestral music (Piano Concerto in F Minor). There is also a considerable amount of choral music, including a number of church cantatas (e.g., "Vom Himmel hoch, da komm ich her" and "O Haupt voll Blut und Wunden") and certain works that reflect his own religion ("Die Nonnen" and an unfinished Requiem Mass). His greatest sacred composition may be his setting of Psalm 100 (Op. 106) for chorus, organ, and orchestra, which he undertook in response to receiving an honorary doctorate from Jena University in 1908.

registration—A register is an organ stop; the choice of which stops to engage constitutes registration. With some exceptions, until the nineteenth century composers rarely specified the registration for organ pieces. Even when the registration is given, an organist must suit the music to the instrument and sanctuary, thus making the art of registration an important facet of organ playing.

Renaissance—French for rebirth, a term applied by historians to the supposed reawakening of individualism and culture in the spirit of the ancient Greeks that ended the MIDDLE AGES. Music historians have applied the term "Renaissance" to the fifteenth and sixteenth centuries (from c.1400 to c.1600), a time dominated at first by Franco-Flemish composers and then by the rise of national styles. The Reformation led by Martin LUTHER occurred during the Renaissance, provoking an equally strong Counter-Reformation movement within the Roman Catholic church. In church music the Renaissance period was the high point for the MASS, the MOTET, and other polyphonic settings of Latin texts; among the great composers were DUFAY, OCKEGHEM, JOSQUIN, WILLAERT, LASSUS, PALESTRINA, and BYRD.

Reproaches—See IMPROPERIA.

Requiem Mass—The liturgical service for the dead (Missa pro defunctis) of the Roman Catholic church, properly celebrated on the day of burial and on the anniversary of an individual's death, and always on All Souls' Day. Since it contains texts from both the PROPER and the ORDINARY, the Requiem is a plenary Mass. The term "Requiem Mass" has also been loosely applied to nonliturgical works in honor of the dead, often of Protestant origin, by composers such as Heinrich SCHUETZ, Johannes BRAHMS, and Benjamin BRITTEN. As a liturgical composition, the Requiem Mass usually (but not always) consists of the following sections (the texts from the Mass Ordinary being in capital letters):

1. Introit: "Requiem aeternam"
2. KYRIE ELEISON
3. Gradual: "Requiem aeternam"
4. Tract: "Absolve, Domine"
5. Sequence: "Dies irae"
6. Offertory: "Domine Jesu Christe"
7. SANCTUS (BENEDICTUS)
8. AGNUS DEI

9. Communion: "Lux aeterna"

10. Responsory (for solemn occasions): "Libera me, Domine"

Like other liturgical services, the music for the Requiem Mass can be a unified setting by one composer, or a selection of different musical settings, sometimes in widely different styles. Early settings were composed in plainchant. Polyphonic settings began in the fifteenth century, apparently the earliest one that survives being that by Johannes OCKEGHEM. Many major composers since that time have written at least one Requiem Mass, among them PALESTRINA, VICTORIA, MOZART, BERLIOZ, and VERDI. The requiems of Berlioz and Verdi are Romantic compositions for the concert hall rather than the church. In the twentieth century there has been a return of religious restraint—even to the use of the church modes—in works such as the *Requiem* by Maurice DURUFLÉ. (See example 35.)

respond—A RESPONSORY, or the refrain of a responsory; a short choral answer to a prayer or reading by a priest, as in the Roman Catholic Office.

response—Short choral answers by the congregation or the choir to readings (called VERSICLES) by the celebrant in the various Christian liturgies.

responsorial—A manner of singing in which a soloist begins and a choir responds. In Gregorian chant responsorial singing is often employed in PSALMODY.

responsory—Two types of Gregorian CHANT that are traditionally sung in a RESPONSORIAL manner have been distinguished as the great (*responsoria prolixa*) and small (*responsoria brevia*) responsories. Both of them alternate verses (sung by a soloist) and RESPONDS (sung by a choir), and they often close with the lesser DOXOLOGY. Great responsories have an important place at MATINS and at VESPERS on solemn feasts, while small responsories occur frequently in the OFFICE.

rhythmic modes—Soon after the inception of polyphony in Western church music, there arose the problem of different voice-parts performing together in time and being notated. The solution was a system of six standardized rhythmic modes, which paralleled, to some extent, basic poetic meters. The following table defines the note values used in modern transcriptions:

EXAMPLE 35. Maurice Duruflé, "Kyrie," *Requiem* (meas. 1–4)

Mode 1—quarter-note, eighth-note;
Mode 2—eighth, quarter;
Mode 3—dotted quarter, eighth, quarter;
Mode 4—eighth, quarter, dotted quarter;
Mode 5—dotted quarter-notes;
Mode 6—eighth-notes.

In practice, as in the organum "Viderunt omnes" by LEONIN, the modes are often mixed and smaller note-values must be introduced. (See example 19.)

ricercare (or ricercar)—An Italian word used by composers to designate an instrumental composition (often an organ piece) that either functions as a PRELUDE (or a TOCCATA), and offers a free, sometimes homophonic style, or it features imitative counterpoint, perhaps on more than one theme. The ricercare was a predecessor of the FUGUE. It was often used in the church by composers such as FRESCOBALDI.

Rituale—The Latin name for the Roman Catholic liturgical book that contains the texts for ceremonies performed by a priest, including baptism, marriage, and extreme unction.

Roman Catholic church music—Music in the Holy Catholic and Apostolic church has always been regarded as an important aspect of ritual. The reader who wishes to obtain an overview of the music is strongly advised to begin with the articles entitled MASS and OFFICE and to consult the cross-references provided in them. The paragraphs below are also intended as references to subjects treated elsewhere in this volume.

In the early Roman Catholic church, CHANT served as handmaiden to the liturgical word. When POLYPHONY was introduced, Gregorian chant—as CANTUS FIRMUS—became the foundation for the major polyphonic genres of ORGANUM, early MOTET, and settings of sections of the MASS. Virtually all of the great early composers of Western music learned and practiced their art in the church, among them MACHAUT, DUFAY, JOSQUIN, LASSUS, and PALESTRINA. Although the Catholic church was threatened by the Lutheran Reformation, its music and liturgy continued to flourish and had a significant impact on the Lutheran service. Music, especially in the form of ORATORIO, played an important part in the late sixteenth- and early seventeenth-century resurgence of Catholicism that has become known as the Counter-Reformation.

Names of significant composers of Catholic church music after 1600 may be found in the genre articles for MASS, MOTET, MAGNIFICAT, REQUIEM, and ORGAN MUSIC. A list arranged by historical period follows: Baroque—FRESCOBALDI, CARISSIMI, CHARPENTIER, COUPERIN, GRIGNY; Classical—HAYDN, MOZART; Romantic—SCHUBERT, BERLIOZ, VERDI, FRANCK, BRUCKNER, REGER; Twentieth Century—POULENC, MESSIAEN, PENDERECKI.

In the late sixteenth century, Spanish missionaries brought Roman Catholic church music to the American Southwest, where it occasionally reached a high standard. In the eastern United States publications of Catholic church music did not appear until the late eighteenth century; the earliest ones often contained an assortment of Protestant hymns. Not until the efforts of the CECILIAN MOVEMENT were felt in the United States in the second half of the nineteenth century was there a revival of plainchant and the great repertory of Catholic Renaissance music. It had little impact, however, beyond very large churches. The founding early in the twentieth century of the Society of Saint Gregory of America and, soon after, the establishment of the influential bulletin the *Catholic Choirmaster* were also significant for American Catholic church music. None of these developments was as important as two decrees issued in 1964: "Directives for the Use of the Vernacular at Mass" and "A Memorandum on Music for the Vernacular Liturgy." They encouraged the congregation to sing during the service, allowed women to sing in choral groups, and permitted instruments in the service. The result has been a wave of music heavily influenced by folk and popular idioms; it is to be hoped that the great Catholic musical heritage will not henceforth be confined to concerts, classrooms, and recordings.

Romantic period—A term used by historians to refer to the period between about 1825 and 1890 (or up to 1900 or 1915). It is also loosely used to mean the nineteenth century, and like many of the terms used for historical periods, does not bear close examination very well. During this time, a great deal of the best church music was composed for the concert hall rather than for the church service, as is seen in the works of SCHUBERT, BERLIOZ, VERDI, and BRAHMS. More likely to be heard in churches was the music of Samuel WESLEY, Lowell MASON, Felix MENDELSSOHN, Samuel Sebastian WESLEY, César FRANCK, Anton BRUCKNER, Charles STANFORD, John MAUNDER, Horatio PARKER, and Max REGER.

Rorem, Ned (1923-)—Like a number of excellent contemporary American composers whose careers and reputations were achieved outside the rather provincial realm of church music, Rorem has composed challenging music for the church that brings both choirs and congregations into contact with the idiom of contemporary music. His training was begun in Chicago with Leo SOWERBY in 1938 and 1939, continued in the East at the Curtis Institute and at the Julliard School of Music (as well as with Virgil Thomson), and was completed in Paris with Arthur Honegger. His reputation has been based, perhaps too narrowly, on his highly successful song cycles, among them *Poems of Love and the Rain* (1963), *Sun* (1967), and *War Scenes* (1969); their quality and quantity brought him recognition as the leading American song composer of his time. His achievement, however, has been of a much wider scope, including symphonic music, chamber music, operas, and choral music. His music for use in the church includes works for soloist as well as for chorus. Among the former are "A Psalm of Praise" and "A Song of David" (both from 1945), *A Cycle of Holy Songs* (1951), "A Christmas Carol" (1952), and "The Lord's Prayer" (1957). The music for church choir includes "Miracles of Christmas" (1959), "Praises for the Nativity" (1970), "Praise the Lord O My Soul" (1982), and a number of MOTETS; of particular note are such unaccompanied choral works as "Christ the Lord Is Ris'n Today" and "Sing My Soul His Wondrous Love" (both 1955), "O magnum mysterium" (1978), and *Three Christmas Choruses* (1978). Also composed for the church service are *Prayers and Responses* (1960), *Proper for the Votive Mass of the Holy Spirit* (1966), *Canticles* (1971), and *Missa Brevis* (1974). The interest in combining vocal and instrumental forces on a larger scale that characterized Rorem's later years yielded such noteworthy works as "Lift up Your Heads" (1963) and various other settings of sacred texts.

sacra rappresentazione—A "sacred presentation" in Italian of a religious event or story. One of a number of related terms, among them *dialogo, misterioso,* and *storia,* that refer to the dramatization with scenery of a biblical, hagiographical, or sometimes an allegorical subject. Sacred plays of this nature, with musical interludes in such forms as *laude* or spiritual madrigals, were written by the eminent Florentine patron Lorenzo de Medici. The sacra rappresentazione originated in the thirteenth-century LAUDA, reached its highest point during the RENAISSANCE, and declined in the BAROQUE PERIOD. Renaissance examples were often performed in three- or four-part polyphony by groups of singers representing the individual characters, including perhaps a narrator. The emergence of monody in the late Renaissance transformed the genre, as in the best-known composition by the name, the *Rappresentatione di anima, e di* corpo (The Representation of the Soul and the Body; Rome, 1600) by Emilio de' Cavalieri. Historically, the genre served as a forerunner of both ORATORIO and opera.

Sacramentary—An early Roman Catholic liturgical book containing the CANON and the proper COLLECTS and PREFACES for the MASS.

salutation—A form of greeting ("the Lord be with you") and response ("and with thy spirit") taken into the early Christian liturgy from the Hebrew and eventually used to introduce parts of the service such as the COLLECT and the BENEDICTION. (See also SURSUM CORDA.)

Salve Regina—Latin for "Hail, Queen." The words begin an antiphon in honor of the Virgin Mary. The chant is sung at COMPLINE during part of the church year. Many composers have created polyphonic settings, among them being DUNSTABLE, OCKEGHEM, and JOSQUIN.

Sanctorale—The Latin term referring to the Proper of the Saints. The chants for the Sanctorale follow the Proper of the Time in the liturgical books.

Sanctus (Benedictus)—Part of the ORDINARY of the MASS and perhaps its oldest acclamation, the Sanctus serves as a response to and conclusion for the PREFACE. In the early church it was sung by everyone, but the earliest chant melodies (which appear in tenth-century manuscripts) seem to reflect performance by trained singers. Musical settings were often elaborate and structurally complex, with repetition or variation of the "Hosanna" when it recurs, and frequent use of thematic relationship between the "Pleni sunt caeli" and "Benedictus qui venit" sections. Polyphonic settings, especially after 1650, find composers setting the "Benedictus" as a separate section or movement featuring a lyrical style and perhaps solo singing within a larger overall design.

Sanctus, sanctus, sanctus,	Holy, holy, holy,
Dominus Deus Sabaoth.	Lord God of hosts.
Pleni sunt caeli	Heaven and earth are
et terra gloria tua.	full of your glory.
Hosanna in excelsis.	Hosanna in the highest.
Benedictus qui venit	Blessed is He who comes
in nomine Domini.	in the name of the Lord.
Hosanna in excelsis.	Hosanna in the highest.

Sarum Use —A modification of the Roman Catholic liturgy that was widely adopted in England until its abolition in 1559. Its influence was preserved to some extent in the BOOK OF COMMON PRAYER and also in the polyphonic compositions that used its melodies as CANTUS FIRMI.

Scarlatti, Alessandro (1660–1725) —The leading Italian composer of vocal music in the late seventeenth and early eighteenth centuries, the composer is best known for his many operas (approximately one hundred), secular cantatas (at least six hundred), and oratorios (approximately forty). As a young man, Scarlatti composed Latin oratorios for the Oratorio del Crocifisso in Rome and served for a time as maestro di cappella in the Roman church of San Girolamo della Carita. He was, therefore, in direct contact with the traditions of these important oratories (prayer halls). During his subsequent years as an opera composer in Naples, he maintained his connections with such leading Roman patrons of music as Cardinal Benedetto Pamphilj and Cardinal Pietro Ottoboni. When he escaped political turmoil in Naples by returning to Rome from 1703 to 1708, Scarlatti not only composed numerous oratorios for Roman patrons, but served briefly as maestro di cappella at the important Oratorio della Vallicella. As a mark of his fame, the composer was granted the title of *Cavalieri* by the pope in 1716.

Alessandro Scarlatti was the most significant Italian composer of ORATORIOS after the time of CARISSIMI. Of his approximately forty oratorios, somewhat more than half are extant; only two of them are in Latin. Among the oratorios in Italian, about half depict biblical or historical events in the same manner—though more concisely—as opera. A chorus is seldom employed, a narrator not at all. A second type of oratorio used by Scarlatti follows the same structure of recitative, aria, and occasional duet, but features allegorical characters. Scarlatti was foremost among the composers who used the new elements of style developed in Baroque opera to transcend the musical and aesthetic limitations previously observed in Italian oratorio. When, after about 1700, he chose to stress the varied emotional states of the characters rather than the events of the religious story, he transformed the nature of the genre. The change in the nature of oratorio was reflected in its purpose and its place of performance: the important oratorios of Scarlatti's second stay in Rome were no longer devotional experiences for oratories or seminaries, as had been the case in his youth, but were Lenten entertainments for the private residence of Prince Ferdinando Ruspoli. (See example 27.)

The remainder of Scarlatti's church music consists of about eighty MOTETS, ten MASSES (some of them composed in the conservative manner, or *stile antico*, that Baroque composers reserved for church music), a number of Christmas cantatas, two MAGNIFICATS, and one PASSION. Among the very few of these works that have been published, two are particularly worthy of mention. The *Passio secundum Johannem* (Saint John Passion) of about 1680 displays the earnest style of the young composer, whereas the *Messa di Santa Cecilia* of 1720 offers the grand style of an old master in a multimovement work for five soloists, five-part chorus, string orchestra, and continuo.

Samuel Scheidt (1587–1654) — Scheidt was a prominent figure among the first Baroque generation of German composers. Like his leading German compatriots, he combined traditional mastery of counterpoint with the new features of the Italian style, making use in particular of the basso continuo and concertato style. Unlike SCHUETZ and Schein, however, Scheidt was a virtuoso organist and a noteworthy composer of instrumental as well as vocal music. From about 1608 to 1609 he studied with the great organist-composer SWEELINCK, a Netherlander, whose style had considerable influence upon his music. Scheidt's entire professional career was centered in Halle, where he served as a church organist and then as court Kapellmeister for the Elector of Brandenburg. The period from 1625 to 1638, when the Thirty Years' War forced the Elector to leave the city, were lean years for Scheidt. Until the return of his patron, he served for some years as Halle's municipal director of music.

As a keyboardist and a court musician, Scheidt composed secular as well as sacred music. Both kinds appeared in his *Tabulatura nova* of 1624, with which he became the first German to publish keyboard music in open score. Among the church music in the first two volumes are eight sets of variations on CHORALE melodies, one of them the well-known "Da Jesus an dem Kreuze stund" (Jesus Hung There on the Cross) (See example 29.) Volume three contains only liturgical music, including CANTUS FIRMUS settings of the Kyrie, Gloria, and Credo for the MASS, and versions of the MAGNIFICAT and the BENEDICAMUS for VESPERS. Not until 1650 did Scheidt publish another volume of organ music, the simple four-voice settings of chorale melodies that make up the *Tabulatur-Buch hundert geistlicher Lieder und Psalmen* (Tablature Book of One Hundred Sacred Songs and Psalms).

Among the sacred vocal works composed by Scheidt are two MASSES, one a MISSA BREVIS; six MAGNIFICATS (in vol. 3 of *Geistliche*

Concerte); and a collection of MOTETS in eight voices entitled *Cantiones sacrae* (1620). Approximately half of the motets are chorale settings. In addition, there are many sacred concertos. Twelve large-scale vocal concerti were published in 1622 with instrumental parts and basso continuo. After the departure of the Elector and the dispersal of his musicians, four volumes of small-scale *Geistliche Concerte* were published, usually requiring just three or four soloists and accompanied simply by basso continuo. Many of these are chorale settings, those in volume 3 being organized according to the church year. *Liebliche Krafft-Bluemlein* (1635) is a collection of works for two voices with basso continuo. Some of the sacred concerti by Scheidt, especially certain of the chorale concerti, point clearly to the later church CANTATA.

schola cantorum—Latin words referring to a school (or a choir) of church singers, especially to the group that sang at the papal court in Rome until its function was assumed in the late MEDIEVAL PERIOD by the papal chapel. The term also was chosen in 1894 by Vincent d'Indy and others as the name for an institution devoted in part to church music.

Schubert, Franz (1797–1828)—A renowned composer of art songs (*Lieder*), Schubert has often been regarded as the first composer of the ROMANTIC PERIOD. The rest of his music, however, principally the symphonies, piano sonatas, and chamber music, links him firmly with the Classical tradition of Haydn, Mozart, and the young Beethoven. As a child, Schubert learned to play the violin, piano, and organ; in 1808 he won a place as a choirboy in the Imperial Court Chapel, where his musical training continued and eventually included composition lessons from Antonio Salieri. In his short lifetime the composer was not able to secure a post commensurate with his extraordinary musical gifts, having instead to serve occasionally as a schoolteacher and as a private music master for a noble family. His fame did not become widespread until long after his death.

Schubert's church music stems directly from that of HAYDN and MOZART. According to the scholar Alfred Einstein (*Schubert: A Musical Portrait*), Schubert's excessive allegiance to tradition caused his church music to veer at times uneasily between conventional and spontaneous expression. Owing perhaps to the sacrosanct nature of the liturgical text, Schubert permits the music to dominate his settings, seldom seeking to fuse words and music as he does in the art songs. At times, especially in the early works, the music can seem too predictable, even perfunctory. Nevertheless, the composer provided a number of useful liturgical settings, some of them well within the reach of modest choirs, as well as a smaller group of works that fully represent his genius. Among the best of Schubert's shorter liturgical works are two settings of the OFFERTORY "SALVE REGINA," the first from 1815 (revised in 1823) and the second from 1819, both for soprano and orchestra; and the offertory entitled "Intende voci orationis meae" (1828), for tenor, chorus, and orchestra.

Three unusual religious compositions by Schubert are not liturgical in function. In *Lazarus* (1820), an Easter CANTATA left incomplete in the middle of act 2, he was able to sustain a high level of dramatic urgency by having the arias grow directly from the recitative, which is accompanied throughout by an orchestra treated with unusual care. Alfred Einstein felt that the first act of *Lazarus* was "a perfect work of art." In 1826 Schubert composed a Mass on a German text by J. P. Neumann for organ, wind instruments, and a mixed choir (a later revision requires only male voices). Perhaps because of the vernacular text, he appears to have felt free to use his song-like manner to stress the human qualities of the words. The composition unfolds in eight movements and an epilogue: Kyrie, Gloria, Evangelium and Credo, Offertorium, Sanctus, Benedictus, Agnus Dei, and Amen and The Lord's Prayer. Finally, in 1828, for the synagogue in Vienna, he set Psalm 92 in Hebrew for baritone and mixed chorus.

There are six complete settings of the MASS Ordinary by Schubert and one short REQUIEM (1818), which his brother Ferdinand passed off as his own. Four of the Masses are early works, composed between 1814 to 1816: Mass in F (1814), Mass in G (1815), Mass in B-flat (1815), and Mass in C (1816). In these early Masses, the influence of Mozart, as in the BENEDICTUS and the AGNUS DEI of the Mass in F, and of Haydn, as in the Mass in G, prevail; nevertheless, a truly Schubertian lyricism occasionally emerges. That quality in the KYRIE and Agnus Dei of the Mass in G, along with its modest performing requirements, has resulted in its frequent performance. All of the Masses reveal Schubert's curious lack of respect for the Mass text, which results in inadmissible repetitions and omissions. For some reason, perhaps his own unorthodox religious beliefs, he omits in each of his settings of the CREDO the words "Et unam Sanctam catholicam et apostolicam ecclesiam" (And one, holy, Catholic, and apostolic church). Modern editions ordinarily correct the textual difficulties as best they can.

The last two Masses reveal a more ambitious Schubert. His Mass in A-flat (1819–1822), which was composed during the same years as Beethoven's *Missa Solemnis*, aspires to similar heights and, indeed, occasionally reaches them. Even more than in his Mass in E-flat, the composer brings into play a wealth of musical imagery and technical devices, including ANTIPHONAL choral effects, unaccompanied choral passages, and solo voices versus chorus, as well as the expected grand fugues. As in the earlier Masses, certain passages of text—among them "Et incarnatus est" and "Crucifixus"—inspired the composer's finest music. Tonal and harmonic subtleties permeate the composition, which unfolds on a large scale in the following unusual series of third relationships: A-flat major, E major, C major, F major/f minor, A-flat major.

More traditional in its tonal relationships is Schubert's liturgical masterpiece, his Mass in E flat of 1828, for soloists, mixed chorus, and a large orchestra that includes trumpets, horns, and trombones. The composition is essentially a choral Mass, the quartet of soloists being reserved for a few special moments: "Et incarnatus est" in the Credo; "Benedictus" as part of the SANCTUS; and "Dona nobis pacem" in the Agnus Dei. Although there remain large sections clearly modelled upon or inspired by earlier composers, such as the enormous fugues that close the GLORIA and the Credo, the composer integrates fugue-like passages more successfully among a larger number of sections that could only be his own. Particularly noteworthy in terms of structure is the composer's willingness to sacrifice liturgical propriety for the sake of greater musical unity, as in the Gloria, where he brings back the opening text and music after the "Gratias"; then, after a contrasting section, the opening music returns again with the words "Quoniam tu solus sanctus." Nevertheless, as a Mass for the concert hall, Schubert's Mass in E-flat constitutes one of the finest nineteenth-century settings of the text.

Schuebler Chorales—A collection of six CHORALE PRELUDES for organ by J. S. BACH; five of them are arrangements of arias from the composer's church CANTATAS. The collection takes its name of popular reference from its publisher, Johann Georg Schuebler. It appeared in about 1748 and contains BWV numbers 645 to 650.

Schuetz, Heinrich (1585-1672)—The leading German composer of church music in the early BAROQUE PERIOD, Schuetz synthesized the new Italian styles of the continuo madrigal, monody, and CONCERTATO with the traditional German grasp of counterpoint; through his compositions and his efforts as a teacher, he helped launch a golden age of Protestant church music that lasted a century. Schuetz's career took wing under the patronage of Landgrave Moritz of Cassel, who placed the boy in his own academy and sent him to Venice from 1609 to 1612 to study composition and organ playing with Giovanni GABRIELI. After Schuetz returned to Germany, his reputation led to an invitation from the Elector of Saxony in Dresden, who maintained the largest and most significant chapel of musicians in Protestant Germany. The composer soon became acting KAPELLMEISTER at the court, eventually (probably in 1619) acquired the formal title, and remained in the Elector's service for the rest of his life. He was to leave Germany again, first (in 1628 and 1629) to renew his knowledge of Italian music by consulting with Monteverdi in Venice, and then (from 1633 to 1645) to escape the worst periods of the Thirty Years' War in Saxony by serving intermittently at the court in Copenhagen.

The major portion of Schuetz's extant compositions were published under his supervision. Economic reasons, caused principally by war, prevented the publication of a substantial number of works, and at least half of these have been lost or destroyed by fire. Most of the approximately five hundred extant works are set to biblical texts. Schuetz seldom used chorale texts (or CHORALE melodies) and the practice of setting contemporary sacred poetry did not become typical Protestant practice until after his time. In addition, although many of his works were used in court religious services, not many of them were specifically liturgical. German texts predominate, even among the sacred works. Indeed, the composer's extraordinary skill in capturing the speech inflections and accents of his native language is at the heart of his success as a composer. Over the years, the exuberance heard in his approach to the subjective texts of his youth changed to a more disciplined and sophisticated attitude that was also reflected in his choice of texts.

Foremost among the works of Schuetz stand his collections of MOTETS, his ORATORIO-like compositions, and his PASSIONS. His first publication of sacred music—*Psalmen Davids*, Op. 2 (1619)—established him immediately as one of the leading composers of the time; it consists of twenty-six concertato motets in the Gabrieli tradition, set on German psalm texts for two, three, four, and more vocal and instrumental choruses, along with solo voices and basso continuo. Not until part 3 of the *Symphoniae sacrae* (1650) did Schuetz return to such large-scale works, now setting them on New Testament as well as Old Testament German texts that cover a wide range of emotions. Subtitled "Deutsche Concerte," this highly influential collection contained twenty-one large works for three to six solo voices, independent instrumental parts and passages, and usually a single (but sometimes double) choir, as in the awe-inspiring "Saul, was verfolgst du mich?" (Schuetz-Werke-Verzeichnis [SWV] 415).

Smaller-scale motets in the concertato manner occupied much of the composer's attention during the war years. Part 2 of *Symphoniae sacrae* (1647) contains twenty-seven compositions on German texts for two or three solo voices and usually a choice of instrumental accompaniment; dedicated to the King of Denmark, they were completed some years before their publication and in several cases represent revisions of earlier works. Even smaller in scale are the *Kleine geistliche Konzerte* (Little Sacred Concerti) of 1636 and 1639, in which one to five solo voices are accompanied only by basso continuo; contrapuntal writing plays a significant role in many of the fifty-five compositions, with the prominent exception of such solo monodies in oratorio style as the well-known "Eile mich, Gott zu erretten" (Hasten, Lord, to Deliver Me; part 1, SWV 282).

The composer's mastery of the small-scale Latin motet was demonstrated in his Opus 4, a collection of thirty-five compositions (with five more in an appendix) entitled *Cantiones sacrae* (1625). Composed in a style like that of the continuo madrigal, some of the four-voice settings (mostly SATB) are based on the psalms, and some are nonbiblical. Italian influence is also prominent in the twenty Latin motets that make up the first part of *Symphoniae sacrae* (1629); composed for one to three voices and specific obbligato instruments, the motets could be used in either the Lutheran or the Roman Catholic service. (See example 6.) In "Fili mi, Absalon" (SWV 269) Schuetz employs a solo bass accompanied by four trombones and continuo to express the lament of King David on the death of his beloved but rebellious son.

It appears that Schuetz designed only one collection of motets specifically for church, rather than court, use – the *Geistliche Chormusik* of 1648. Dedicated to the choir of the church of Saint Thomas in Leipzig, it is made up of twenty-nine motets for five to seven voices, arranged to fit specific occasions in the church year. At times, it draws upon traditional chorale tunes. The eminent musicologist Friedrich Blume wrote that this collection stands at the peak of Protestant motet composition in the seventeenth century. Despite the wide variety of styles found in these motets, the composer's restraint and avoidance of subjective interpretation in them appears to represent his support for traditional contrapuntal values in church music, which was still in the process of accepting the German language in the service. Although many motets from the publications described above could serve a variety of purposes in the Lutheran liturgy, two comparatively modest collections intended for use in the daily routine of the choristers of the Chapel Royal might prove more useful – the Becker Psalter (Op. 5, 1627; revised edition 1640) and *Zwoelf geistliche Gesaenge* (Twelve Sacred Songs; Op. 13, 1657). Both offer four-voice settings of German texts, those of the Psalter being largely simple homophonic settings of the composer's own melodies to metrical versions of the Psalms. Another useful collection is his music for the burial service (*Musikalische Exequien*, 1636), in which a Missa Brevis in six voices is set between motets for double choir on quotations from the Bible. Both movements of the Missa Brevis interpolate biblical (but nonliturgical) texts and are shaped by musical factors; the Kyrie, for example, begins "Nacket werde ich" (Naked shall I also return) and unfolds structurally in six sections that are clearly articulated by the use of timbre, texture, and style. Finally, there is a German Magnificat (SWV 494) by Schuetz; composed for a double choir of eight voices with basso continuo, it dates from the last year of his life.

Schuetz composed large-scale sacred works of a dramatic but unstaged kind over the last five decades of his career. The term employed for most of them was *historia*, since they relate stories taken from the Bible. The earliest one, whose abbreviated title is *Historia der Auferstehung Jesu Christi* (Easter Oratorio, 1623), represents a combination of liturgical German practice and the subjective style the composer had learned in Venice. On the one hand, he borrowed the German Easter text, the plainsong formula for the Evangelist, the ideas for the opening and closing choruses, and the practice of setting the parts of Jesus, Mary Magdalene, and the others for two voices from a setting for Dresden by Antonio Scandello in 1568; on the other, the scale of the composition is expanded, instruments are required, the recitative becomes expressive in the manner of monody at appropriate moments, the choruses call for six voices and double choir, and the countermelody to the soloists may be omitted or performed instrumentally. The *Historia der Geburt Jesu Christi* (Christmas Oratorio, SWV 435) by Schuetz relies less upon liturgical tradition than upon the musical unity provided by an arch-like, large-scale structure and a means of expression reliant upon tone-painting of a symbolic kind. One of the greatest compositions of the seventeenth century, it was published (in part) in 1664 and consists of expressive recitatives, eight colorful concertato motets with OBBLIGATO instrumental parts, and a final chorus.

Towards the end of his long career, Schuetz composed three settings of the Passion that stand apart from any that had preceded or would follow. They differ markedly from his own short Passion oratorio entitled *Die sieben Worte unsers Jesu Christi am Kreuz* (The Seven Last Words, 1645); in it, the seven short episodes for the Evangelist and Jesus—both of whom are accompanied by instruments—are enclosed by an inner frame of identical instrumental movements and an outer frame of hymns for five-voice chorus. In the three Passions (SWV 479–81) composed by Schuetz in his eighties, he uses no instrumental accompaniment, as in the traditional Renaissance Passion (which had grown out of the customary recitation of the Gospel story during Holy Week). Drawn respectively from Luke, John, and Matthew (the one based on Mark is now regarded as not being by Schuetz), they employ only solo singers and a four-voice chorus. The narration and the dialogue are not unlike plainsong, and yet they are of uncompromising and inimitable originality, a personal synthesis of sixteenth- and seventeenth-century practices in setting the Passion. The complete mastery of tradition and its thorough assimilation into the profoundly expressive personal style that is found in the finest works of Schuetz would not be matched in German sacred music until the time of J. S. Bach.

seconda prattica—The "second practice," a new technique of setting words and treating dissonance that was employed by early Baroque composers, foremost among them Claudio Monteverdi.

Senfl, Ludwig (c.1486–c.1543)—A Swiss composer who occupied a significant place in German musical life of his time, Senfl was an outstanding composer of church music. His career was spent largely in the service of two great royal patrons. From 1496 until the death of Emperor Maximilian I in 1519, Senfl served the imperial court, first as a choirboy, later as the successor to Heinrich ISAAC as court KAPELLMEISTER. His finest hour may have come during the last Reichstag held by Maximilian in 1518, at which time he surely met Martin LUTHER. After his dismissal by the successor to the throne, a routine occupational hazard of the time that had enormous impact on both musical life and on the lives of court musicians, Senfl assumed leadership of the chapel of Duke Wilhelm of Bavaria, a post he occupied until his death.

Senfl's concern for composing polyphonic music for the Mass PROPER began with his work as copyist for Isaac's great *Choralis constantinus*, a task that prepared him to compose the portion of that work left incomplete. He also composed a large number of his own Proper settings. In addition, Senfl composed seven settings of the Mass ORDINARY, a cycle of MAGNIFICATS for each mode, and a considerable number of Latin MOTETS built upon the tradition of JOSQUIN des Prez. Although he was a Catholic, the composer expressed his sympathy with the Lutheran Reformation in various ways, not least in a small number of German motets and a few LIEDER on religious texts.

sepolcro—Italian for "sepulchre." A seventeenth-century Viennese musical genre written on the subject of the PASSION story and represented dramatically with scenery and costumes in the court chapel in front of a representation of the holy sepulchre. Except for the dramatic action and its one-part structure, a *sepolcro* resembles an ORATORIO; it was sometimes referred to as a SACRA RAPPRESENTAZIONE.

sequence—With reference to church music, the sequence (*sequentia*) was an extraliturgical addition to the Roman Catholic MASS that flowered from the tenth through the thirteenth centuries and eventually became part of the liturgy. The sequence began as a textual and then musical TROPE at the end of the ALLELUIA. So popular did it become that, by the sixteenth century, sequences had been appointed for almost every day in the LITURGICAL YEAR. Finally, action was taken at the COUNCIL OF TRENT to limit the number of sequences to four: "Dies Irae" (Day of Wrath; from the REQUIEM MASS), "Victimae paschali laudes" (Praises to the Paschal Victim; from the Easter Mass), "Veni sancte spiritus" (Come, Holy Spirit), and "Lauda Sion salvatorem" (Zion, Praise), all of which received polyphonic settings by such great composers as PALESTRINA and LASSUS. Another sequence popular with composers was added to the liturgy in the eighteenth century, the "STABAT MATER dolorosa" (The Grieving Mother Stood...). Not all sequences vanished when they were removed from the liturgy; some became sources for German CHORALES.

Service—From the seventeenth century, the term "Service" has been used to refer to polyphonic musical settings of all or most of the invariable texts from the three principal services of the Anglican liturgy: MORNING PRAYER, HOLY COMMUNION, and EVENING PRAYER. When all three are composed, usually in a common key, they are referred to as a "Full Service." However, a polyphonic setting of any one of them alone is called a "Service." Other terms include "Great Service," meaning that the composer has used considerable contrapuntal complexity in his setting, and "Short Service," meaning that the musical treatment is basically chordal and syllabic. A "Verse Service" features some accompanied solo singing, in addition to choral singing. In setting the liturgy composers have usually emphasized the CANTICLES listed below:

	MORNING PRAYER	
Psalm 95:	"O come let us sing"	("VENITE")
hymn:	"We praise thee"	("TE DEUM")
or Daniel 3:	"All ye works"	("BENEDICITE")
Luke 1:68–79:	"Blessed be the Lord"	("BENEDICTUS")
or Psalm 100:	"Be joyful in the Lord"	("JUBILATE Deo")

	HOLY COMMUNION	
	"Lord, have mercy"	("KYRIE")
	"I believe in one God"	("CREDO")
	"Holy, holy, holy"	("SANCTUS")
	"Lamb of God"	("AGNUS DEI")
	"Glory be to God"	("GLORIA in excelsis")

	EVENING PRAYER	
Luke 1:46–55:	"My soul doth magnify"	("MAGNIFICAT")
or Psalm 98:	"O sing unto the Lord"	("Cantate Domino")
Luke 2:29–32:	"Lord, now lettest thou"	("NUNC DIMITTIS")
or Psalm 67:	"God be merciful"	("Deus miseratur")

Among the numerous significant composers who have composed Services are Thomas TALLIS, William BYRD, Orlando GIBBONS, Henry PURCELL, Samuel Sebastian WESLEY, and Ralph VAUGHAN WILLIAMS.

Seven Last Words—The last utterances of Christ, which have been gathered from the New Testament and used as a text for compositions on the PASSION by such noteworthy composers as Heinrich SCHUETZ (*Die sieben Worte*) and Charles Gounod (*Les sept paroles*). The text also received an inspired instrumental setting in 1785 by Franz Joseph HAYDN, who subsequently arranged it as an ORATORIO. Probably no setting has been as popular for so long as the one composed in 1867 by Theodore Dubois, most performances of it undoubtedly being in English.

Sext—The fifth of the CANONICAL HOURS, usually celebrated at noon.

shofar (also *shophar or sofar*, meaning *"hollow"*)—An ancient Jewish instrument that, because of its relation to the sacrifice of Isaac, was usually made from a ram's horn. The account is found in the Torah reading for the second day of the new year. Although the instrument can produce only two tones (which can, however, be awe-inspiring), calls blown on the shofar remain significant in Hebrew worship. (Scriptural references to the shofar are found in Leviticus 25:8–10, Numbers 21:27 and 229:1, Psalms 98:6, Exodus 19:19 and 24:7, Amos 3:6, and Isaiah 27:13.)

sinfonia—An Italian word meaning "symphony." It was used in the BAROQUE PERIOD to refer to an instrumental piece that introduced a large-scale composition, such as an opera, an ORATORIO, or a church CANTATA.

singing school—In the American colonies during the eighteenth century the singing of HYMNS and PSALMS was taught in singing schools, a custom that had no little influence upon the formation of church choirs and choral organizations.

Sistine Chapel—The principal chapel in the Vatican and the chapel most used by the pope. It was built for and named after Pope Sixtus IV and remains in use today.

Solesmes—A Benedictine monastery in the French town of Solesmes. A number of monks from Solesmes have taken part in editing significant publications of CHANT and developing important theories of chant interpretation.

sonata da chiesa—A "church sonata," one of the principal types of instrumental music in the BAROQUE PERIOD. Two types in particular flourished: the trio sonata (usually composed for two violins and violoncello) and the solo sonata (usually for solo violin and violoncello). In both types, the bass part would normally receive a keyboard realization, probably by an organist. As established by Arcangelo Corelli, the usual form of the *sonata da chiesa* consisted of (1) a slow opening movement in the tonic key employing quadruple meter and often featuring dotted rhythms; (2) a fast movement, again in the tonic, often in duple meter and freely imitative in texture; (3) another slow movement, possibly in a closely related key, usually in triple meter; and (4) a fast closing movement in the tonic key, often of a lighter character, as expressed in a compound duple or quadruple meter. (See example 36.)

Sowerby, Leo (1895–1968)—One of the leading American composers of church music in the twentieth century, Sowerby did not confine himself to that medium but composed in a wide variety of genres. Recognition of his gift for composition came as early as 1913, when his *Violin Concerto* was performed by the Chicago Symphony Orchestra. It was followed by chamber and orchestral scores, among them a wind quintet, two string quartets, two piano and two organ concertos, and five symphonies, as

EXAMPLE 36. Arcangelo Corelli, "Adagio," *Trio Sonata da chiesa,* Op. 3, no. 2 (meas. 1–6)

well as more than three hundred art songs. His style reflected his considerable interest in French music of the time, but he also used elements from jazz and folk music. From 1925 until 1962, Sowerby taught composition at the American Conservatory in Chicago and, from 1927, also served as organist and choirmaster at Saint James Cathedral there. During his last years he founded and directed the College of Church Musicians in Washington, D.C.

As choirmaster at an Episcopal cathedral, Sowerby naturally composed a good deal of liturgical music, including several communion SERVICES and many CANTICLES. In addition, there are several CANTATAS, many organ works (often based on hymn tunes), and more than one hundred ANTHEMS, most of the texts for them being drawn from the Bible, the BOOK OF COMMON PRAYER, or approved Episcopal HYMNODY.

spiritual—A type of American religious folk song, the spiritual has been variously attributed to exclusively African-American origins (the "black" spiritual), and to mixed white and black sources (the "white" spiritual). It has also been called plantation song, folk hymn, religious ballad, and CAMP-MEETING song. George Pullen Jackson has produced evidence that certain black spirituals, such as the popular "Roll, Jordan, Roll," derive from white camp-meeting songs. Certain spirituals may have originated from the adaptation of religious texts to secular folk tunes (as in the Renaissance process called CONTRAFACTUM). A great deal of research remains to be done. Despite their folk origins, spirituals were heard for many years in sophisticated arrangements for the concert hall or the church service, for example, in the touring performances of the Jubilee Singers from Fisk University or recital performances by well-known solo singers. Although the popularity of the spiritual continued to increase among white audiences throughout the first half of the twentieth century, black churches had already turned to the GOSPEL SONG.

Stabat Mater—The opening words of a Roman Catholic SEQUENCE whose subject is the mother of Christ standing in anguish at the foot of the cross. The sequence was removed from the liturgy by the COUNCIL OF TRENT, but was reinstituted by the pope in 1727. It has inspired compositions by such composers as JOSQUIN, PALESTRINA, Alessandro SCARLATTI, SCHUBERT, Rossini, Liszt, VERDI, and PENDERECKI.

Stanford, Charles Villiers (1852–1924) — Stanford was one of the major figures in the late nineteenth-century revival of English music after a long period of foreign domination. Irish-born, he acquired his advanced musical training at the Royal College of Music in England and in the German cities of Leipzig and Berlin. Upon his return to England, he became professor of composition at the Royal College of Music in 1883 and then professor of music at Cambridge University in 1887. Through these important positions, which he held for the rest of his life, he became the revered teacher of several generations of significant English composers, among them Ralph VAUGHAN WILLIAMS and Herbert HOWELLS. In addition, he conducted the London Bach Choir and participated as conductor and composer at all of the English choral festivals. He served for a time as a cathedral organist as well. After a long career and many honors, he was buried in Westminster Abbey next to the last English composer who had achieved such eminence, Henry PURCELL.

Although he composed in a wide variety of mediums, including the symphonic, the chamber, and the operatic, Stanford achieved his most enduring successes in choral and church music. The ORATORIOS, which are said to be a step above the provincial English standards of the era, and certain of the works on liturgical texts, among them the *Requiem* (1897), the *Te Deum* (1898), and the *Stabat Mater* (1907), were composed for festival rather than church performance and require soloists, chorus and orchestra. Among the functional church works are six Morning, Communion and Evening SERVICES, more than twenty ANTHEMS (e.g., "I Heard a Voice from Heaven" and "While the Shepherds Watched"), a number of MOTETS and HYMNS, and more than fifty organ works, as well as various settings of the MAGNIFICAT and NUNC DIMITTIS. In spite of a basic conservatism in style, Stanford brought to his church music the fruits of his symphonic training, thus surpassing the typical English church composers of the time with his bolder treatment of melody and harmony, his greater variety of texture, including unison passages and sections (even entire works) in *a cappella* manner, and his powerful organ accompaniments.

stile antico — Italian for "ancient style;" music composed in the style of PALESTRINA (or according to late RENAISSANCE precepts), was perceived by the first and later generations of BAROQUE composers as being "in the old style."

stop (organ stop) — See ORGAN.

Stravinsky, Igor (1882–1971) — From his sudden emergence as a major composer in his Parisian ballets to his unexpected adoption of the serial technique towards the end of his career, perhaps none of the surprises the Russian-born Stravinsky sprang upon the music-loving public was more difficult to comprehend than the corpus of religious works that increasingly marked his creative journey after 1926. Following a spiritual crisis and an intense religious experience in Padua at the seven-hundred-year anniversary celebrations of Saint Anthony in 1926, Stravinsky returned to active profession of faith in the Russian Orthodox church. Between 1926 and 1934, he composed three sacred works for this church, whose language is Church Slavonic and whose music must be sung by unaccompanied voices; in Latin, the language of their revision in 1949, the titles of these choral works are "Pater noster," "Credo," and "Ave Maria." Given the restrictions of language and medium in his church and his acknowledged aversion to unaccompanied choral music, it should not be surprising that so few of Stravinsky's works are suitable for liturgical use. Only two remain to be cited, a short "Anthem" (1962) on a text by T. S. Eliot ("The dove descending breaks the air") and a Roman Catholic MASS that was first performed in 1948. In Stravinsky's setting, which calls for men's and children's voices accompanied by ten mixed wind instruments, the Mass ORDINARY unfolds in an austere, frequently chant-like manner that avoids nonfunctional vocal or musical display.

In spite of his relatively few liturgical compositions, the composer deeply respected such sacred genres as the MASS and the MOTET. In *Conversations* (Doubleday, 1959), he says that "these are not simply defunct forms, but parts of the musical spirit in disuse" (p. 141). Their place was taken in his career by a significant number of religious but nonliturgical works. The first major one, a direct result of his conversion experience, was the cantata-like *Symphony of Psalms*, which was written on commission for the fiftieth anniversary of the Boston Symphony Orchestra in 1930 (revised in 1948). Verses from Psalms 38, 39, and 150 (as given in the Latin of the Vulgate Bible) served as the composer's texts, establishing a sequence of repentance, faith, and praise. The original titles of the three movements, later suppressed, were "Prelude," "Double Fugue," and "Allegro symphonique." In style, the contrapuntal texture for chorus and orchestra points to the period of Bach, most clearly in the second movement. Also contributing to the consciously anti-Romantic character of the work are the frequent chant-like melodies for chorus of boys and men and, in the absence of violins and violas, the predominantly wind sonorities. Both the sonorities and the chant-like style first explored in the *Symphony of Psalms* were to find a subdued echo in the composer's *Mass* of 1948. (See example 37.)

Between 1951 and 1961 Stravinsky, now a citizen of the United States, added four significant works to his growing list of religious compo-

EXAMPLE 37. Igor Stravinsky, "Psalm 39," *Symphony of Psalms II* (meas. 52–56)

sitions. Two of them are on Latin texts from the Vulgate Bible. Commissioned by the city of Venice, *Canticum sacrum* (1956), an oratorio-like composition for tenor, baritone, chorus, and orchestra, was apparently constructed on the symmetrical plan of Saint Mark's Cathedral; its five movements frame with choruses of exhortation two eloquent solo arias around a central sermon on the cardinal virtues of faith, hope, and charity. The composer's recent interest in the serial technique found expression in the inner movements, especially the densely contrapuntal sermon. *Threni* (1958), the result of yet another commission from Venice, represents Stravinsky's first completely serial composition. A setting of selected portions from the Lamentations of Jeremiah for six solo voices with subordinate chorus and orchestra, it reveals Stravinsky's unique approach to serialism in its use of repeated notes and phrases to emphasize certain pitches. English works on religious texts from the ninth decade of Stravinsky's career were *Cantata* (1952), a chamber piece in a modified serial style, and *A Sermon, a Narrative and a Prayer* (1961), a cantata-like composition set mostly to New Testament texts. In the latter, composed for alto and tenor soloists, speaker, mixed chorus, and orchestra, the composer's increasingly assured use of serialism results in fragmentation of melody, rhythm, and instrumentation.

It was Stravinsky's philosophy that the essential aim of music was "to promote a communion, a union of man with his fellow man and with the Supreme Being" (*Poetics of Music in the Form of Six Lessons*, 1939, as translated in the Harvard University Press dual language edition of 1970, p. 146). In 1962, his television dance-drama entitled *The Flood* failed to convey his religious message to the wider public and probably set back recognition of his stronger sacred works. The same year brought a commission from Israel that resulted in a sacred cantata for baritone and chamber orchestra entitled *Abraham and Isaac* (1964). Here the composer found inspiration in yet another language, Hebrew words drawn from the twenty-second chapter of Genesis.

Throughout his career the subject or the occasion of death inspired some of Stravinsky's finest music. In several instances a religious composition was his response, as in the *Introitus* (1965) from the Roman Catholic Requiem Mass that he composed after the death of T. S. Eliot; the setting calls for male voices, piano, harp, two timpani, two tam-tams, viola, and double bass. For his own approaching death, the composer turned to selected texts from the same source in a setting for soloists, chorus, and orchestra. *Requiem Canticles* (1966), which does not constitute a complete liturgical Requiem, was sung at Stravinsky's funeral in 1971. In his *Dialogues and a Diary* of 1963 (Doubleday, p. 23), Stravinsky wrote intriguingly that he "would have been more suited for the life of a small Bach, living in anonymity and composing regularly for an established service and for God.... The small Bach might have composed three times as much music."

suffrages—Prayers of intercession in the Anglican liturgy.

Sursum corda—Latin words from the SALUTATION which begins with "Lift up your hearts" and is answered by "We lift them up unto the Lord." In the Roman Catholic liturgy these words begin the PREFACE in the EUCHARIST.

Sweelinck, Jan Pieterszoon (1562–1621)—The last in the long Renaissance line of important composers in the Netherlands, Sweelinck achieved eminence in both secular and sacred music. Although his reputation stems principally from the organ works and his role as organ teacher of many significant German composers, among them Samuel SCHEIDT, at least as much of his attention was occupied with vocal music, which constitutes the larger part of his output. According to one of his students, Sweelinck served for forty-four years (from the age of fifteen) as organist at the Oude Kerk in Amsterdam. Since the Calvinists would not permit the organ to be used during the church service, the composer was employed by the city to provide music daily for an hour each morning and another hour each evening. If a service was to be given, it took place before, between, or after the periods of music.

Perhaps the composer's greatest achievement was his polyphonic setting of the PSALTER, which was published in four parts over the course of his life. According to Randall Tollefsen (in *The New Grove Dictionary*, vol. 18, p. 408), these psalm settings, most of them in five voices, were not intended for church use but for a group of music-loving citizens. The Geneva Psalter served as Sweelinck's source for CANTUS FIRMI, to which he applied various standard polyphonic techniques of the period. The *Cantiones sacrae*, another significant collection of the composer's sacred music that would not have been used in public worship services, was published in 1619; it consists of thirty-seven MOTETS on texts from the Catholic liturgy and demonstrates Sweelinck's mastery in the absence of a cantus firmus.

Approximately seventy keyboard compositions by Sweelinck are extant; none were published during his lifetime. They range from the discipline of variations, some of them on CHORALE themes, to the freedom of his TOCCATAS, and include as well noteworthy FANTASIAS that occupy an important place in the development of the Baroque FUGUE. (See example 13.)

symphonia — Latin for "symphony"; a term used by Giovanni GABRIELI and succeeding composers to designate motet-like compositions for two or more choirs and instruments; an example is his collection of *Symphoniae sacrae* that was published posthumously in 1615. (See also SCHUETZ.)

Tallis, Thomas (c.1505–1585) — Tallis was the leading English church composer of his generation and one of the first to compose for the new ANGLICAN LITURGY. Although his works are predominantly vocal, Tallis served almost his entire career as an organist, spending perhaps as many as forty-eight years in the CHAPEL ROYAL. Except for a few early hymn settings using CANTUS FIRMI, however, there is virtually no organ music by the composer. The sixteenth century was a stormy time for church music in England, a situation reflected in the variety of Tallis's works. For the period before the break with Rome and again during the reinstitution of Catholicism in the reign of Mary Tudor, there are three Latin MASSES, approximately thirty MOTETS, six settings of RESPONSORIES for major feasts, seven HYMNS for the OFFICE in ALTERNATIM structure, and two LAMENTATIONS. For the new liturgy of the Church of England, there are three Anglican SERVICES, approximately twenty ANTHEMS, and some psalm settings for popular PSALTERS. Some of the Latin motets from the composer's earlier years were given English words to make them suitable for the new state religion. According to Paul Doe (*The New Grove Dictionary*, vol. 18, p. 543), two of Tallis's most sumptuous works come from the time of Queen Mary: the *Missa Puer natus est nobis* in seven voices and the ANTIPHON "Gaude gloriosa Dei mater" (Rejoice, Glorious Mother of God) in six voices.

Seldom did the mature Tallis compose on such a large and expansive scale. The later works in general conceal the composer's mastery in his restrained, basically syllabic treatment of the texts, as in the famous Lamentations for MATINS on Maundy Thursday. The influence of the Anglican reformers, such as Archbishop Cranmer, on the composers in the CHAPEL ROYAL, among them Thomas Tallis, is perhaps reflected in the style of the composer's church music. When he chose, Tallis could challenge the most modern of the madrigal-influenced younger composers, as in two motets from 1572, "Derelinquat impius" (Let the Wicked Forsake His Way) and "In jejunio et fletu" (Fasting and Weeping). Indeed, his incredible forty-voice motet entitled "Spem in alium" (Hope in Any

Other) must have been as impressive then as it remains today; it may have been his last major choral composition.

Taverner, John (c.1490–1545) — Little is known of the composer's youth. Not until about 1524 can he be located as a lay clerk of the choir at the collegiate church of Tattershall. In 1526, he became the first instructor of choristers in the large choir of Cardinal College at Oxford. Political changes dictated a further move to the English parish church of Saint Botolph in Boston for the years from about 1530 to about 1537, after which he appears to have retired in comfortable circumstances. Taverner's church music includes eight MASSES in four, five and six voices; miscellaneous settings of parts of the Mass ORDINARY, three MAGNIFICATS; and approximately twenty-five MOTETS, most of them votive ANTIPHONS. All of the Masses are shortened by omission of the KYRIE and parts of the CREDO. The Mass in four voices on the folk tune "Western Wynde" is Taverner's best-known composition; secular tunes seldom received that treatment in Renaissance England. The composer's later music apparently reflects the altered conditions that Henry VIII brought about in English church music. Such was Taverner's reputation and quality of output that certain of his works were modified for use in the new ANGLICAN LITURGY.

Te Deum — A shortened reference to "Te Deum laudamus," which is Latin for "We praise thee, O God." In the Roman Catholic liturgy it is sung at the end of MATINS on Sundays and feast days; in the Anglican liturgy, during MORNING PRAYER. Among the Renaissance composers who set the text were PALESTRINA and LASSUS; later composers have included HAYDN, BERLIOZ, BRUCKNER, VERDI, BRITTEN, and PENDERECKI.

Telemann, Georg Phillip (1681–1767) — An amazingly prolific German contemporary of J. S. Bach, Telemann was widely regarded during his lifetime as the leading composer in Germany. Unlike Bach, Telemann changed with the times and adopted the new aesthetic and style of pre-Classical music. He also took a new attitude towards his profession, refusing to accept the restrictions that kept music of the theater separate from ecclesiastical music. Telemann became a self-taught musician after being orphaned in 1685, and he continued to accept new challenges throughout his life. Sent to Leipzig University to study law, he founded a collegium musicum there and gave regular concerts. Soon he was musical director at the Leipzig Opera, then organist at the Neue Kirche. In 1705, he became court Kapellmeister at Sorau, where he had to master the fashionable French style. At Frankfurt am Main he assumed the duties of municipal director of music and church Kapellmeister. Finally, in 1721, he settled in Hamburg as school cantor at the Johanneum and musical director of Hamburg's five main churches. According to Martin Ruhnke in *The New Grove Dictionary* (vol. 18, p. 650), "For each Sunday he was expected to write two cantatas and for each year a new Passion. Special cantatas were required for induction ceremonies, and oratorios for the consecration of churches...." In addition, despite opposition from the city council, he took part in opera performances; indeed, he not only composed operas for the Hamburg Opera, but also served as its musical director from 1722 to 1738. He established public concerts in the city as well, and attempted to reach yet a wider public through his many publications of music for domestic music-making.

Statistics given by Martin Ruhnke indicate that Telemann composed 1,043 church CANTATAS encompassing a wide variety of types. Most of them require at least four voices, and many are accompanied by strings and woodwinds; cantatas written for feast days call for brasses as well. In keeping with his desire to make music available for the public, Telemann took the unusual step of publishing complete cycles of church cantatas in 1726, 1732, 1744, and 1748. Of particular interest is the fact that he reduced the instrumental requirements in these cantatas to make them more widely accessible. The composer set forty-six liturgically proper PASSIONS, of which twenty are extant. He also composed six Passion ORATORIOS on free poetic texts. Other kinds of church music by this prodigious composer include eleven MASSES on CHORALE tunes, four short Masses, two MAGNIFICATS (one in Latin and one in German), seventeen psalm settings, twenty-six MOTETS, a number of sacred songs and canons, and some CHORALE PRELUDES and FUGUES for organ.

Temporale—A Latin term referring to the Proper of the Time, whose feasts commemorate events in the life of Jesus.

Tenebrae—The Roman Catholic service that is composed of MATINS and LAUDS on Thursday, Friday, and Saturday of Holy Week, so named because it ends *in tenebris* (in darkness). Musical settings of texts from the Tenebrae were frequent during the Renaissance; three of the greatest composers represented were PALESTRINA, LASSUS, and VICTORIA. Since that time, attention has centered on the LAMENTATIONS of Jeremiah, one of the most noteworthy settings being that of François COUPERIN.

Terce—The fourth of the CANONICAL HOURS in the Roman Catholic OFFICE.

testo—Italian for "text"; used to refer to the narrator in an ORATORIO or PASSION. In Latin, the appropriate term is *Historicus*.

Thompson, Randall (1899–1984)—A leading American composer of choral music both sacred and secular, Thompson devoted much of his life to college teaching and administration. After receiving his training at Harvard University, he taught at Wellesley College (1927–1929 and 1936–1937) and the University of California at Berkeley (1937–1939). From 1939 to 1941 he served as director of the Curtis Institute of Music in Philadelphia, followed by five years as head of music at the University of Virginia. Finally, after two years at Princeton University, he returned to Harvard until his retirement in 1965. Fellowships, awards, and honorary doctorates marked Thompson's career. His sacred vocal music—only a portion of his output—ranks among the best composed in the twentieth century. Basically diatonic and traditional in style, yet expressive and strongly rhythmic, it is unfailingly sensitive to the words and rewarding for both singers and listeners. Among the small-scale works, the ANTHEM entitled *Alleluia* (1940), for four-voice chorus, retains a richly deserved popularity in church services of many different traditions. The larger works include a MASS (the Mass of the Holy Spirit, 1957), a REQUIEM (1958), and a PASSION (according to Saint Luke, 1965), as well as extended settings of biblical texts such as *A Peaceable Kingdom* (for unaccompanied mixed choir in eight voices on a text from Isaiah, 1936).

tiento—A Spanish term referring to a keyboard (sometimes organ) piece that may be of a technical and idiomatic nature, like a TOCCATA; improvisatory, like a PRELUDE or FANTASIA; or sometimes contrapuntal, like a RICERCARE. Two important composers of tientos were Antonio de Canezon (1510–1566) and Juan Bautista Jose Cabanilles (1644–1712).

Titcomb, H. Everett (1884–1968)—An outstanding American composer of ANTHEMS, Titcomb was able to write functional church music of quality and still appeal on a basic level to musically unsophisticated congregations and volunteer church choirs. His productivity and popularity were rooted in skillful thematic development, effective use of varied choral devices, well-written organ accompaniments, and an unusual capacity for contrast—characteristics that may be heard to advantage in such favorite anthems as "Behold Now, Praise the Lord." In addition to his many anthems composed on Scriptural texts, the composer also drew successfully upon traditional hymn texts, as in "Ride On, Ride On in Majesty" and "Eternal Praise." The popular hymn-anthem entitled

"The Lord's My Shepherd" features both a Scriptural text and a traditional hymn tune in a setting that reveals the composer's ability to capture moods of reflection as well as exaltation. Among the works that best reflect Titcomb's range as a composer are *Eight Short Motets* (1934), a group of pieces composed in a Renaissance-like style for *a cappella* chorus for use during the greater festivals of the church year, and a powerful English setting of the *Te Deum* (1944).

Titelouze, Jehan (c. 1562–1633)—The first important composer of organ music in France, Titelouze was a priest who held the position of organist at the Cathedral of Rouen from 1588 until the end of his life. Born in the Spanish Netherlands, he became a French citizen in 1604. Such was his renown as a musician, as an expert in organ construction, and as a poet that he was named a canon at the cathedral in 1610. His organ compositions consist of VERSETS based on Gregorian CHANT for performance during the service in alternation with the choir. In the twelve *Hymnes de l'Église* of 1623, Titelouze either uses the plainchant melody as a CANTUS FIRMUS (usually in the bass) or paraphrases it and creates successive points of imitation. His collection entitled *Le Magnificat* (1626) offers eight cycles of versets, one for each of the church modes. Only the odd-numbered verses of the MAGNIFICAT text are used in the composer's settings, which employ the Gregorian chant phrases as a source for short imitative sections. With its firm basis in the church modes and its conservative use of the imitative texture of the High Renaissance, the organ music of Titelouze remains perfectly suited to a functional purpose in the church service.

toccata—Derived from the Italian word *toccare* (to touch), the toccata first appeared in the early sixteenth century in a form not unlike the RICERCARE and the TIENTO. Not until later in the century did it take on the alternation of scalar and chordal passages with imitative ones that characterize the genre in the hands of the Italian organists, the finest of whom was FRESCOBALDI. (See the entry for that composer and example 15.) From the Italians, the toccata was taken up by South German composers and, finally, by such great North German organist-composers as BUXTEHUDE and J. S. BACH. (See example 38.) By the late Baroque period, the toccata had become an entire movement of improvisatory character preceding an extended FUGUE, a model that has inspired countless subsequent composers. (See also ORGAN MUSIC.)

Tomkins, Thomas (1572–1656)—The last in the distinguished line of English Renaissance composers, Tomkins composed more anthems and

EXAMPLE 38. J. S. Bach, "Toccata," Toccata and Fugue in D Minor, BWV 565 (meas. 20–21)

services for the Anglican church than TAVERNER, TALLIS, BYRD, or GIBBONS. Although it represents something of an unfashionable backwater in an era dominated by the Italian and Italian-influenced styles of monody and concertato, the best of the composer's music exhibits a high degree of contrapuntal and structural skill in the service of English sacred music. Musical ability abounded in the Tomkins family during the years before the Commonwealth: Thomas's father was a church organist before becoming a vicar, and his half-brothers (by his father's second wife) — who eventually joined Thomas in the Chapel Royal — included John (organist at Saint Paul's Cathedral), Giles (organist at Salisbury Cathedral), and Robert (a viol player). Thomas, who was probably appointed to the Chapel Royal in about 1620, served as organist of Worcester Cathedral from about 1596 to 1646, when public worship was restricted and the organs removed from the cathedral. His son Nathaniel (another organist) most likely prepared his father's music for posthumous publication in the collection entitled *Musica Deo Sacra* (London, 1668).

Nearly one hundred ANTHEMS were printed in *Musica Deo Sacra,* most of them based upon texts drawn from the Book of Psalms. They represent a wide variety of styles and forms, ranging from ordinary use in the Communion Service or the Burial Service to exceptional use at Christmas or at other special occasions. The full anthems are written for as many as twelve voice-parts ("O Praise the Lord") and as few as three, with the larger settings dating from earlier in the composer's career. Particularly noteworthy is the group of five-voice anthems; among them are two of Tomkins's best known and most expressive works: "When David Heard" and "When David Mourned." The composer's sensitivity to these biblical texts is reflected in skilled tone-painting and in subtle use of contrasting textures and sonorities. As an organist, Tomkins himself accompanied the solo voice or voices in his forty-one verse anthems, which were intended to ornament the greater feast days of the church year. In addition to taking advantage of the greater opportunities for textural contrast offered by the verse anthem, the composer also achieves variety by using thematic contrast and recurrence and, as in "My Shepherd Is the Living Lord," by not using the chorus simply to repeat the words just sung by the soloist. Another striking technique that often occurs in this group of works is the use of melodic sequence as a means of intensifying the mood.

Among the five SERVICES by Tomkins, the finest is probably the third; its breadth and vocal requirements indicate that it must have been composed for the considerable resources of the Chapel Royal. The First and Second Services are generally referred to as "Short Services" (although the second has some verses in its "Te Deum"), whereas the Fourth and Fifth Services require the organ to accompany solo singing. Although a fair amount of Tomkin's organ works are extant, they are conservative and do not equal his vocal music in significance.

Tonary (in Latin, *tonarium, tonarius, tonale*)—A liturgical book in which CHANTS are classified by church mode.

tonus peregrinus—A Latin term for an irregular (literally, "wandering") psalm tone that differs from the traditional eight psalm tones by changing its reciting tone after the mediation. (See PSALM-TONE.)

tract—In the Roman Catholic liturgy the tract, which is part of the Mass PROPER, replaces the Alleluia in the REQUIEM MASS and on certain days of the church year.

transcription—A term used in church music principally to designate a version for organ of an operatic or symphonic composition. During the late nineteenth and early twentieth centuries, an enormous amount of secular music of all kinds was transcribed for the organ and performed during the church service.

Tridentine—An adjective referring to the COUNCIL OF TRENT.

Trisagion—A Greek word meaning "thrice holy." A chant sung originally in the Eastern Christian church that came to be sung as part of the Roman Catholic IMPROPERIA.

trope—An addition of either words or notes (or sometimes both) to an existing Gregorian CHANT. The chant items that were most frequently troped were the INTROIT, KYRIE, GRADUAL, ALLELUIA, and OFFERTORY. Troping embellished the liturgy with increasing frequency until the twelfth century, when the practice began to decline. A remnant of it may still be seen in the manner in which Masses are labelled for convenience by trope words that had at one time been added to their Kyries, as in *Missa "Cunctipotens dominator."* (See example 9f.)

troper (Latin, *troparium*)—A liturgical book containing largely TROPES and SEQUENCES, as well as other MEDIEVAL accretions to the Roman Catholic liturgy.

Tudor church music—Music composed for the English royal family of that name, including principally Henry VII, Henry VIII, and Elizabeth I. During the reign of the Tudors, the CHAPEL ROYAL served as a focal point for patronage of an impressive number of excellent musicians and a high level of musical life, both secular and sacred. Among the leading English composers of the time were John TAVERNER, Thomas TALLIS, and William BYRD.

tune book—A collection of tunes published in eighteenth- or nineteenth-century New England for the singing of PSALMS. The tunes included folk songs and native American melodies, as well as European tunes. Among the most influential early tune books was *An Introduction to the Art of Singing Psalm-Tunes,* which was published in Boston in 1721.

Vater unser—German words for "Our Father who art in heaven..." (in

Latin, "Pater noster"). The sixteenth-century CHORALE melody that set these words became a popular CANTUS FIRMUS for CHORALE PRELUDES by German composers of the BAROQUE PERIOD, among them Samuel SCHEIDT, Dieterich BUXTEHUDE, and J. S. BACH.

Vatican II (or Second Vatican Council) — Summoned by Pope John XXIII, the Second Vatican Council met intermittently from 1962 to 1965 and brought about the replacement of Latin by vernacular languages in the Roman Catholic liturgy, and the publication of a new MISSAL (1970) and a new BREVIARY (1971). Recommendations were made for music that would involve the entire congregation and for music that could be performed by small choirs.

Vaughan Williams, Ralph (1872–1958) — Noteworthy particularly as a symphonist, a composer of choral music and art songs, and a devoted collector of English folk songs, Vaughan Williams saw church music as another avenue through which a composer could fulfill a useful role in society. He was significant in bringing English church music, and English music in general, into the mainstream of early twentieth-century musical activity. He also contributed to an elevation of musical taste in the church through his work as an editor and composer of hymn tunes. Not in any sense a prodigy, the young Vaughan Williams studied composition at the Royal College of Music in London and at Cambridge University under Parry, Wood, and STANFORD. He also studied abroad with Bruch and Ravel. Just as significant may have been his lifelong friendship and practice of reciprocal criticism with Gustav Holst. Although he was briefly a church organist, he held no other church posts and never became a professing Christian; nevertheless, a rich vein of mysticism put him in touch with things spiritual, and his extraordinarily long tenure as principal conductor with the Leith Hill Musical Festival gave him occasions for composing choral music on religous texts.

Among Vaughan Williams's relatively few church works stands one complete SERVICE in D Minor for the Anglican Church, a setting for four-voice chorus and organ with an additional part to be sung in unison by the congregation. There are also two independent settings of the TE DEUM, one accompanied by orchestra since it was composed for the Coronation of King George VI. More serviceable are several hymns and certain of his MOTETS and ANTHEMS. While he was doing editorial work on *The English Hymnal* (1906) and *Songs of Praise* (1925), Vaughan Williams composed some new hymn tunes, including the well-known "Sine nomine" (For All the Saints) and "King's Weston" (At the Name of Jesus). There are also highly effective hymn arrangements, such as "All Hail the Power of Jesus' Name" (on the tune "Miles Lane") and "The Old Hundredth Psalm Tune"; because both of these were composed for festival performance, they originally required full orchestra. Among the most noteworthy motets and anthems are "O Clap Your Hands" (1920), for six-voice choir, organ, brass, and percussion, and "O How Amiable" (1934), in which the organ is given most of the difficult passages. There remains what is perhaps the composer's finest church composition, a Mass in G Minor (c.1922) for the Roman Catholic liturgy. Set for unaccompanied double chorus and four soloists, it displays neo-modal harmony, a wide variety of textures, and a love for cross-relations typical of the source of its inspiration, the music of William BYRD.

Vaughan Williams composed a considerable amount of concert music and some stage music on religious texts or themes. The larger works include an ORATORIO on the subject of life after death (*Sanctas Civitas*, 1925), a CANTATA whose message is a plea for peace (*Dona Nobis Pacem*, 1936), and a Christmas cantata entitled *Hodie* (1953). For Christmas there is also a *Fantasia on Christmas Carols*, composed in 1912 for the Hereford Festival. Another composition of occasional music is the cantata-like *Benedicite*, one of three choral works composed in 1930 for the Leith Hill Festival. Among the dramatic compositions on religious themes are two ballets — a folk dance on a number of Christmas carols (*On Christmas Night*, 1921) and a masque for dancing on William Blake's *Illustrations of the Book of Job* (*Job*, 1930). Finally, in 1951, came the performance of *The Pilgrim's Progress*, a morality opera in a prologue, four acts, and an epilogue. Inspired by Bunyan's famous allegory, it reveals the depth of national commitment of a composer who often sought inspiration in specifically English tradition.

velorio — A Spanish word referring to a wake or another Latin-American religious observance; distinctive musical traditions have evolved for some observances.

Venite — The opening Latin word of the invitatory psalm (Psalm 95: "Venite exsultemus"), which is sung during MATINS.

Verdi, Giuseppe (1813–1901) — Without equal in his mastery of Italian opera, which was his preoccupation from 1839 to 1893, Verdi composed very little music to religious texts; indeed, he was a rigorous critic of the church and a decidedly unconventional believer. Although he came to music through the church, studying with and functioning as a small town organist and composing adolescent motets for the local cathedral, only very late in his life did he occasionally turn his attention to sacred music. Like that of a number of his renowned contemporaries of the Romantic period, his sacred music was most successful when he disregarded liturgical propriety and function and expressed himself with all the force of his accumulated operatic experience. Among the greatest of his works in operatic style is his REQUIEM MASS of 1874, which was composed in honor of the Italian patriot and writer Alessandro Manzoni. The starkly dramatic liturgical text serves as one of Verdi's best librettos, a vehicle to express through great solo and choral singing and a large orchestra his own vision of the Last Judgment. As in his operas, the appeal is popular, not sectarian, and he is certainly not mindful of institutional sanctity. The MOTU PROPRIO issued by Pope Pius X in 1903 is the response of the institution to what it regarded as unbridled Romantic excess.

Verdi's other religious music was composed on a smaller scale. In 1880, he wrote an unaccompanied PATER NOSTER (1880) for five-part chorus and an aria for soprano and strings entitled "Ave Maria"; both are based on free Italian paraphrases of the Latin texts by Dante. Finally, during the years between and after *Otello* and *Falstaff*, the *Quattro pezzi sacri* (Four Sacred Pieces) appeared, one after another, with no relationship other than religious texts to bind them. The first, an "Ave Maria" in four voices without accompaniment, represents Verdi's solution for using a unique scale (example 39); the second offers a beautiful setting of Dante's "Laudi alla Vergine Maria" for unaccompanied four-voice women's chorus. In the STABAT MATER, written for four-part chorus and orchestra, Verdi evinces greater respect for the liturgical text than usual, but once again interprets in dramatic accents the anguish of the subject. The eighty-year-old composer desired that the third of the sacred pieces, his TE DEUM for double chorus and orchestra, a typically individual and thoroughly worthy setting of the liturgical canticle, be buried with him.

verse anthem—See ANTHEM.

verset—A verset is a short organ piece that replaces a verse of Gregorian CHANT in the service. By the practice known as *in* ALTERNATIM, organ versets replaced the odd-numbered verses of the items of the Mass ORDI-NARY, the MAGNIFICAT, and other chants as desired. Versets may use the appropriate chant melody as a CANTUS FIRMUS or they may be independent pieces. They must often have been improvised. (See ORGAN MASS.)

versicle—A phrase or sentence of the Roman Catholic liturgy that is sung by a priest, to which the choir or congregation responds. (See RESPONSE.)

EXAMPLE 39. Giuseppe Verdi, "Ave Maria," *Four Sacred Pieces* (meas. 49–54)

In the Anglican church, a series of such exchanges make up PRECES, SUFFRAGES, and RESPONSES.

Vesperale—A modern liturgical book containing the Roman Catholic chants for VESPERS, and sometimes for COMPLINE.

Vespers—The seventh of the Canonical Hours, Vespers is held in the evening (*ad vesperas* in Latin) and is one of the richest services in the Office for music. Among its texts are the MAGNIFICAT, the BENEDICAMUS DOMINO, and various PSALMS, all of them frequently set by composers.

Victimae paschali laudes—The opening Latin words (meaning "Praises to the Paschal victim") of the SEQUENCE that is sung as part of the Mass PROPER for Easter.

Victoria, Tomas Luis de (1548–1611) –The greatest Spanish composer of the Renaissance, Victoria was the composer who most nearly challenged PALESTRINA's supremacy in late sixteenth-century Rome. In an era when composers wrote in all genres as a matter of course, he achieved his reputation exclusively in church music. Born in or near Avila, Spain, where he learned music as a choirboy, Victoria was sent, probably in 1565, to the Jesuit Collegio Germanico in Rome in order to further his education as a singer. There he must have known, perhaps even studied with, Palestrina. He served for some years beginning in 1569 as a singer and organist at the Roman church of Santa Maria di Monserrato, and then from 1573 as maestro di cappella of the Collegio Germanico. Following his ordination to the priesthood in 1575, he became chaplain at San Girolamo della Carita from 1578 to 1585. After more than twenty years in Rome, during which he published several volumes of church music, he requested and received permission to return to Spain, where he served until 1603 as chaplain to the widow of Emperor Maximilian II (and sister of King Philip II). When she died, he remained as choirmaster and then organist at the convent of Descalzas Reales in Madrid for the remainder of his life, in preference to several cathedral posts.

Most of Victoria's music was composed specifically for liturgical use. There are twenty settings of the MASS Ordinary, all of them published during his lifetime. Fifteen are PARODY MASSES, eleven of them on compositions of his own (mostly motets); four are PARAPHRASE MASSES; and one (*Missa "Quarti toni"*) is virtually free of pre-existing material. There are also two Masses for the dead, one of them part of a six-voice setting of the *Officium defunctorum* that was composed for the funeral of his patroness in 1603. In his Masses, the composer generally avoided the expressive tone-painting and mystical fervor that distinguishes certain of his famous motets, striving rather for a devotional attitude and conciseness of expression. The finest of the Masses, such as *Missa "O quam gloriosum"* and *Missa "Vidi speciosam"*, reveal considerable freedom and imagination in the use of borrowed material. In contrast to the style of Palestrina, Victoria achieves clarity of structure through frequent cadences and an almost tonal use of harmony. Instrumental doubling of the vocal parts also appears to be characteristic of Spanish practice. Among the composer's later Masses are four polychoral ones, after the Venetian rather than the Roman model.

Justly famous among Victoria's works is his music for Holy Week, published in 1585 as *Officium Hebdomadae Sanctae*. Included are nine LAMENTATIONS, eighteen RESPONSORIES, and two PASSIONS that have been performed in the Sistine Chapel during Holy Week for more than three hundred years. Among the other liturgical works are eighteen MAGNIFICATS, some of them among his finest compositions, thirteen ANTI-PHONS, eight polychoral psalms, and more than thirty-two hymns. In his forty-five or so MOTETS, as in the admirable Christmas motet "O magnum mysterium," the composer's style can be seen at its most flexible in the service of the text. More fervent in expression is the well-known, four-voice "O vos omnes" (O, All You). Its conventional ABCB form features: (A) an opening section that closes with a stirring declamatory phrase for the words "Behold and see"; (B) an intense madrigalian refrain ("If there be any sorrow like unto my sorrow") characterized by stepwise descent, a repeated-note motive terminating in the interval of a minor second, and the striking melodic leap of a diminished fourth; (C) a climactic plea ("Behold and see my sorrow") in which the voices climb to their highest ranges; and (B) the return of the affective refrain. (See example 40.)

vigil—Certain of the most important feasts of the liturgical year are preceded on the night before by a liturgical service known as a vigil. The vigil for Easter begins after sunset on Holy Saturday and ends with a midnight MASS.

voluntary—An organ piece composed or improvised for the Anglican service, which it generally introduces or follows. During the service, a voluntary might be played before the first lesson, or between the end of MORNING PRAYER and before HOLY COMMUNION. Voluntaries vary widely in style, ranging from imitative works in the Renaissance to sonata-like forms in the Classical period. Among the leading composers of the voluntary were William BOYCE and Samuel WESLEY.

votive antiphon—A reference to any one of the four ANTIPHONS for the Blessed Virgin Mary. (See MARIAN ANTIPHON.)

votive Mass—A special MASS that is held in honor of an individual (such as the Blessed Virgin Mary) or for a certain occasion (such as the consecration of a bishop).

Walther, Johann Gottfried (1684–1748)—J. G. Walther contributed to the history of music as a distinguished composer of church music as well as a theorist and a musicologist. His *Musicalisches Lexicon* of 1732 remains unsurpassed as a contemporary, encyclopedic source of knowledge about music, musicians, musical life, and music bibliography. It

EXAMPLE 40. Tomas Luis de Victoria, "O vos omnes" (meas. 40–48)

was the first major German publication of its kind, and the first in any language to include both terms as well as biographical information about musicians. Walther's extensive knowledge of music theory had already been documented in a treatise entitled *Praecepta der musicalischen Composition,* a manual that includes an explanation of how a composer should express the affections of his text appropriately in music.

As a composer of church music, Walther ranks among the finest of his era. Although nearly all of his sacred vocal music has been lost, there remain more than one hundred CHORALE PRELUDES, ranging from simple settings for manuals only to fully worked-out CHORALE PARTITAS and chorale FUGUES. In volume 20 of *The New Grove Dictionary*, George Buelow finds Walther's "sensitivity in the affective connotations of the chorale preludes, his rich harmonic variety, the brilliant keyboard technique rooted in motivic counterpoint, and the strength of the contrapuntal ideas" comparable to the mastery of his great contemporary, J. S. BACH.

Wesley, John (1703–1791)–An Anglican clergyman of considerable importance as the founder of Methodism and as a powerful figure in the surge of English and American HYMNODY in the eighteenth century. His brother Charles (1707–1788) contributed to the Methodist movement as a distinguished hymn writer. Methodism began in the meetings of a religious group formed by John Wesley at Oxford in 1729. He carried it with him to the British colonies in America, where it eventually became enormously successful. His recognition of the power of music played an important role in the success of his movement. Like Martin LUTHER, he sought tunes that the congregation could sing heartily, and saw nothing wrong with adapting popular or even operatic songs for his purpose. In 1737, he published the *Collection of Psalms and Hymns*, the first of a series of similar popular hymn books.

Wesley, Samuel (1766–1837)–A gifted English composer of as yet limited recognition, Samuel Wesley was the son of the noted hymn writer (Charles) and the nephew of the founder of Methodism (John). He appears in contemporary accounts as the finest organist of the time, already able at age seven to play a psalm tune during the worship service. As a composer, he wrote his first ORATORIO (*Ruth*) at age eight. Nicholas Temperley (in *The New Grove Dictionary*, vol. 20, p. 359–60) has high praise for the composer's symphonic music, keyboard sonatas, and organ concertos, as well as for his organ music and, in particular, for his five Latin MASSES and approximately fifty MOTETS: "In this music Wesley forged a personal sacred style, building upon a deep knowledge and understanding of Renaissance and Baroque music that was unique among composers of his day." Among the motets singled out for special praise are "Confitebor tibi Domine" (1799), for soloists, chorus, and orchestra; "In exitu Israel" (1810), for eight-voice chorus and organ; "Omnia vanitas" (1827), for five-voice chorus; and "Tu es sacerdos" (1827), for six-voice chorus. Wesley's music for the Anglican liturgy, including a Morning and Evening SERVICE and approximately thirty ANTHEMS, seldom reaches the same heights. Another of his enthusiasms, his love for the music of J. S. Bach, is reflected in some of his approximately fifty organ VOLUNTARIES; the best of them also represent vintage Wesley. Besides playing Bach in the church service, he edited some of Bach's music for publication and presented some works in concert, including the Mass in B Minor. Wesley also composed some thirty sacred songs and, late in his life, many HYMNS. His influence as a teacher was felt through the noteworthy career of his son Samuel Sebastian.

Wesley, Samuel Sebastian (1810–1876) – Son and pupil of SAMUEL WESLEY, he was the outstanding organist of his time and a composer able to rise above the mediocre standard that kept English cathedral music provincial. Wesley's career was spent, except for seven years in a parish church, as a cathedral organist. His outstanding achievement was his Morning and Evening SERVICE in E Major. Among the nearly forty ANTHEMS, the most consistently successful are the short ones for full choir. There are also many excellent harmonizations of hymn tunes and a few organ compositions that represent the composer at his best.

white spiritual – See SPIRITUAL.

Willaert, Adrian (c.1490–1562) – A Netherlander who served from 1527 until his death as maestro di cappella at Saint Mark's Cathedral in Venice, Willaert contributed greatly to the rise of Venice to musical leadership in Italy. His antiphonal psalm settings firmly established the use of divided choirs (*cori spezzati* in Italian) as the chief distinguishing characteristic of Venetian church music. He was also a noteworthy madrigalist and a leader in the use of expressive chromaticism.

Foremost among Willaert's church music are his MOTETS, almost 175 in number, ranging from ANTIPHONS and sections of the Mass PROPER to HYMNS, SEQUENCES, and psalms. There are also nine MASSES, most of them early works. The composer's Franco-Flemish heritage is particularly clear in his sequence-motets, among them "Veni Sancte Spiritus" and "Victimae paschali laudes," while his psalm settings for double chorus reveal his unique fusion of traditional imitative counterpoint with the Venetian love for richness of harmony and tone color. Eight works for divided choirs, including "De profundis" and "Confitebor tibi," appear in a psalm collection of 1550 which was published jointly with Jaquet of Mantua. Willaert's later works are characterized by an increasing concern for expressing the accentuation as well as the meaning of the text and, as in the five-voice Vespers motet "O crux splendidor," by his preference for a polyphonic texture free of the constraints of a CANTUS FIRMUS. His most famous publication, entitled *Musica nova*, appeared in 1559; it contained both motets and madrigals, an unusual combination in the period, and confirmed his position as a leader in both genres.

Willan, Healey (1880–1968)—Born and educated in England, Willan emigrated to Canada in 1913 and became an important figure in musical life there. For many years he taught at the University of Toronto and the Toronto Conservatory, making an indelible mark as a teacher. His secular works, which were composed in a rich post-Romantic style, cover a wide range of genres, including two symphonies, a piano concerto, several works for band, a small group of chamber pieces, some songs, and an opera. Far more numerous are the church compositions, most of them composed for Saint Mary Magdalene Church, where he served as organist and choirmaster for many years. There are MASSES, Communion SERVICES, MOTETS, organ music, more than sixty ANTHEMS (some of them hymn-anthems), as well as Christmas CANTATAS and other miscellaneous pieces. In contrast to the post-Romantic richness of the larger works, Willan cultivated a more restrained manner in the functional church music; the anthems became simpler in style as time passed. Much of his church music reflects in its greater use of modality and melodic subtlety his love of plainchant and of Renaissance polyphony.

Zimmermann, Heinz Werner (1930–   )—A German composer noteworthy for using certain jazz instruments and rhythms in his church music in an attempt to breathe new life into that great tradition. His career began when, after four years of study with Wolfgang Fortner, he became teacher of composition at the Heidelberg Church Music Institute. Subsequently, he has served as both principal and teacher of composition at the Spandau Church Music School in Berlin and has also taught at Oxford University and in the United States. Jazz made its appearance in Zimmermann's music as early as 1954 in his "Geistliches Konzert," a three-movement solo cantata for baritone and eleven jazz soloists. In 1956, in the foreword to Psalm 113 ("Lobet, ihr Knechte des Herrn"), an introit motet for a chorus of mixed voices in five heavily syncopated parts with double-bass, he wrote, "I am conscious of the fact that this rhythm . . . has parallels in the dance music of our day—as does the harmony. . . . These motets . . . are rooted firmly in the tradition of Protestant church music and are concerned with the advancement of that tradition through new expressive means." Zimmermann's most ambitious composition in this style may be his five-movement *Psalmkonzert* (1957), written for bass-baritone, five-part mixed chorus, unison boys' choir, three trumpets, vibraphone, and double bass. Here, the composer explains that he uses a jazz technique because "it is the only kind of contemporary music that can still express joy." Nevertheless, in the opinion of Adam Adrio (writing under "Renewal and Rejuvenation" in Friedrich Blume's *Protestant Church Music* [Norton, 1974], p. 448), Zimmermann seems to be "aware of the irreconcilable gulf between religious and secular forces" by the manner in which he depends upon the "symbolic power" of a chorale melody to unify the otherwise unintegrated elements of the traditional motet and jazz.

In more recent years the composer has added to his list of works, among others, a complete Vesper setting (1962) for five mixed voices, vibraphone, harpsichord, and double bass; a *Missa Profana* (1968) for soloists, chorus and jazz group; a *Magnificat* (1970) for chorus, vibraphone, harpsichord, and double-bass; and a setting of Psalm 113 (1973) for chorus, organ, and double-bass. Although nearly all of his works have been for voices, there are some organ pieces, including a number of chorale partitas and chorale preludes, as well as some organ works not set on chorale cantus firmi.

American Publishers of Church Music

Abingdon Press
201 Eighth Avenue South
P.O. Box 801
Nashville, TN 37202

Agape IL
380 South Main Place
Carol Stream, IL 60187

Augsburg Fortress, Publishers
426 South Fifth Street
P.O. Box 1209
Minneapolis, MN 55440

Baker Book House
6030 East Fulton
Ada, MI 49301

Behrman House
  Publishers, Inc.
235 Watchung Avenue
West Orange, NJ 07052

Belwin Mills Publishing
  Corporation
15800 N.W. 48th Avenue
P.O. Box 4340
Miami, FL 33014

Boosey & Hawkes, Inc.
200 Smith Street
Farmingdale, NY 11735

Boston Music Company
116 Boylston Street
Boston, MA 02116

Broadman Press
127 Ninth Avenue North
Nashville, TN 37234

Brodt Music Company
P.O. Box 9345
Nashville, TN 37234

Cambiata Press
P.O. Box 1151
Conway, AR 72032

Cambridge University Press
40 West 20th Street
New York, NY 10011

Chorister's Guild
2834 West Kingsley Road
Garland, TX 75041

Concordia Publishing House
3558 South Jefferson Avenue
St. Louis, MO 63118

Deseret Book Company
40 East South Temple
P.O. Box 30178
Salt Lake City, UT 84130

Dover Publications, Inc.
180 Varick Street
New York, NY 10014

Faith Publishing House
920 West Mansur
Guthrie, OK 73044

Firm Foundation Publishing
  House
P.O. Box 17200
Pensacola, FL 32522

Carl Fischer, Inc.
56–62 Cooper Square
New York, NY 10003

Harold Flammer, Inc.
% Shawnee Press
Delaware Water Gap, PA 18327

Galaxy Music Corporation
131 West 86th Street
New York, NY 10024

Gonzaga University Press
Spokane, WA 99202

The Frederick Harris Music
  Company
529 Speers Road
Oakville, ON L6K 2G4 Canada

Herald Press
616 Walnut Avenue
Scottdale, PA 15683

Hope Publishing Company
380 South Main Place
Carol Stream, IL 60188

Jensen Publications, Inc.
2880 South 171st Street
P.O. Box 13819
Milwaukee, WI 53213

Edwin F. Kalmus
Miami-Dade Industrial Park
Box 1007
Opa Locka, FL 33054

Neil A. Kjos Music Company
4380 Jutland Drive
San Diego, CA 92117

Lawson-Gould Music
  Publishers
% G. Schirmer
24 East 22nd Street
New York, NY 10012

Lorenz Corporation
501 East Third Street
P.O. Box 802
Dayton, OH 45401

Edward B. Marks Music
  Corporation
1619 Broadway
New York, NY 10019

Thomas Nelson, Inc.
Nelson Place at
  Elm Hill Pike
P.O. Box 14100
Nashville, TN 37214

Novello Company, Ltd.
Fairfield Road
Borough Green
Sevenoaks,
Kent TN 15 8 DT
England

Organ Literature Foundation
45 Norfolk Road
Braintree, MA 02184

Oxford University Press, Inc.
200 Madison Avenue
New York, NY 10016

C. F. Peters Corporation
373 Park Avenue South
New York, NY 10016

Plymouth Music Company, Inc.
170 Northeast 33rd Street
Ft. Lauderdale, FL 33334

Polanie Publishing Company
643 Madison Street, N.E.
Minneapolis, MN 55413

Theodore Presser Company
Presser Place
Bryn Mawr, PA 19010

E. C. Schirmer Music
  Company, Inc.
138 Ipswich Street
Boston, MA 02215

G. Schirmer, Inc.
24 East 22nd Street
New York, NY 10012

Shawnee Press, Inc.
Waring Drive
Delaware Water Gap, PA 18327

Summy-Birchard Music
  Company
180 Alexander Road
P.O. Box 2072
Princeton, NJ 08540

Willis Music Company
7380 Industrial Road
Florence, KY 41042

Word, Inc.
P.O. Box 1790
Waco, TX 76703

World Library of Sacred
  Music
3815 Willow Road
P.O. Box 2701
Schiller Park, IL 60176

A P P E N D I X   I I
Societies and Organizations Associated with Church Music

American Choral Directors Association
P.O. Box 6310
Lawton, OK 73506
    Serves the needs of choral directors at all levels, including churches; encourages choral composition by offering commissions; publishes *The Choral Journal*.

American Choral Foundation
130 West 56th Street
New York, NY 10019
    Advises and educates choral musicians; publishes *American Choral Review*.

American Guild of Organists
Suite 1260
475 Riverside Drive
New York, NY 10015
    Advances the cause of organ and choral music; publishes the monthly journal *American Organist*.

Association of Anglican Musicians
Trinity Cathedral
Spring at 17th Streets
Little Rock, AR 72206
    Actively encourages composers to create works for the church; supports equitable compensation and benefits for professional church musicians; publishes *A Guide for the Selection and Employment of Church Musicians*.

Choristers Guild
2834 West Kingsley Drive
Garland, TX 75041
    Primarily serves the needs of children's choir directors in churches
and schools.

Church Music Association of America
548 Lafond Avenue
Saint Paul, MN 55103
    Serves those involved in Roman Catholic liturgical music;
encourages composers to write for the church according to the criteria
of the Second Vatican Council; publishes the quarterly journal *Sacred
Music.*

Church Music Publishers Association
P.O. Box 333
Tarzana, CA 91356
    Furnishes information concerning publications by twenty-six Chris-
tian music publishers on request.

Drinker Library of Choral Music
Free Library of Philadelphia
Music Department
Logan Square
Philadelphia, PA 19103
    Supplies copies of choral music to choral organizations, generally
in English translation.

Fellowship of United Methodists in
Worship, Music, and Other Arts
P.O. Box 840
Nashville, TN 37202
    Provides resources, training, and project ideas to upgrade local
church worship programs.

Gospel Music Association
38 Music Square West
Nashville, TN 37203
    Promotes gospel music throughout the world.

Gregorian Institute
 of America Publications, Inc.
7404 South Mason Avenue
Chicago, IL 60638
 Provides a choral subscription service for parishes; publishes
anthems, psalms, Masses, etc.

Guild of Temple Musicians
6636 North Talman
Chicago, IL 60645
 Preserves Jewish musical tradition; publishes a continuing *Bibliography of Jewish Music*.

The Hymn Society of America
National Headquarters
Texas Christian University
Fort Worth, TX 76129
 Promotes the composition of new hymns and hymn-tunes relevant
in contemporary society; supports an ongoing *Bibliography of American
Hymnody*; publishes a quarterly journal entitled *The Hymn*.

Immanuel Bible Foundation
1301 South Fell Avenue
Normal, IL 61761
 Serves as a nondenominational Christian Service Center; operates
a music lending library.

Moravian Music Foundation
P.O. Drawer Z, Salem Station
Winston-Salem, NC 27108
 Publishes editions of music, books of research, and catalogs of
Moravian music.

National Association
 of Pastoral Musicians
225 Sheridan Street, N.W.
Washington, DC 20011
 Supports Roman Catholic parish musicians of all kinds; publishes
Pastoral Music Magazine.

National Oratorio Society
6686 Brook Way
Paradise, CA 95969
Promotes the performance of oratorios and maintains a collection of oratorio scores.

North American Liturgy Resources
10802 North 23rd Avenue
Phoenix, AZ 85029
Specializes in resources for worship and religious education, particularly in the medium of contemporary music; publishes music, records, tapes, and books.

Organ Literature Foundation
45 Norfolk Road
Braintree, MA 02184
Issues an annual catalog of organ books and records.

Presbyterian Association of Musicians
The Joint Office of Worship
1044 Alta Vista Road
Louisville, KY 40205
Publishes the quarterly journal *Reformed Liturgy and Music*.

Religious Arts Guild
25 Beacon Street
Boston, MA 02108
Provides complete worship services focused upon drama, music, and poetry; operates a lending library of anthems for Unitarian Universalist societies.

APPENDIX III

A Selected List of Sacred Music Periodicals

Accent on Worship, Music, the Arts
Lutheran Society for Worship,
  Music, and the Arts
Valparaiso University
Valparaiso, IN 46483

American Choral Review
American Choral Foundation
251 South 18th Street
Philadelphia, PA 19103

American Organist
American Guild of Organists
475 Riverside Drive
Suite 1260
New York, NY 10015

Canticle
209 West 11th Street
Port Angeles, WA 98362

Choir Herald
Lorenz Publishing Company
501 East Third Street
Box 802
Dayton, OH 45401

Choir Leader
Lorenz Publishing Company
501 East Third Street
Box 802
Dayton, OH 45401

The Choral Journal
American Choral Directors
  Association
Box 6310
Lawton, OK 73506

*Church Music: An Annual
  Publication of Church Music
  in America*
Concordia Publishing House
3558 South Jefferson Avenue
St. Louis, MO 63118

Church Musician
Southern Baptist Convention
Sunday School Board
127 Ninth Avenue North
Nashville, TN 37203

Contemporary Christian Music
CCM Publications, Inc.
25231 Paseo de Alicia
Suite 201
Laguna Hills, CA 92653

The Diapason: Devoted to the
   Organ, the Harpsichord,
   the Carillon, and
   Church Music
American Institute of Organbuilders
Scranton Gilette Communications,
   Inc.
380 Northwest Highway
Des Plaines, IL 60016

Gospel Choir
Southern Baptist Convention
Sunday School Board
127 Ninth Avenue North
Nashville, TN 37234

The Hymn: A Journal of
   Congregational Song
The Hymn Society of America
Texas Christian University
P.O. Box 30854
Fort Worth, TX 76129

Journal of Church Music
Lutheran Church in America
Fortress Press
2900 Queen Lane
Philadelphia, PA 19129

Journal of Synagogue Music
Cantors Assembly, Inc.
150 Fifth Avenue
New York, NY 10011

Letter
Choristers Guild
2834 West Kingsley Drive
Garland, TX 75041

Methodist Church Music Society
   Bulletin
Methodist Church Music
   Society
17 First Avenue
St. Anne's Park
Bristol BS4 4DU, England

Modern Liturgy Magazine
160 East Virginia Street
P.O. Box 290
San Jose, CA 95712

Moravian Music Journal
Moravian Music Foundation,
   Inc.
20 Cascade Avenue
Winston-Salem, NC 27127

Music Leader
Southern Baptist Convention
Sunday School Board
Church Music Dept.
127 Ninth Avenue North
Nashville, TN 37234

Music Ministry
201 Eighth Avenue South
Nashville, TN 37203

Organ Portfolio
Lorenz Publishing Company
501 East Third Street
Box 802
Dayton, OH 45401

Organist
Lorenz Publishing Company
501 East Third Street
Box 802
Dayton, OH 45401

Pastoral Music
National Association of Pastoral
  Musicians
225 Sheridan Street, N.W.
Washington, DC 20011

Reformed Liturgy and Music
The Joint Office of Worship
Presbyterian Association of
  Ministers
Drayton Avenue
  Presbyterian Church
2441 Pinecrest Drive
Ferndale, MI 48220

Response
Lutheran Society for Worship,
  Music, and the Arts
Valparaiso University
Valparaiso, IN 46383

SAB Choir
Lorenz Publishing Company
501 East Third Street
Box 802
Dayton, OH 45401

Sacred Music
Church Music Association of
  America
548 Lafond Avenue
St. Paul, MN 55103

Sacred Organ Journal
Lorenz Publishing Company
501 East Third Street
Box 802
Dayton, OH 45401

*Singing News: The Printed Voice
  of Gospel Music*
The Singing News
Box 18010
Pensacola, FL 32523

Sounds
Gospel Recordings, Inc.
122 Glendale Boulevard
Los Angeles, CA 90026

*Stanza: Newsletter of the Hymn
  Society of America*
The Hymn Society of America
Texas Christian University
Fort Worth, TX 76129

Volunteer Choir
Lorenz Publishing Company
501 East Third Street
Box 802
Dayton, OH 45401

Young Chorister
Lorenz Publishing Company
501 East Third Street
Box 802
Dayton, OH 45401

Young Musicians
Southern Baptist Convention
Sunday School Board
127 Ninth Avenue North
Nashville, TN 37243

I N D E X

Compositions Discussed and/or Exemplified, Arranged by Composer

David Poultney is professor of musicology at Illinois State University and has been a church organist for most of the mainstream American churches. He studied with Hans T. David and Louise Cuyler at the University of Michigan, where he received his Ph.D. in 1968. Poultney is the author of *Studying Music History: Learning, Reasoning, and Writing about Music History and Literature* (Prentice-Hall, 1983).

The paper used in this publication meets the minimum requirements of American National Standard for Information Sciences — Permanence of Paper for Printed Library Materials, ANSI Z39.48-1984.

Text and cover design by Interface Studio, Northbrook, Illinois.

Music examples set by Philip Feo Music Preparation, Norridge, Illinois.

Composition by Interface Studio in English Times and Helvetica Condensed on a MCS 10, using a Agfa Compugraphic 9600 typesetter.

Printed on 50-pound Glatfelter, a pH-neutral stock, and bound in a Holliston Roxite B Vellum Finish cloth by Edwards Brothers, Inc.